# Teaching the Dimensions of Literacy

# Teaching the Dimensions of Literacy

Stephen B. Kucer

*Washington State University—Vancouver*

Cecilia Silva

*Texas Christian University*

**LEA** LAWRENCE ERLBAUM ASSOCIATES, PUBLISHERS
**2006** Mahwah, New Jersey                          London

| | |
|---|---|
| Senior Acquisitions Editor: | Naomi Silverman |
| Assistant Editor: | Erica Kica |
| Cover Design: | Kathryn Houghtaling Lacey |
| Textbook Production Manager: | Paul Smolenski |
| Full-Service Compositor: | TechBooks |
| Text and Cover Printer: | Hamilton Printing Company |

This book was typeset in 10/12 pt. Times Roman, Italic, Bold, Bold Italic. The heads were typeset in Times Roman, Italic, Bold, Bold Italic; Zapf Humanist, Bold, Italic, and Bold Italic.

Lawrence Erlbaum Associates, Inc., Publishers
10 Industrial Avenue
Mahwah, New Jersey 07430
www.erlbaum.com

**Library of Congress Cataloging-in-Publication Data**

Kucer, Stephen B.
  Teaching the dimensions of literacy / Stephen B. Kucer, Cecilia Silva.
    p.  cm.
  Includes bibliographical references and index.
  ISBN 0-8058-5020-1 (pbk. : alk. paper)
  1. Language arts.   2. Reading.   3. English language—Composition and exercises—Study and teaching.   4. Literacy.   I. Silva, Cecilia.   II. Title.
  LB1576.K835   2005
  372.6—dc22

                                        2005010260

Books published by Lawrence Erlbaum Associates are printed on acid-free paper, and their bindings are chosen for strength and durability.

Printed in the United States of America
10  9  8  7  6  5  4  3  2  1

To Clare Silva
who touched our lives with her love,
guided our goals with her knowledge,
and edited our words with her green felt-tip marker.

# Brief Contents

# Contents

## II:   Strategy Lessons

# Preface

In many respects, literacy instruction has moved full circle from the 1950s. The current emphasis on phonics and spelling taught in a segmented and sequential fashion reflect the type of teaching and learning many of us baby boomers remember from our youth. Paradoxically, this emphasis on code cracking in the schools comes at the same time that our understanding of literacy has greatly expanded. As well as cracking the code, it is now recognized that literacy also involves the dimensions of making meaning, critically using reading and writing in varied contexts, and ongoing linguistic, cognitive, and sociocultural development.

In *Teaching the Dimensions of Literacy*, we attempt to capture this expanded view of literacy. We do this in two ways. First, by providing a conceptual framework for understanding literacy in all of its complexity. Second, we present a wide variety of instructional strategy lessons to promote complex literacy learning in our students.

We are indebted to a number of individuals for this book. First, we give thanks to those who have written strategy lessons that have been adapted for use in *Teaching the Dimensions of Literacy*. It is our hope that we have been faithful to the spirit of their lessons in our modifications. We also are grateful to our university students and the classroom teachers who used many of these strategy lessons with their students and gave us feedback as to their usefulness. The feedback was invaluable. Once again, Tim Gerken assisted with the construction of many of the figures found throughout the book.

A special note of gratitude goes to the two reviewers of our book, Mary Heller, Kansas State University, and Sally M. Oran, Northern Arizona University. Their insights and suggestions for revisions significantly strengthened the contents of the book. Finally, we thank our editor, Naomi Silverman, who was continually supportive and enthusiastic throughout the entire writing and publishing process.

# Teaching the Dimensions
# of Literacy

# I

# Exploring the Dimensions
# of Literacy

The first three chapters of this book set forth the conceptual foundation for teaching and learning the dimensions of literacy. The chapters reflect the belief that literacy instruction involves more than passively following and implementing a series of recipes. Rather, teaching is a conscious, reflective, and constructive process whereby teachers enact instruction based on their knowledge of their discipline, in this case the reading and writing processes, and knowledge of their children. In an age of standardized curricula and standardized tests, more than ever we are in need of teachers who are capable of taking on the responsibility for promoting the literacy learning of their children. This is only possible if practioners have a deep understanding of what reading and writing entail linguistically, cognitively, socioculturally, and developmentally. The following three chapters are intended to provide such an understanding.

# 1

# Introduction

The ongoing debate and controversy concerning how best to teach our children to read and write shows no signs of dissipating (e.g., Coles, 2000; Cunningham, 2001; Ehri, Nunes, Willows, Yaghoub-Zadeh, & Shanahan, 2001; Luke, 1998). These disputes, which are played out in both academic and public arenas, might lead a casual observer to the conclusion that little is actually known about literacy instruction. Despite these debates, or perhaps because of them, our understanding of literacy has increased dramatically over the last several decades. In fact, it might be argued that it is just this explosion in knowledge that has contributed, at least in part, to the disputes. This is because scholars with an interest in literacy oftentimes focus on or privilege one dimension of literacy learning to the detriment or exclusion of the others. The result may be classroom literacy instruction that narrows or constricts both the teacher's and the children's understanding of literacy teaching and learning. However, as Ed Young reminded us in *The Seven Blind Mice* (1992), "knowing in part may make a fine tale, but wisdom comes from seeing the whole."

Compounding the problems associated with the limited scope of this "fine tale"—literacy instruction—is the fact that the tale changes over time. "What's hot and what's not" or what is in and out of fashion has been the butt of jokes as well as scholarship. *Reading Today*, a publication of the International Reading Association, for example, publishes a yearly article that identifies literacy issues that are "in" and "out" for the year. To a certain extent, however, critiques of changes in education as representing mere fads are unfair. On the other hand, when literacy is narrowly conceived, oftentimes what appears to be advances in instruction represent little more than a shift in focus rather than an expanded understanding of literacy development. Unlike other scientific discoveries, these shifts in instructional focus may not significantly improve the lives of teachers and students.

If literacy teaching and learning are to be effective, it is important that we move from a fine tale to wisdom. It has been well established that literacy is dynamic and multidimensional in nature (e.g., Bernhardt, 2000; Gee, 1996; Kucer, 2005; Luke 1995, 1998; New London Group, 1996). Becoming literate—a never-ending process—reflects learning to manage or juggle these various dimensions. As illustrated in Fig. 1.1, every act of real-world use of written language involves four dimensions: linguistic, cognitive, sociocultural, and developmental.

At the center of the literacy act is the cognitive dimension, the language user's exploration, discovery, construction, and sharing of meaning. Even in those circumstances where there is no intended "outside" audience, such as in the writing of a diary or the reading of a novel for pure enjoyment, there is an "inside" audience, the language user himself or herself. Regardless of the audience, the generation of meanings always involves the employment of various mental

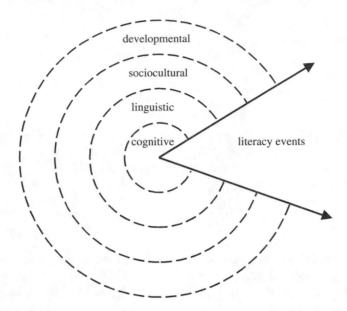

FIG. 1.1.   Dimensions of literacy.

processes and strategies, such as predicting, revising, and monitoring. Similarly, this cognitive dimension seems to transcend languages. Readers employ these mental processes and strategies when reading whether reading in their first or second language (Chamot & El-Dinary, 1999).

Surrounding the cognitive dimension is the linguistic, the language vehicle through which meanings are shared. Literacy depends of various systems, such as graphophonemics, syntax, and semantics, and English-proficient language users have a well-developed understanding of how these systems operate. Although these understandings may be implicit—the rules for the language systems, for example, are not consciously verbalized—the understandings are explicitly demonstrated every time the individual engages in a literacy event. When readers or writers put eye or pen to paper, they must coordinate these transacting language systems with the meanings being constructed.

Literacy events, however, are more than individual acts of meaning making and language use. Literacy is a social act as well. When individuals read or write, they bring not only their own personal experiences, but also the experiences of the various social groups in which they hold membership. Our gender, ethnicity, and socioeconomic status, for example, all impact how we understand or interpret any article we might read in the *New York Times*. We never read or write alone; our social identities are always sitting on our shoulders.

Finally, encompassing the cognitive, linguistic, and sociocultural dimensions is the developmental. Each literacy event reflects those aspects of literacy that the individual does and does not control in any given context. Potentially, development never ends, it continues to unfold as individuals encounter communicative situations that involve using the literacy dimensions in new and novel ways. These experiences offer the opportunity for additional literacy learning that results in developmental advancements.

Although defined separately, reading or writing calls on the individual to utilize knowledge of the four dimensions of literacy in a transactive, symbiotic manner. Each dimension informs and is informed by the others. The challenge faced by the individual is to juggle and integrate both the constraints and possibilities offered by each dimension. Rarely in the national debates over literacy instruction, however, are reading and writing addressed in such a multidimensional and textured manner. If literacy use inside school is to reflect literacy use outside school, it is imperative that teaching and learning reflect the varied nature of the reading and writing processes. Instructional wisdom calls us to help our students develop literacy in all of its richness and complexities.

## HIGHLIGHTING VERSUS ISOLATING THE TEACHING AND LEARNING OF THE DIMENSIONS OF LITERACY

Identifying and defining the dimensions of literacy is a relatively easy task. As we shall see in the following chapter, there is a plethora of research that can guide us in this endeavor. The real challenge is in the development of curricular and instructional strategies that promote the teaching and learning of the dimensions. Historically, instruction in general, and literacy instruction in particular, has tended to take complex processes, divide them into bits and pieces, and present them in a scoped and sequenced manner. Instruction of this type is so pervasive as to have become a cultural norm of schooling. Alternatives are oftentimes deemed to be deviant and receive social sanctions (Wolfe & Poynor, 2001).

The problem with this type of instruction is twofold. First, when literacy is taken apart, the individual pieces may operate differently than when they are part of the whole. It is well established, for example, that teaching children to spell in isolation from the writing process is largely ineffectual (Wilde, 1992, 1997). The children may, in fact, learn the words for the test on Friday, and then will turn around and misspell the words in their stories on Monday. Or, children may be taught to sound out the individual letters in words on flash cards and then discover that this kind of fine-grain analysis is not required when reading the words within the context of a story.

Second, proficiency requires the ability to juggle all of the dimensions as the literacy event unfolds. Readers and writers are called to consider and use their knowledge of the dimensions simultaneously. When literacy is learned piecemeal, many learners are confronted with the difficulty of putting the pieces back together. As John Dewey (1938) reminded us many years ago, the manner in which something is learned impacts the manner in which it can be used. We have far too many students who have mastered the pieces yet still struggle to use reading and writing outside of the school walls. The last thing needed is for us to take the four dimensions of literacy, divide each into a set of skills, and then to teach these skills in isolation. We have been down that path far too often.

The problems related to breaking instruction into small parts become more complex when working with English language learners (ELLs) in English as a second language (ESL) or bilingual settings. Common sense might dictate that in order to make literacy development easier for second language learners it might be a good idea to begin reading instruction by teaching the small parts—for example, letter names and sounds. In reducing the complexity of this instructional task, however, one also reduces the levels of support available to a reader in order to make predictions and construct meaning. Left with the task of recognizing a simple letter, the reading act becomes a meaningless task.

Rather than isolating the dimensions, a more effective response is to highlight them. In such instructional contexts, students are engaged in real-world, meaningful, and authentic literacy activities. All dimensions are available and operating together. Special attention or emphasis, however, is given to a particular aspect of literacy within the whole. Repeated reading, a strategy in which students read a particular text a number of times, is a good example of such highlighting. In the first reading, students are encouraged to respond to the meanings being generated as they interact with the text. Initially, the focus is on understanding and reacting to the ideas of the author. In subsequent readings, students might be asked to focus on a particular linguistic dimension of literacy, such as how the author structured his or her meanings or what the various sounds that a letter sequence such as <ho> represents. Cognitively, the students may be asked to identify words they did not recognize and be taught how to use context to predict unknown words. In all of these instructional examples, students are able to draw upon all of the dimensions of literacy while at the same time giving special attention to one of them.

## OVERVIEW

The idea for this book was conceived as I was completing the first edition of *Dimensions of Literacy: A Conceptual Base for Teaching Reading and Writing in School Settings* (Kucer, 2001). In this book, I laid out what we know theoretically about literacy. Rather than a book on instruction, it was a book that explored what it means to be a reader and writer in today's society. The intention was to provide teachers with an in-depth understanding of literacy that might serve as a base for instruction. As this book came to fruition, I began to realize that a companion book was in the making. In this companion, various instructional strategies would be identified and developed that would promote literacy learning in the various dimensions. A colleague, Cecilia Silva, with whom I had written previously, agreed to join me in this endeavor and bring her considerable expertise in bilingual and biliteracy education.

The book is organized around the four dimensions of literacy. In the second chapter, we review conceptually the linguistic, cognitive, and sociocultural dimensions. The chapter represents a synthesis of the theoretical *Dimensions of Literacy* book. Readers familiar with this book will find that chapter 2 summarizes much of its contents; readers unfamiliar with the book and who desire more in-depth knowledge might wish to read it. The relationship between development and instruction is explored separately in chapter 3. Development and instruction are given their own chapter because they concern teacher mediation and student learning, the heart of the educational enterprise.

The remaining chapters present a variety of strategy lessons that assist teachers to promote and students to develop knowledge about the linguistic, cognitive, and sociocultural dimensions of literacy. Each strategy begins with a description of the literacy concept to be highlighted. Materials necessary for the lesson are then identified, followed by general into, through, and beyond procedures for implementing the strategy. Sample materials that have been used with a variety of students frequently conclude the discussion of the strategy lesson.

Because of the wide range of students for whom the strategy lessons are appropriate, the lessons are necessarily general in nature. Lessons will need to be modified and adapted for particular groups of students. The chapter on development and instruction provides guidelines for how such modifications can be accomplished. When warranted, we also provide possible variations that teachers might want to consider for particular learners.

In the final chapter, we explore how teaching and learning the dimensions of literacy might look in the evolving life of the classroom. The focus here is on the curriculum and ways in which literacy can be integrated with such disciplines as science, social science, and literature. It makes little sense to teach literacy in all of its richness and at the same time to divorce it from the very content that makes reading and writing possible.

# 2

# The Multiple Dimensions of Reading and Writing

In this chapter and the next, we examine more closely the dimensions of literacy—linguistic, cognitive, sociocultural, and developmental—and the multiple forms and functions that literacies can take on. Our purpose here is to understand what proficient literacy users are able to do with print so as to teach children to do the same. These abilities or competencies can perhaps best be conceptualized in terms of the reader or writer as: (1) code breaker and code maker (linguistic dimension), (2) meaning maker (cognitive dimension), (3) text user and critic (sociocultural dimension), and (4) scientist and construction worker (developmental dimension). Similar distinctions are made by Luke (1995) and Freedbody and Luke (1990).

To facilitate understanding, each of the four dimensions is addressed somewhat separately. In actuality, however, they are embedded in one another, as represented in Fig. 1.1 in the previous chapter. Each dimension impacts and is impacted by all the others. Additionally, the dimensions are experienced, learned, and used in tandem. Real-world literacy always involves all four of the dimensions operating together. We need, therefore, to resist the notion that particular dimensions, such as the linguistic, are taught and learned before other dimensions, such as the sociocultural. Scope and sequence charts are antithetical to the teaching and learning of the dimensions of literacy.

Readers and writers are typically unable to consciously and explicitly talk about much of their dimensional knowledge, but are able to employ this knowledge when transacting with print. Many readers of this book, in fact, lack explicit knowledge about much of the information addressed in this chapter. However, they demonstrate implicit knowledge every time they put eye or pen to paper. This is in contrast to school knowledge, which typically children must be able to explicitly "talk about" in very direct ways in order for it to be recognized or "counted" as knowledge. Such a distinction between implicit and explicit knowledge is important to recognize as we examine the nature of literacy and consider ways to help children develop the implicit knowledge that undergirds all literacy use.

## THE LINGUISTIC DIMENSION: THE READER AND WRITER AS CODE BREAKER AND CODE MAKER

The linguistic dimension represents all the reader or writer understands about how language operates as a vehicle for communication. Smith (2004) called this visible aspect of language the surface structure of the text, in contrast to the deep structure, which is the meaning that "hides" behind the print. Meaning, therefore, is at the heart of language and its use.

In the process of making meaning through written language, the individual understands, at least implicitly, that language is made up of various systems or cues (Goodman, 1996), such as semantics, syntax, and graphophonemics. The systems of language are used by the individual to construct meaning through written discourse. Based on experiences—or lack thereof—in various communicative contexts, the individual may control particular systems more or less than others. We briefly discuss these various systems of language or codes, moving from the most general to the most specific, and provide examples of each.

## The Pragmatic System

The pragmatic system represents the language user's understanding of the various functions, uses, and intentions that language can serve. It governs which forms of language are appropriate in particular contexts. Just as furniture has various functions—to sit or lie on, to eat or write on, to place items in—language also serves various purposes. Proficient readers and writers have implicit knowledge of these functions and when and how to employ them in appropriate ways and contexts. As the most powerful system, all language systems are embedded within, and governed by, the pragmatics of the situation. The purpose underlying the use of literacy will influence the type of text read or written, the organization of the text, the meaning and structure of the sentences within the text, the words selected, and so on.

A number of researchers have delineated various taxonomies for the functions that language can serve (Goodman, 1996; Halliday, 1973; Heath, 1983; Smith, 1977). Halliday's functions have perhaps received the most attention and are presented in Table 2.1. Halliday has proposed that the text produced during a language event always fulfills at least one of seven functions, although in many cases multiple purposes are served.

The instrumental or "I want" function is the use of literacy to obtain things, to satisfy material needs, for example, an order form or a shopping list. It is the language of requests—or demands. The regulatory or "Do as I tell you/How it must be" function is the use of literacy to control the behavior, feelings, or attitudes of others. A note to one's child to clean up her room or laws passed by the U.S. Congress to govern human behavior are examples of using literacy in a regulatory manner. Literacy used to interact with others, to form, maintain, and dissolve personal relationships, represents the interactional or "Me and you/Me against you" function of language. Letters and e-mails to friends and family, many greeting cards, letters to Abby or Ann Landers, and postcards sent while on vacation are typically interactional in nature.

The personal or "Here I come" function is the use of literacy to express individuality or the sense of self. Autobiographies, journals, and diaries frequently express the personal function of language. The heuristic or "Tell me why" function is the use of literacy to explore the environment and world. Scientists and other types of researchers often make use of this function. In contrast, the use of reading and writing to create new worlds and to leave the here and now is the imaginative or "Let's pretend" function. Reading for enjoyment or the writing of creative stories or poems are examples of the imaginative use of literacy.

The final function of language is the informative, the "I've got something to tell you" function. It is the use of literacy to communicate or discover information that is not already known. The effective and efficient use of literacy involves the use of print for various purposes and functions. It is therefore critical that schools provide students with a range of literacy activities so they have the opportunity to develop proficiency with all of these functions. In chapter 6, we present a number of literacy activities that engage students in all of the seven functions of language just discussed.

**TABLE 2.1**

The Pragmatic System of Language

The Functions, Uses, and Intentions of the Language User as He or She Relates to
Particular Contexts

*Instrumental*
(I want)
Literacy used as a means of getting things; satisfying material needs.

*Regulatory*
(Do as I tell you/How it must be)
Literacy used to control the behaviors, feelings, or attitudes of others.

*Interactional*
(Me and you/Me against you)
Literacy used to interact with others; forming and maintaining personal relationships;
establishing separateness.

*Personal*
(Here I come)
Literacy used to express individuality and uniqueness; awareness of self; pride.

*Heuristic*
(Tell me why)
Literacy used to explore the environment; to ask questions; to seek and test knowledge.

*Imaginative*
(Let's pretend)
Literacy used to create new worlds.

*Informative*
(I've got something to tell you)
Literacy used as a means of communicating information to someone who does not
possess that information.

**TABLE 2.2**

The Text Type System of Language

Particular Discourse Forms With Distinguishing Features and Patterns

narration, exposition, poetry, drama

## Text Type, Genre, and Text Structure

As illustrated in Tables 2.2, 2.3, and 2.4, text types—narrative, exposition, poetic, dramatic—
are expressed through particular genres and text structures and reflect particular features,
patterns, and content. Narratives are realized through such genres as novels, short stories,
mysteries, and folktales. Research papers, newspapers, magazines, as well as many textbooks
are genres within the expository text type. Finally, the poetic text type can be expressed through
epic and soliloquy genres and the dramatic through comedies and tragedies.

**TABLE 2.3**

The Genre System of Language

A Class of Texts Marked by Distinctive Styles, Forms, or Content Within a Text Type

novels, short stories, mysteries, folktales/fairy tales
(narration)

research papers, directions, essays, medical reports, editorials
(exposition)

epics, sonnets, odes, elegies
(poetry)

tragedies, comedies, romances
(drama)

**TABLE 2.4**

The Text Structure System of Language

The Total Organization of Meanings Across a Text Type

Temporal Order: time order
Attribution: idea development
Adversative: compare/contrast
Covariance: cause/effect
Response: problem/solution

Text types and genre are expressed in a variety of corresponding structures. Temporal texts, commonly associated with narratives and dramas, organize ideas by time or when they occur. The rules used to structure ideas in this manner are commonly referred to as story grammars. Although a number of story grammars have been generated (e.g., Mandler & Johnson, 1977; Rumelhart, 1975; Thorndyke, 1977), as conceived here, a story consists of an explicit or implicit setting (characters, time, location) and a number of episodes. Episodes involve an event that initiates a response in the form of a goal set by the protagonist and an attempt to achieve the goal. The attempt is followed by the consequence of achieving or not achieving the goal and the reaction of the protagonist to the consequence.

Attributions, oftentimes expressed through expositions, involve the development of factual, conceptual, and generalizable knowledge. Typically, facts are organized by concepts and concepts by generalizations, and they are arranged by order of importance or significance. Adversatives involve the comparing and contrasting of ideas in which similarities and differences are noted. Covariance structures demonstrate how particular events occur (effects) or come into being because of other events (cause). Finally, response structures present a problem with a number of possible solutions or, conversely, several problems that can be resolved by a single solution. Adversatives, covariances, and responses are frequently found in expositions. Narratives, however, can also make use of covariance and response structures.

At this point, a cautionary note is warranted. The characteristics assigned to each text type, genre, and structure are best understood in terms of dominance (Beaugrande, 1984). Consequently, any text may actually contain a mix of types and structures. An expository text, such as that found in the social sciences, may include the kind of sequenced events that typically are found in literary narrative discourses as well as information in an attributive form. Or, a problem-solution–structured scientific text may in many ways resemble the structure of temporal ordered discourse of a literary novel.

**TABLE 2.5**

The Semantic System of Language

The Meaning Relationships Among Morphemes Within the Sentence

*Agent*
One who causes or performs an action:
*Jan* sailed the boat.

*Action*
The behavior taken:
Jan *sailed* the boat.

*Object*
Someone or something receiving an action:
Jan sailed the *boat*.

*Locative*
Place or locus of an action or entity:
Jan sailed the boat into the *harbor*.

*Experiencer*
An animate object experiencing a temporary or durative state:
Jan felt *hungry* after the sailing.

*Instrument*
A force or object involved in a state of action:
Jan cut her sandwich with a *knife*.

*Goal*
Desired or obtained endstate:
Jan wanted a *sandwich* for lunch.

*Entity*
A person or thing having distinct or particular characteristics:
The *sailor* was late for the race.

*Possession*
A relationship between an object and a possessor:
That is *Jan's* sailboat.

*Attribution*
Characteristics of an entity, object, agent, or action that could not be known
from its class characteristics alone:
Jan's sailboat is *red* and *white*.

*State*
A condition of being:
Jan *wants* a bigger sailboat.

*Beneficiary*
One who is the inheritor of a relationship:
*Jan* received a sailboat for her birthday.

## Semantic

The semantic system of language governs the meaning relationships among words within the sentence. Just as texts reflect a rule-governed organization of meaning across sentences and paragraphs, sentences reflect a rule-governed organization of meaning among words. The roles assigned to the words in a sentence establish each word's relationship to other words within the structure. Table 2.5 illustrates the more common roles that words can play, followed by an example of each.

**TABLE 2.6**

The Syntactic System of Language

The Knowledge of Grammatical or Structural Arrangements Within the Sentence

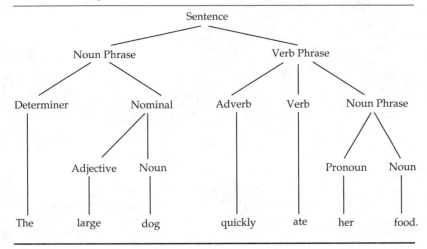

**TABLE 2.7**

The Morphemic System of Language

The Knowledge of Wordness—the Smallest Meaning-Bearing Unit of Language

| | | |
|---|---|---|
| cat + s | laugh + ed | look + ing |
| box + er + s | run [n] er | re + search |
| pre + view | re + statement | un + doubt + ed + ly |

## Syntactic

The syntactic system of language reflects the rules that govern the grammatical arrangements of words within the sentence. As indicated in Table 2.6, a sentence is typically composed of a noun phrase and a verb phrase. A noun phrase may include a determiner (e.g., the) and a nominal composed of an adjective (e.g., large) and a noun (e.g., dog). Similarly, the verb phrase includes a verb (e.g., ate) that may be modified by an adverb (e.g., quickly). The verb phrase may also include a second noun phrase with a pronoun (e.g., his) and a noun (e.g., food). In English, determiners and adjectives usually precede nouns and adverbs precede verbs. As can be readily observed, there exists an intimate relationship between the semantic role and syntactic assignment of words within a sentence.

## Morphological

Morphemes are the smallest meaning-bearing units of language. Morphological knowledge reflects the language user's understanding of "wordness" in terms of meaning, semantic role, and syntactic category. As illustrated in Table 2.7, there are two basic types of morphemes: unbound and bound. Unbound or free-standing morphemes are individual elements that can stand alone within in a sentence, such as <cat>, <laugh>, <look>, and <box>. They are essentially what most of us call words. Bound morphemes are meaning-bearing units of language, such as prefixes and suffixes, that are attached to unbound morphemes. They cannot stand alone.

**TABLE 2.8**

Connective or Signal Morphemes

A Special Class of Morphemes that Indicate Conceptual Relationships Among Various
Ideas Across the Text

| Connective/Signal | Indicated Relationship |
|---|---|
| Also, again, another, finally, furthermore, likewise, moreover, similarly, too | Another item in the same series |
| Afterwards, finally, later, on, next, after | Another item in a time series |
| For instance, for example, specifically | Another example or illustration of what has been said |
| Accordingly, as a result, consequently, hence, then, therefore, thus, so | A consequence of what has been said |
| In other words, that is to say, to put it differently | A restatement of what has been said |
| All in all, altogether, finally, in conclusion, the point is | A concluding item or summary |
| But, however, on the other hand, on the contrary | A statement opposing what has been said |
| Granted, of course, to be sure, undoubtedly | A concession to an opposing view |
| All the same, even though, nevertheless, nonetheless, still | The original line of argument is resuming after a concession |

**TABLE 2.9**

The Relationship Between Connectives or Signal Morphemes and Text Structures

| Text Structure | Typical Connective or Signal |
|---|---|
| Temporal order (time order) | Time, not long after, now, as, before, after, when |
| Adversative (compare/contrast) | However, but, as well as, on the other hand, not only . . . but also, either . . . or, while, although, unless, similarly, yet |
| Response (problem/solution) | Because, since, therefore, so that, consequently, as a result, this led |
| Covariance (cause/effect) | To, so that, nevertheless, thus, accordingly, if . . . then |
| Attribution (idea development) | To begin with, first, second, next, then, finally, most important, also, in fact, for instance, for example |

Their attachment modifies the unbound morphemes in such things as number or syntactic category. Adding the bound morpheme <s> to the unbound morpheme <cat> changes the noun's number; the addition of the <ed> to <laugh> changes tense. Similarly, the addition of <er> to <run> changes the verb to a noun. As noted in the previous discussion, beyond their individual meanings, morphemes also play various syntactic (e.g., nouns, verbs, adjectives) and semantic roles (e.g., agents, actions, objects) within the sentence itself.

Relationships among ideas across sentences within a text are indicated by morphemes known as connectives or signals. (See Table 2.8.) They connect ideas as well as signal or mark these connections by their very existence. Connectives can signal such relationships as time, opposition, concession, and summary (Just & Carpenter, 1987). Readers use connectives to build relationships among ideas in what they are reading; similarly, writers use these morphemes to highlight or mark their organizational patterns.

Not surprisingly, particular types of connectives are frequently found within particular types of text structures. Some of these correspondences are shown in Table 2.9. For example, the

**TABLE 2.10**

The Orthographic System of Language

The Knowledge of Spelling Patterns or Relationships Among Letters

| ead; eet; qu; cei; pho | but not | qtp; rzf; ltg |
|---|---|---|

**TABLE 2.11**

The Graphophonemic System of Language

The knowledge of letter/sound relationships; relationships between letters and sounds; how twenty-six letters are related to approximately forty-four sounds.

When there are two vowels side by side, the long sound of the first vowel is heard and the second vowel is usually silent.

morphemes <time>, <not long after>, and <now> frequently are represented within temporal order (time order) discourse. The morphemes <however>, <but>, and <as well as> are oftentimes found within adversative (compare/contrast) texts. Authors use such morphemes to cue their readers to the types of conceptual relationship being expressed.

**Orthographic**

The orthographic system of language represents the rules for spelling within the language. These orthographic rules determine not only how words are spelled in a conventional sense, but also what spelling patterns are common within the language. As illustrated in Table 2.10, the letter patterns <ead>, <eet>, <qu>, <cei>, and <pho> are frequently found in English words and we can readily think of frequently used words that reflect these patterns. On the other hand, the letter sequences <qtp>, <rzf>, and <ltg> are uncommon in the English spelling system.

**Graphophonemic**

The graphophonemic system expresses the rules for relating letters and sounds within the language. (See Table 2.11.) It is on this system of language that much of the debate over beginning reading instruction is centered. In English, this relationship involves 26 letters and approximately 44 sounds. The challenge in English is that there are far more individual sounds in the spoken language that must be systematically linked to a much more limited number of letters. A rule system for the linking of letters and sounds must account for this discrepancy. Consider for a moment the variations found in the relationship between letters and sounds in English that are illustrated in Table 2.12.

Two attempts at generating a rule system that accounts for letter–sound relationships in English are particularly noteworthy as well as revealing. Berdiansky, Cronnel, and Koehler (1969) examined the letter–sound relationships in 6,092 one- and two-syllable words in the comprehension vocabularies of 6- to 9-year-old children. In attempting to generate rules for the relationships of the 6,092 words, the researchers immediately encountered the problem of deciding what was a rule and what was an exception. If a rule was required to account for every instance of a particular letter–sound relationship represented among the 6,092 words, with few if any exceptions, a tremendous number of rules were required. For example, a common phonic rule taught to children is that "when two vowels go walking"—for example, <read>—"the first vowel does the talking." Therefore, in the written word <read>, the <e> represents a long sound and the letter <a> is not heard. However, in some contexts, the word <read> is

**TABLE 2.12**

Letter–Sound Relationships in English

- One letter represents several different sounds.
  &lt;c&gt; ----&gt;     /cat/
                    /ice/
- One group of letters represents several different sounds.
  &lt;gh&gt; ----&gt;     /rough/          &lt;ph&gt; ----&gt;     /telephone/
                    /through/                        /haphazard/
                    /ghost/                          /shepherd/
- One sound is represented by several different individual letters.
  /j/ ----&gt;          &lt;gem&gt;
                    &lt;jeep&gt;
- One sound is represented by individual as well as groups of letters.
  /f/ ----&gt;          &lt;telephone&gt;
                    &lt;fun&gt;
- One sound is represented by a group of letters.
  /ch/ ----&gt;        &lt;choice&gt;       /e/ ----&gt;       &lt;eat&gt;
  /th/ ----&gt;        &lt;the&gt;          /t/ ----&gt;       &lt;butter&gt;

**TABLE 2.13**

Letter–Sound Relationships

|                                | *Consonants* | *Vowels* | *Total* |
| ------------------------------ | ------------ | -------- | ------- |
| Letter–Sound Correspondences   | 83           | 128      | 211     |
| Rules                          | 60           | 106      | 166     |
| Exceptions                     | 23           | 22       | 45      |

pronounced /red/, an exception to the rule. Numerous other examples to this rule exist, such as <chief>, <build>, and <said>. On the other hand, if fewer rules were generated, a large number of exceptions existed. These exceptions become, in fact, additional rules to be learned. Because there was a symbiotic relationship between rules and exceptions, attempts to limit one resulted in an increase in the other.

Ultimately, the researchers decided that each rule needed to account for a particular letter–sound relationship in at least 10 words from the corpus. Table 2.13, modified from Smith (1994, p. 139), summarizes the major findings of this research. For the 6,092 one- and two-syllable words, 211 letter–sound relationships were found (83 for the consonants, 128 for the vowels). One hundred sixty-six rules existed (60 for the consonants, 106 for the vowels), each representing at least 10 instances of the given letter–sound correspondence. Accompanying these rules were 45 exceptions (23 consonants, 22 vowels).

As is readily apparent, any attempt to teach and or learn all of the rules and exceptions as the sole basis for reading and spelling development would be difficult at best. What is also interesting is that the rule-governed nature of the letters in the English alphabet varies across consonants and vowels. Letter consonants are much more consistent in the sounds they represent, whereas letter vowels are far are more variable. This accounts for the much greater number of letter–sound correspondences found with the vowels as well as the greater number of rules necessary to account for these correspondences.

In a classical second study examining the relationship between letters and sounds, Clymer (1996) identified 45 phonic rules or generalizations that were taught to children in four basal readers. Clymer's intent was to discover the degree to which the phonic generalizations taught to children were useful, that is, whether they supported the child in correctly pronouncing unknown words. Interestingly, in his review of the basal series, Clymer found that there was a lack of consensus among publishers as to which generalizations were to be taught; generalizations that were common across the four basal readers were minimal.

After the generalizations were identified, Clymer developed a word list that included all of the words introduced in the four basals as well as the words from the Gates Reading Vocabulary for the Primary Grades. The list contained 2,600 words. Each generalization was then applied to all words in the list that were relevant to the generalization. For example, the first generalization stated that when two vowels are side by side, the first vowel "says its name" and the second vowel is silent. All words in the word list containing two adjacent vowels were located and the generalization applied to each word's pronunciation. The degree to which the generalization generated the correct pronunciation was computed as a percentage and labeled the "percent of utility." The findings of this study are presented in Table 2.14.

As the findings demonstrate, a significant number of the phonic generalizations taught to children fail to apply. Further compounding the issue is that many generalizations fail to account for a variety of English dialects. Even when the generalization can be applied, it may lead to a pronunciation that is at variance from the reader. In such cases, the child may apply the generalization correctly, yet still fail to recognize the word. Clymer concluded by noting that if the criteria of 75% application is set to determine the usefulness of any generalization, only 18 are helpful: 5, 8, 10, 16, 20, 21, 22, 23, 25, 28, 29, 30, 31, 32, 40, 41, 44, and 45. This research has been largely corroborated by Emans (1967) and Bailey (1967).

This variability between letters and sounds in English has led many educators to lament the English spelling system. Some have even called for a new or modified alphabet to solve the numerous orthographic irregularities (Venesky, 1980). However, the irregularity of English spelling may not be as irregular as it appears if we move beyond a strictly alphabetic analysis of the language.

Two columns of words are found in Table 2.15. The first column consists of homophones: words that sound alike but that in this case are spelled differently. In oral language, if these words were said in isolation, it would be difficult to know which particular word was being spoken. In the second column are words that contain identical parts. These parts represent different sounds but are spelled the same. For example, the <s> in <dogs>, <cats>, and <horses> makes three distinct sounds: /z/, /s/, and /uz/; the <g> in <sign> is silent but heard in the word <signature>. Take a few minutes to analyze the two lists of words. Try and generate a spelling rule for the difference in spelling for words that sound alike (group one) and the continuity of spelling for word parts that sound different (group two).

If you were able to generate a spelling rule for each column, you discovered that the relationship between letters and sounds in English orthography is not based solely on the alphabetic principal. Meaning also plays a critical role. The group of words in the first column are spelled differently even though they have identical pronunciations because of the influence of meaning. The words in the first column are different morphemes and represent different meanings. Consequently, their spelling represents not so much a link with spoken language as it does a link to meaning. Spelling in English marks meaning as much as it marks sound. The general rule in English is that when words sound alike but have different meanings, the words are spelled differently. Put another way, English orthography, when possible, accommodates meaning rather than sound (Chomsky, 1970).

On the other hand, when there are elements of meaning that are shared by various words, the tendency of the English language is to maintain a shared spelling. The <s> is pronounced differently in <dogs>, <cats>, and <horses> yet spelled the same way because <s> at the end of nouns typically signifies plurality. Similarly, the <g> in <sign> may not be heard yet is

**TABLE 2.14**

The Utility of 45 Phonic Generalizations

| *Generalization | No. of words conforming | No. of exceptions | Percent of utility |
|---|---|---|---|
| 1. When there are two vowels side by side, the long sound of the first one is heard and the second is usually silent. | 309 (bead)[†] | 377 (chief)[†] | 45 |
| 2. When a vowel is in the middle of a one-syllable word, the vowel is short. | 408 | 249 | 62 |
|     middle letter | 191 (dress) | 84 (scold) | 69 |
|     one of the middle two letters in a word of four letters | 191 (rest) | 135 (told) | 59 |
|     one vowel *within* a word of more than four letters | 26 (splash) | 30 (fight) | 46 |
| 3. If the only vowel letter is at the end of a word, the letter usually stands for a long sound. | 23 (he) | 8 (to) | 74 |
| 4. When there are two vowels, one of which is final e, the first vowel is long and the e is silent. | 180 (bone) | 108 (done) | 63 |
| *5. The r gives the preceding vowel a sound that is neither long nor short. | 484 (horn) | 134 (wire) | 78 |
| 6. The first vowel is usually long and the second silent in the digraphs *ai, ea, oa,* and *ui.* | 179 | 92 | 66 |
|     ai | 43 (nail) | 24 (said) | 64 |
|     ea | 101 (bead) | 51 (head) | 66 |
|     oa | 34 (boat) | 1 (cupboard) | 97 |
|     ui | 1 (suit) | 16 (build) | 6 |
| 7. In the phonogram *ie,* the *i* is silent and the *e* has a long sound. | 8 (field) | 39 (friend) | 17 |
| *8. Words having double e usually have the long e sound. | 85 (seem) | 2 (been) | 98 |
| 9. When words end with silent e, the preceding a or i is long. | 164 (cake) | 108 (have) | 60 |
| *10. In *ay* the y is silent and gives a its long sound. | 36 (play) | 10 (always) | 78 |
| 11. When the letter *i* is followed by the letters *gh,* the *i* usually stands for its long sound and the *gh* is silent. | 22 (high) | 9 (neighbor) | 71 |
| 12. When a follows w in a word, it usually has the sound a as in *was.* | 15 (watch) | 32 (swan) | 32 |
| 13. When e is followed by w, the vowel sound is the same as represented by *oo.* | 9 (blew) | 17 (sew) | 35 |
| 14. The two letters *ow* make the long o sound. | 50 (own) | 35 (down) | 59 |
| 15. *W* is sometimes a vowel and follows the vowel digraph rule. | 50 (crow) | 75 (threw) | 40 |
| *16. When y is the final letter in a word, it usually has a vowel sound. | 169 (dry) | 32 (tray) | 84 |
| 17. When y is used as a vowel in words, it sometimes has the sound of long *i.* | 29 (fly) | 170 (funny) | 15 |
| 18. The letter a has the same sound (δ) when followed by *l, w,* and *u.* | 61 (all) | 65 (canal) | 48 |
| 19. When a is followed by r and final e, we expect to hear the sound heard in *care.* | 9 (dare) | 1 (are) | 90 |
| *20. When c and h are next to each other, they make only one sound. | 103 (peach) | 0 | 100 |
| *21. *Ch* is usually pronounced as it is in *kitchen, catch,* and *chair,* not like *sh.* | 99 (catch) | 5 (machine) | 95 |
| *22. When c is followed by e or i, the sound of s is likely to be heard. | 66 (cent) | 3 (ocean) | 96 |

(continued)

## TABLE 2.14 (*Continued*)

| *Generalization | No. of words conforming | No. of exceptions | Percent of utility |
|---|---|---|---|
| *23. When the letter *c* is followed by *o* or *a* the sound of *k* is likely to be heard. | 143 (camp) | 0 | 100 |
| 24. The letter *g* often has a sound similar to that of *j* in *jump* when it precedes the letter *i* or *e*. | 49 (engine) | 28 (give) | 64 |
| *25. When *ght* is seen in a word, *gh* is silent. | 30 (fight) | 0 | 100 |
| 26. When a word begins *kn*, the *k* is silent. | 10 (knife) | 0 | 100 |
| 27. When a word begins with *wr*, the *w* is silent. | 8 (write) | 0 | 100 |
| *28. When two of the same consonants are side by side only one is heard. | 334 (carry) | 3 (suggest) | 99 |
| *29. When a word ends in *ck*, it has the same last sound as in *look*. | 46 (brick) | 0 | 100 |
| *30. In most two-syllable words, the first syllable is accented. | 828 (famous) | 143 (polite) | 85 |
| *31. If *a, in, re, ex, de*, or *be* is the first syllable in a word, it is usually unaccented. | 86 (belong) | 13 (insect) | 87 |
| *32. In most two-syllable words that end is a consonant followed by *y*, the first syllable is accented and the last is unaccented. | 101 (baby) | 4 (supply) | 96 |
| 33. One vowel letter in an accented syllable has its short sound. | 547 (city) | 356 (lady) | 61 |
| 34. When *y* or *ey* is seen in the last syllable that is not accented, the long sound of *e* is heard. | 0 | 157 (baby) | 0 |
| 35. When *ture* is the final syllable in a word, it is unaccented. | 4 (picture) | 0 | 100 |
| 36. When *tion* is the final syllable in a word, it is unaccented. | 5 (station) | 0 | 100 |
| 37. In many two- and three-syllable words, the final *e* lengthens the vowel in the last syllable. | 52 (invite) | 62 (gasoline) | 46 |
| 38. If the first vowel sound in a word is followed by two consonants, the first syllable usually ends with the first of the two consonants. | 404 (bullet) | 159 (singer) | 72 |
| 39. If the first vowel sound in a word is followed by a single consonant, that consonant usually begins the second syllable. | 190 (over) | 237 (oven) | 44 |
| *40. If the last syllable of a word ends in *le*, the consonant preceding the *le* usually begins the last syllable. | 62 (tumble) | 2 (buckle) | 97 |
| *41. When the first vowel element in a word is followed by *th, ch*, or *sh*, these symbols are not broken when the word is divided into syllables and may go with either the first or second syllable. | 30 (dishes) | 0 | 100 |
| 42. In a word of more than one syllable, the letter *v* usually goes with the preceding vowel to form a syllable. | 53 (cover) | 20 (clover) | 73 |
| 43. When a word has only one vowel letter, the vowel sound is likely to be short. | 433 (hid) | 322 (kind) | 57 |
| *44. When there is one *e* in a word that ends in a consonant, the *e* usually has a short sound. | 85 (leg) | 27 (blew) | 76 |
| *45. When the last syllable is the sound *r*, it is unaccented. | 188 (butter) | 9 (appear) | 95 |

†Words in parentheses are examples—either of words that conform or of exceptions, depending on the column.

*Generalizations marked with an asterisk were found "useful" according to the criteria.

**TABLE 2.15**

Examining English Orthographic Patterns

| *Group One* | *Group Two* |
|---|---|
| feat — feet | dogs — cats — horses |
| threw — through | walked — hugged |
| tail — tale | sign — signature |
| sea — see | except — exception |
| principle — principal | medicine — medical |
| bare — bear | equate — equation |
| their — there — they're | critical — criticize |
| I — eye | hymn — hymnal |
| to — too — two | bomb — bombard |
| night — knight | solemn — solemnity |
| hour — our | autumn — autumnal |
| son — sun | music — musician |
| blue — blew | logic — logician |
| main — mane | resign — resignation |

**TABLE 2.16**

The Graphemic System of Language

The Knowledge of Letter Shapes and Formations

A a **A a** A a A ɑ A a      <u>but not</u>      g q; b d p

included because of the semantic relationship between <sign> and <signature> in which the <g> is pronounced. A second general rule in English is that when parts of words are related semantically, the spelling is the same for these parts even when the sound varies.

Given the spelling-meaning-sound relationships represented in English, readers need not necessarily go through sound to access word meaning. In fact, an overreliance on sound may actually inhibit the reader's ability to understand. In the two phrases, <the cross-eyed bear> and <the cross I'd bare>, spelling, not sound, indicates the meaning being represented.

The use of a spelling system that is not exclusively based on sound has another advantage. It assures that regardless of what dialect(s) one speaks, the spelling will be the same. Some dialects distinguish between /pin/ and /pen/; others do not. Some dialects pronounce /oil/ and /all/ in the same way, other dialects do not. Given the English spelling system, the pairs of morphemes are spelled differently, even though in some speech communities one would need to use context to distinguish which word is being used. English speakers use the same written language system although they speak different dialects.

**Graphemic**

The graphemic system expresses the rules for the formation of letters within the language. As shown in Table 2.16, each grapheme can be constituted in a variety of ways. Letters, especially when displayed in cursive, reflect a wide range of styles and formations, yet they are still judged to be the same letter. On the other hand, there are other features among letters that demonstrate less variation but represent critical features that distinguish one letter from another. In some ways, for example, the <A>s in Table 2.16 reflect as much variation as that found among <b>, <d>, and <p>. However, the differences among the <A>s are not taken to be critical; they do not represent different letters despite their variation. The differences among <b>, <d>, and <p> are critical; they do contain features that represent different letters.

## THE COGNITIVE DIMENSION: THE READER AND WRITER
## AS MEANING MAKER

An examination of the cognitive dimension of literacy moves us from a focus on the language itself to an examination of the individual who is transacting with the print. A cognitive discussion of literacy concerns those mental processes, strategies, or procedures that the individual engages so as to construct meaning. Because in the construction of meaning there is a transaction between a mind (cognition) and a text (linguistic), this part of the chapter can best be conceived as a psycholinguistic extension of the previous linguistic discussion.

The cognitive dimension is divided into three sections. The first addresses the role of perception in the literacy processes. Second, the cognitive aspects of reading and comprehending are discussed. Finally, the section concludes with a look into the mind of the writer.

### Perception and Literacy

In order to better understand perception and its role in the reading process, we are going to engage you in a series of experiments. In Table 2.17—don't look at it just yet!—eight lines of print are presented. Cover all of the lines of print with a piece of paper or your hand. Then, briefly glance—about one second—at the first line of print, cover it once again, and write down everything that you saw. Move to the second line and do the same thing; continue until all eight lines of print have been looked at.

Now, that you have glanced at each line of print and recorded what you saw, for each line write down the total number of letters that you recorded. For line seven, each group of marks—for example, =/, *&—constitutes an individual letter. If you look at the total number of letters perceived across the various lines of print, you should see a remarkable difference in the numbers. Examine the lines of print and the number of letters perceived and see if you can determine why you were able to read more on some lines than others.

We can use our knowledge of the systems of language to explain the differences in your perception. Our guess is, for example, that you were able to perceive more in line three than in lines two, six, or seven. As illustrated in Table 2.18, there are more or fewer systems of language present in each of these lines of print. Consequently, as more or fewer systems are made available, the reader is able to perceive more or less. If you are able to read Spanish, line five contained numerous systems of language. On the other hand, if you are monoliterate in English, very few systems were available. Typically, biliterate readers of English and Spanish perceive more on line five than do English monoliterates. Therefore, one characteristic of perception, which is an intimate part of the reading process, is that what is being read influences how it is read.

### TABLE 2.17
Perception and Lines of Print

| |
|---|
| 1. BOY    HORSE    DESK    GRASS    COFFEE |
| 2. JKG    YZX    PDU    MVB    DFQ |
| 3. WASHINGTON    D.C.    IS    THE    CAPATAL    OF    THE    UNITED    STATES. |
| 4. THR    ING    HOM    ERS    STR    ION |
| 5. LAPIZ    Y    PAPEL    GATOS    Y    PERROS |
| 6. D    J    E    K    G    I    T    L    G    O    Q    M    C    N    X |
| 7. =/    *&    @#    = -    !~    —)    #%    +^    ($ |
| 8. BACON    AND    EGGS    ICE    CREAM    AND    CAKE |

**TABLE 2.18**

Perception and the Systems of Language

| Line | Available Systems |
|---|---|
| 1. BOY HORSE DESK GRASS COFFEE | graphemes<br>graphophonemics<br>orthographics<br>morphemes |
| 2. JKG YZX PDU MVB DFQ | graphemes<br>graphophonemics |
| 3. WASHINGTON D.C. IS THE CAPATAL<br>OF THE UNITED STATES. | graphemes<br>graphophonemics<br>orthographics<br>morphemes<br>syntax<br>semantics<br>pragmatics |
| 4. THR ING HOM ERS STR ION | graphemes<br>graphophonemics<br>orthographics<br>morphemes |
| 5. LAPIZ Y PAPEL GATOS Y PERROS | graphemes<br>graphophonemics<br>orthographics<br>morphemes<br>partial syntax<br>partial semantics |
| 6. D J E K G I T L G O Q M C N X | graphemes<br>graphophonemics |
| 7. =/ * & @ # =- !~ –) # % +^ ($ | graphemes |
| 8. BACON AND EGGS<br>ICE CREAM AND CAKE | graphemes<br>graphophonemics<br>orthographics<br>morphemes<br>partial syntax<br>partial semantics |

In addition, in line three did you notice the misspelling of <capital>? In our university classes, when we flash this line of print on an overhead projector, many students fail to perceive the misspelling and write the word as it is conventionally spelled. This example of misperception is similar to what happens when we proofread our own writing. It is not uncommon for typographical errors to go unnoticed. Many professional proofreaders actually "read" from bottom to top and from right to left so as to better perceive what is actually on the page. In such instances, all of the systems of language are available, yet there is still misperception. Why this inability to read what is on the page? In order to begin to answer this question, it is necessary to look at more traditional as well as current understandings of perception.

Traditionally, our view of perception was similar to that of a vacuum cleaner sweeping up dirt on a carpet. Whatever the vacuum cleaner—or eye—went over was put into a bag—or brain. Cognitively speaking, perception was conceived as a one-way process in which the print was recorded by the eye, similar to a photograph, and then processed by the brain. Not only was this described perceptual process one-way in nature, it was also rather passive. The eye did little more than record the information available and the brain's role was to simply

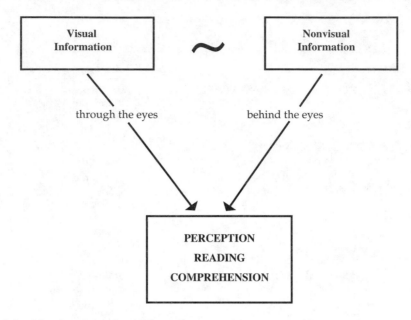

FIG. 2.1.   Visual and nonvisual information.

process whatever it was provided. In a sense, as illustrated later, the print environment largely determined what was perceived.

print → eye → brain → meaning

More recently, however, perception has come to be understood in more transactive and constructive ways. In this understanding, the eye and brain are much more actively and inter-actively involved in information processing. Under the direction of the brain, the eye selectively picks up relevant information from the print environment. What is selected is determined by both the print available and what the brain determines is important or relevant. Then, based on the print selected and contributions by the brain, meaning is constructed. In the previous ex-ample concerning Washington, DC, the misspelling of <capital> may have been misperceived because the brain knows the correct spelling and simply overrode what the eye had selected. Or, the reader knows that Washington, DC, is the capital of the United States. Or, as we will see next, the letter <a> may have been ignored altogether.

Frank Smith (1994) characterized perception as involving an interaction between visual and nonvisual memory. Rather than being a one-way and passive process as described previously, Smith suggested that perception is a very active and constructive process in which nonvisual information—the brain—influences what visual information—the print—is selected by the eye. The relationship between visual and nonvisual information is a reciprocal one. The more the brain knows, the less information the eye needs to select; the eye is required to pick up only information that is unknown to the brain. The brain, therefore, fills in the gaps that the eye creates. Figure 2.1, adapted from Smith (1994, p. 67), illustrates this process. Although perception and reading are the focus here, comprehension has also been included in the figure. As we shall see, much of what we know about perception and reading will be relevant to comprehension as well.

**TABLE 2.19**

Perception and Beginning, Middle, and Ending Letters

- __nce __pon a __ime __here __as a __ittle __oy __amed __enjamin __ho __oved __rom a __mall __arm in__he__idwest__nto a__arge __partment__ouse in __ew __ork __ity.
- Th__re w__re m__re pe__ple li__ing in h__s apar__ment ho__se th__n th__re we__e in t__e en__ire to__n th__t w__s ne__r h__s fa__m.
- Althoug__ Benjami__ di__ no__ wan__ t__ leav__ th__ far__, hi__ mothe__ wa__ offere__ a jo__ i__ th__ cit__ tha__ sh__ wa__ unabl__ t__ refus__.

**TABLE 2.20**

Perception and Vowels and Consonants

- T__m__s w__r__ t__gh f__r f__rm__rs __nd th__y s__mply c__ld n__t m__k__ __n__gh m__n__y t__ p__y __ll __f th__r b__lls.
- __o, ___e__ __o___ ___a__ ___ey __ou___, __a___e__ u__ ___e__ __e__ai__i___ __e__o___l___, a___ __ea__e__ ea___.

Table 2.19 contains three paragraphs from the beginning of a short story. In each paragraph different letters have been systematically omitted. Read each paragraph and monitor how difficult or easy it is to predict the words that contain deleted letters.

Similar to the experiment with the eight lines of print, you most likely found certain words with deleted letters easier to read than others. Stated another way, some parts of words are more salient or informative than others. Typically, the beginning letters in a word are more important than the middle or ending letters. Initial letters are more difficult to predict from context—that is, what comes before and after the letters. When beginning letters are missing, they tend to make reading more difficult than when middle or ending letters are absent.

Ending letters tend to be the second most important letters in a word. Their absence also can cause difficulty when reading, but usually not as much as when beginning letters are omitted. Middle letters are the least salient and oftentimes have minimal impact on perception when they are deleted. In a sense, this means that when perceiving, or reading, not all letters are created equal; some letters are more important to process than others. It was not by chance that when we misspelled <capital>, we selected the middle part of the word. We knew that you would be much less likely to perceive the misspelling in this position than if we had selected a beginning or ending letter. Interestingly, Wilde (1992) found that when young children misspell words, they oftentimes misspell the middle letters more frequently than the beginning or the ending letters. Because beginning and ending letters are more salient or more likely to be perceived by the reader, children tend to first learn to conventionally spell these parts of words.

In Table 2.20, the story continues. Once again, particular letters have been omitted through-out the story. Read the next two parts and, again, monitor the degree of difficulty experienced.

You most likely found the omission of the vowels much less disruptive than the lack of consonants. In fact, it is doubtful that you were able to read much of the story when the consonants were missing. These two experiments, once again, inform us as to the inequality among letters when reading. Returning to the misspelling of <capital>, we selected to misspell

**TABLE 2.21**

Factors Influencing the Reader–Text–Writer Transaction

| *Reader* <-----------------> *Text* <-------------> *Writer* | |
| --- | --- |
| systems of language | systems of language |
| availability of, and flexibility with, the reading strategies | availability of, and flexibility with, the writing strategies |
| background knowledge | background knowledge |
| purpose of reading | purpose of reading |
| ability and willingness to assimilate and/or accommodate during reading | ability and willingness to assimilate and/or accommodate during writing |

the vowel rather than the consonant because we knew that this would be less disruptive to the reading process. Once again, Wilde (1992) found that children tend to correctly spell the consonants in words and experience more difficulty with the vowels.

Now that you have a better understanding of how the perceptual process operates, we turn our attention to the reading and writing processes themselves and explore the cognitive procedures the individual engages so as to construct meaning through print. We begin with a look at the factors that impact the reader/text/writer transaction. This is followed by a theory and model of the reading process and an examination of proficient and less proficient readers and writers.

**Factors Influencing the Reader–Text–Writer Transaction**

All too often we think of reading and writing abilities in somewhat static, monolithic ways. We say, for example, that a child is reading on the "fourth-grade level" or that a child's writing is "below grade level." These grade level designations, however, obscure the fact that one's ability to read or write a particular text is impacted by a number of factors. Most of us have had experiences with students who are able to successfully read a particular story in the basal reader and the very next week struggle with another story on the same "grade level" in the same basal. Such variation is because "ability" is not something that the individual carries around in his or her head. Rather, ability is actually a dynamic relationship between reader, text, and writer. Frequently, when processing problems are experienced, all responsibility is given to only the reader or only the writer. However, because communication is a two-way process, it is necessary to examine the contributions of both individuals to any meaning making event.

As indicted in Table 2.21, this relationship is based on the correspondence between the reader's and writer's language, background knowledge, purpose, strategy availability and flexibility, and the need to assimilate and accommodate. As the correspondence of these factors between the reader and writer vary, so too will reading and writing "ability."

*The Relationship Between the Reader's Language and the Author's Language.* The relationship between the reader's language and the writer's language—systems of language—influences the ease with which the language of a text can be processed. Potentially, shared language systems can result in more effective and efficient text processing. It is important to remember, however, that a similarity in reader–writer language does not necessarily result in fewer reader miscues, only miscues that tend to be more linguistically appropriate. In fact, the number of miscues may actually increases as the reader becomes familiar with the text's language and feels comfortable translating the author's preferred way of expressing an idea to the reader's preferred way. An economist, for example, most likely finds the language used by other economists to be fairly predictable. Economists share a "language" that is used to talk about fiscal matters.

The same influence is found in writing as well. When generating a text for an audience that shares and understands the author's language, the writer need not spend inordinate amounts of time and cognitive energy selecting language forms that will be readily comprehensible to the reader. Rather, linguistic structures commonly used by the writer, and shared by the reader, can be accessed and employed with less difficulty and effort. Our economist most likely finds it easier to write to and for other economists than the general public.

*The Relationship Between the Reader's Background Knowledge and the Author's Background Knowledge.* Readers and writers bring not only their language to the printed page, but conceptual knowledge is brought as well. In general, the more the reader's and author's backgrounds parallel one another—they know similar things—the smoother the construction of meaning is likely to be. For the reader, background knowledge impacts both the quality of the miscues and how a text is ultimately understood. In school settings, this relationship between background knowledge and ease of reading can readily be seen in the use of thematic curricula. When students are first introduced to a thematic unit topic that is unfamiliar to them, they may initially experience some difficulty reading and making sense. However, as students move through the unit and become more knowledge about the topic, as well as the language used, their reading and meaning-making improves. In a sense, the ideas and language become more predictable for the students.

Similarly, for the writer, background knowledge impacts his or her ability to manipulate and translate ideas into written language. If you are writing about a personal experience, accessing and using this knowledge will be relatively easy. Both the meanings and their organization are already arranged in your mind in a time-sequenced structure. However, if the writing task calls for synthesizing information that is not already cognitively integrated, you are more likely to encounter difficulty as pen is put to paper or fingers to computer keyboard.

*The Relationship Between the Reader's Purpose and the Author's Purpose.* Language users do not initiate an engagement with a text without a reason or purpose in mind. These reasons influence the kind of relationship that a reader or writer forms with a text. Returning to our discussion of the functions of language, a reader or writer might, for instance, engage the printed word for an instrumental purpose, to satisfy or obtain material needs. Or the purpose may be to explore the environment, to ask questions and seek knowledge. These purposes have a direct and significant impact on how meaning is ultimately constructed through print.

*The Relationship Between the Reader's Strategy Availability and Flexibility and the Author's Strategy Availability and Flexibility.* Another factor that influences a reader's and writer's transaction with print is the strategies available to the language user and his or her flexibility with these strategies. Strategies are those mental processes that the individual engages so as to create meaning through written discourse. Readers and writers, for example, predict meanings based on the use of various language systems when interacting with print. As reading or writing proceeds, these anticipated meanings are monitored and evaluated in light of subsequent and future meanings. When predictions are found to lack meaning, proficient readers draw on a variety of available strategies to "repair" the gap in meaning. They have access to numerous strategies that can be used to solve the problem. Additionally, as we have already seen in our discussion of the relationship between the reader's and writer's purpose, all texts are not read or written in the same manner. Effective and efficient literacy users know how to vary their processing of print based on their purpose.

***The Relationship Between the Reader's Need to Assimilate and Accommodate and the Author's Need to Assimilate and Accommodate.*** As meaning is constructed, it is not uncommon for the reader and writer to be changed cognitively. That is, what the language user knows when the transaction with print terminates may be qualitatively and/or quantitatively different than when the transaction was initiated. Both readers and writers build knowledge through two basic processes involved in learning: assimilation and accommodation. In some instances, the meanings constructed through print fit within the knowledge structures of the reader or writer; a cognitive congruency exists between the individual and the information. Therefore, the addition of information to the individual's background results in an elaboration or extension of existing knowledge structures. The new knowledge is simply added, or assimilated, to what is already known. In this top-down process, the meanings fit within existing cognitive frameworks.

There are also instances when the information to be generated through print will not easily fit into the language user's available cognitive structures. The reader may lack the knowledge to make sense of the information presented; or the writer, through the very act of writing, may discover new meanings or insights that create disequilibrium with existing knowledge structures. In order for the information to be understood by the reader or writer, a restructuring or accommodation of what is known is required. This bottom-up process results in a modified cognitive framework from which the reader or writer is then able to assimilate the meanings under construction. In general and to varying degrees, both assimilation and accommodation occur during reading and writing.

Given the impact of language, strategies, background, purpose, and assimilation/ accommodation on reading and writing, it should be clear that all acts of literacy are not equal. Reading and writing do not consist of a set of subskills that can be easily isolated, practiced, mastered and then used with the same degree of proficiency from one text to the next. Rather, language performance changes as the relevant factors influencing the literacy processes change.

## Readers Reading

In order to better illustrate how the literacy processes operate, a model of these processes is illustrated in Fig. 2.2. At this point, the model is used to discuss the act of reading. In the next section, our focus is on writing.

As was previously addressed, even before initiated, the reading process is based on a relationship between a reader and a writer. The reader operates within a context of situation, the environment that brings the reader to the text in the first place. The situational context influences the individual's purpose for reading. In turn, the reader's purpose has a direct impact on how the print on the page is sampled. That is, readers vary their relationship with a text as their purpose varies. If the reader is looking for a specific piece of information, scanning may be initiated. In such cases, the reader ignores much of the print, focusing attention only on that information that is being sought. Skimming is employed when the reader is seeking a general understanding of the text. It is not uncommon for the morning newspaper to be skimmed when one is pressed for time before going to work. The reader's purpose is simply to get a "feel" for what has happened in the world, with the hope, perhaps, of a closer reading at the end of the day. Such a close reading is usually initiated when a fuller, more detailed understanding of a text is desired.

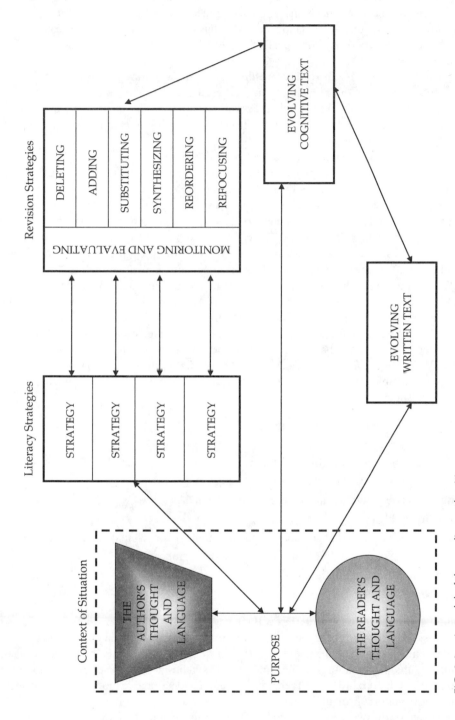

FIG. 2.2.  A model of the reading and writing processes.

If the purpose is to recall the information in a text—rather than simply to fully understand it—the reader may need to process the text several times and engage in recall attempts. School contexts frequently require students to recall what has been read on quizzes or examinations. Finally, the need to memorize will repeatedly focus the reader's attention on the surface level of the discourse.

In general, more proficient readers are flexible in the way they process a text based on their purpose. They vary their reading to fit their needs. Less proficient readers, on the other hand tend to exhibit less flexibility and process all texts in a similar manner, regardless of the purpose for the reading. Unfortunately, schools far too often fail to teach students to vary their reading behaviors based on purpose.

Based on the reader's language and background experiences, as well as the reason for reading, reading is initiated. The reader transacts with the evolving or unfolding written text—we have already discussed in some detail the impact of the text on reader perception—using various strategies to construct mental meanings or an evolving cognitive text. These strategies, represented in Table 2.22, might be understood as being similar to the tools and equipment that a carpenter uses to build a house. The carpenter employs hammers, saws, and rulers to nail, cut, and measure the wood that will form the house. Similarly, the reader samples visual information, predicts meaning, and integrates meanings into a coherent whole.

Throughout the entire process of constructing a mental understanding of the text, the reader monitors and evaluates the meanings being generated. The reader asks such questions as, "Does what I am reading make sense?" "Does it sound like language?" "Does it meet my purpose for reading this text in the first place?" To continue our carpenter analogy, it would be similar to the carpenter looking at what was being built and evaluating whether it reflected what was intended. When the answer to such questions is "no"—that is, the use of the reading strategies has not been completely successful—the reader has a number of options available (Kucer, 1995, p. 23). The reader can:

stop reading and rethink what was read,

reread previous portions of the text,

read ahead to gather more information,

read on to see if there is need to revise,

form a tentative prediction and read on to see if it makes sense

ignore the problem,

seek assistance from an outside source (e.g., dictionary, encyclopedia, another reader),

use text aids (e.g., illustrations, charts, headings and subheadings),

substitute a different meaning, or

stop reading altogether.

A number of transformations in the evolving cognitive text can occur when readers engage in the revision of meanings through rereading, reading on, and so on. Information can be deleted or removed from the mental text or new information added. Existing meanings can be substituted with other meanings or meanings can be synthesized and combined. Readers may also revise through the reordering of relationships among ideas or give more or less prominence to particular meanings through refocusing.

As reflected by the two-way arrows in Fig. 2.2, there are a number of exchanges taking place throughout the process of reading. The transactions between the reader and writer as well as the reader and the literacy and revision strategies have already been noted. Additionally, there is the relationship among the reader, evolving written text, and evolving cognitive text. Initially, the written text drives the reading process. That is, the reader is reliant on the cues laid out

TABLE 2.22
Reading Strategies and Processes

1. **Generates and organizes major ideas and concepts.** Readers understand that the ideas in a text can be ordered in terms of their significance. They know that all ideas are not of equal importance. Readers attempt to get the "big picture" and look for generalizations and concepts and their corresponding or supporting facts and details.

2. **Develops and supports generalizations and concepts with details and particulars.** Readers develop and link details and facts to major ideas and concepts. Generalizations are linked to concepts and facts; facts and concepts are linked to generalizations.

3. **Organizes or integrates meanings across the text into a logical and coherent whole.** Readers pull ideas together so that they form a unified and noncontradictory whole. Facts and details are linked to major ideas, concepts, or generalizations. Major ideas are related to supporting evidence and supporting evidence is related to major ideas.

4. **Samples and selects visual information from the available print.** Readers selectively pick up only that print that is necessary for the formulation of meaning. Word beginnings and endings, consonants, and tops of letters typically provide the most useful information. In many cases, much of the print is ignored.

5. **Uses a variety of linguistic cues.** Readers use a variety of cues or kinds of information to make meaning from what they are reading. Readers select from a range of systems of language: pragmatic, text type, text structure, genre, semantic, syntax, morphology, orthography, graphophonemic, grapheme.

6. **Uses a variety of text aids—for example, pictures, charts, graphs, subheadings.** In addition to the use of linguistic cues, readers utilize text aids. They realize that text aids have been used by authors to facilitate, extend, and organize text meanings.

7. **Uses relevant linguistic and conceptual background knowledge.** In order to generate meaning, readers make use of relevant linguistic and conceptual background knowledge. Readers bring their knowledge of their world and language to the text in order to make meaning from the print. It is through the use of this knowledge that readers are able to determine whether or not what they have read sounds like language, makes sense, and meets their purpose.

8. **Makes meaningful predictions.** Readers make meaningful predictions based on what has been previously read, the visual information sampled and selected, and their background knowledge.

9. **Monitors and evaluates the meanings generated.** Readers continually assess the meanings generated. They ask themselves: "Does this sound like language?" "Does this make sense?" "Does this meet my purpose or intention?"

10. **Revises when meaning is lost or purposes are not realized.** Readers change their predictions or meanings when they answer "no" to the questions: "Does this sound like language?" "Does this make sense?" "Does this meet my purpose or intention?"

11. **Utilizes a variety of strategies when revising.** When revision is initiated, the reader is able to utilize a variety of strategies that are appropriate to what is being read. They may: stop reading and rethink what has been read, reread previous portions of the text, read ahead to gather more information, read on to see if there is a need to revise, form a tentative prediction and read on to see if it makes sense, ignore it, seek assistance from an outside source (e.g., dictionary, encyclopedia, another reader), stop reading, use text aids, substitute a different meaning, sound it out.

12. **Generates inferences or goes beyond the information given.** Writers do not make all meanings explicit in their texts. Rather, they expect readers to be able to go beyond the information given and make unstated connections on their own. Readers generate inferences by building links between their prior knowledge and the information generated from the text.

13. **Reflects on, and responds and reacts to, what is being read.** Reading is an affective as well as a cognitive process. Meanings generated elicit personal reflections, responses, and reactions from the reader. The reader argues, affirms, talks to, laughs, or cries at the meanings that the author is conveying.

14. **Varies the manner in which texts are read based on different purposes.** Readers do not process all texts in the same way. Rather, they vary their reading depending on their purposes, such as to locate specific details, to find the general idea of the text, to understand the entire text, to remember the text, to memorize the text. How a recipe is read to discover what ingredients need to be purchased differs from the reading of a mystery for enjoyment, and both differ from how one reads directions to assemble a bicycle.

by the author to construct an interpretation of the text. However, once the reader begins to develop an initial and tentative understanding—evolving cognitive text—of the written discourse, this understanding begins to impact the reader's transaction with the text. The reader is better able to predict or anticipate both the language and the meanings to be encountered based on what has been previously read. In effect, the reader's background knowledge has been changed by the text already processed and the subsequent text becomes more predictable.

## Biliterate Readers

Reading in two languages is becoming an increasingly common phenomenon in the United States. Regardless of where teachers work, they are encountering students who are bilingual as well as biliterate. Biliterate students are not engaged in altogether different processes when reading in two languages. However, there are a number of factors that are unique to this population, and understanding how these factors impact the reading process can help teachers promote the literacy development of bilingual students in their classrooms.

By its very nature, the bilingual population is extremely varied. Bernhardt (2000) noted that second language reading is "a diverse, complicated, and frustrating landscape to traverse, let alone explain or predict" (p. 791). This variation manifests itself in such things as whether or not students first learn to read in their home language (other than English) and then learn to read in the language of the school (English) or whether they first learn to read in English and only later learn the written form of their home language. There is also the issue of whether their home language is maintained at school as the English language is introduced or if the school language becomes a substitute for the home language. Additionally, the degree of oral proficiency in both the first and second language impacts the literacy processes. According to Bernhardt, two critical variables in second language literacy are the degree to which the first language has been developed in oral and written form as well as the linguistic similarity between the two languages.

To address all the possible variations, unfortunately, is beyond the scope of this chapter. The focus here is on comparing and contrasting the cognitive processes used when individuals are proficient readers—efficient and effective—in their home (first) language and in the English (second) language. However, because of the varied circumstances and experiences encountered by bilingual students, care needs to be taken not to overgeneralize the findings from the biliteracy research.

In general, there is a positive and supportive relationship between the processes and strategies used in the first and second languages (Allen, 1991; Buck, 1977; Carrasquillo, Kucer, & Abrams, 2004; Fitzgerald, 1995; Jimenez, Garcia, & Pearson, 1995, 1996; Weber, 1996). Individuals who are proficient in two written language systems are frequently able to successfully employ strategies used in the first language for use in the second language. In both languages, readers monitor their processing through such metacognitive procedures as evaluating, revising (e.g., rereading, reading on, substituting), and predicting upcoming meanings and structures. Biliterates make inferences, draw conclusions, and ask questions. In English as well as in the home language, readers draw on their background knowledge of content and the systems of language to make sense of the ideas being encountered. Vocabulary items that are similar in both languages—cognates—such as the Spanish word "producto" for the English word "product" are also relied on in the making of meaning. Except for the use of cognates, proficient biliterate readers employ the same basic strategies discussed in Table 2.22.

Interestingly, not only do biliterates employ similar strategies in the two languages, but they frequently have a unitary view of reading. According to Jimenez and colleagues (1996), biliterate students typically discuss their reading processes and learning to read in a first and second language as two sides of the same coin. As stated by one student in their research, "There aren't really any differences [between reading in English and Spanish]; I mean they're both based on the same thing, how you understand it, how you read it, how you take it, and how you evaluate it and all that" (p. 99). Others have made similar observations (e.g., Cummins, 1988, 1991; Freeman & Freeman, 1994).

There are similarities in reading in two languages, but some consistent differences are also evident. Biliterates may translate—code switch—from one language to the other, and this translation occurs in both directions. Occasionally, miscues made in English can be attributed to the use of syntactic knowledge of the first language. The reader may predict a word order that reflects the language with which the reader is most comfortable. This is especially the case when the reader has a strong spoken command of the first language and less of a command of the second. However, as readers develop oral proficiency in the second language, they typically develop increased reading fluency in the second language as well (Bernhardt, 2000).

Although readers successfully employ a wealth of available strategies when reading in both languages, the extent to which monitoring and revision strategies are necessary may vary. It is not uncommon for biliterates to encounter unknown vocabulary more frequently than monolinguals. Like proficient monolinguals, proficient biliterate readers are able to apply various strategies to determine the meanings of these words. However, the repeated need to engage these revision strategies may impact the degree to which the reader is able to comprehend the text. The cognitive energy required to make such repairs may limit the attention the reader is able to apply to understanding the overall meanings of the text. This is in contrast to monolingual readers who typically encounter fewer unknown words and therefore may find it less necessary to engage in revision.

The need for additional monitoring and revision is not language specific, however. The content and structure of the text, as well as opportunities to read in the language under consideration, determine the need to monitor and repair, not whether the text is in the reader's first or second language. It is not uncommon for the biliterate reader's first oral and written language to be one other than English. However, if the school setting does not honor and maintain the reader's home language, and if academic subjects are encountered largely in English, monitoring and repair may be more frequent in the child's home language than in English.

Interestingly, in her review of the research on biliterates, Fitzgerald (1995) found that regardless of the language being read, unfamiliar content had a more significant impact on the biliterate reader than unfamiliar text structure. Weber (1996), Allen (1991), and K. Goodman and Y. Goodman (1978) reported similar findings concerning the relationship between background and linguistic knowledge more generally. As previously noted, background knowledge tends to "trump" or have a dominating influence on the reading process. More importantly, Weber also found that it was through direct experience with the concepts at hand, rather than simply through the introduction of vocabulary words, that biliterate readers can be provided with the necessary background knowledge to effectively process the English written discourse.

Similar patterns are found when proficient bilingual students reading in English are compared and contrasted with proficient monolingual students reading in English. Both groups engage metacognitive strategies and monitor for meaning. They generate inferences, recall superordinate ideas, and focus more on content than on function words. At times, however, the bilingual readers did not use context as effectively as monolingual readers and monitored their comprehension more slowly. These differences, however, may be developmental; that is, with time and experience, the bilingual students will come to use context as effectively as the monolingual readers. More importantly, they will be proficient in reading two languages rather than one.

**TABLE 2.23**

Pat

1. Pat slowly got up from the mat, planning the escape. Pat hesitated a moment and thought. Things were not going well.

2. What was most bothersome was being held, especially since the charge had been weak. Pat considered the present situation.

3. Pat was aware that it was because of the early roughness that the penalty had been so severe—much too severe from Pat's point of view. The situation was becoming frustrating; the pressure had been grinding for too long. Pat was being ridden unmercifully.

4. Pat was getting angry now and felt it was time to make the move. Success or failure would depend on what Pat did in the next few seconds.

## Readers Comprehending

In this section, we shift from a focus on the reading process to that of comprehension. The goal of any reader is to understand the text being encountered, and there are a number of principles that impact how a text is understood. Once again, you will be engaged in a series of demonstrations to help you more fully discern what is involved in the process of constructing meaning when the reader puts eye to print.

In Table 2.23, a short story about a character named Pat is presented in four parts. This story has been adapted from Anderson, Reynolds, Schallert, and Goetz (1977). Divide the left-hand side of a piece of paper into four sections, numbered from one to four. Cover all but the first part of the text, read the first part, and then write a one- or two-sentence interpretation for what is happening. Support your interpretation using information from the story. Uncover and read the second part. Does your initial understanding still make sense? If it does, support it with additional information from the story. If your interpretation no longer is viable, generate and support a new one. Using this procedure, continue throughout the four parts of the story.

If your responses are like those of other readers', you discovered a number of things about the process of comprehending. One facet of comprehension is that the prior experiences of the reader, sometimes called *schemata,* exert a powerful influence on how a text is understood Kintsch, 1998; Smith, 2004; Weaver, 2002). In fact, Rumelhart (1980) called schemata "the building blocks of cognition" (p. 33). Simply defined, schemata are complex structures of information that represent the individual's past encounters with the world. They contain the reader's knowledge of objects, situations, and events, as well as knowledge of processes, such as reading, washing clothes, or home buying.

One viable interpretation for the text is that Pat is a wrestler involved in a wrestling match. Many individuals who never considered this interpretation have little knowledge of this sport. For these readers, wrestling was never an option. One of the more interesting interpretations we have encountered had Pat as a horse who was being "broken" for riding. Although we had used the text numerous times, this interpretation was a first. To support this interpretation, many readers stated that they had grown up on ranches and breaking horses was a common event in such contexts. When one considers that one of us was teaching at the University of Wyoming, the students' response is not all that surprising.

In reading Pat, you probably also made a number of changes to your predictions as you encountered new information. A critical aspect of the comprehending process is that the building of meaning is predictive and hypothetical, and involves constant monitoring and updating. The reader is building a world of meaning partially based on the print encountered. The reader, therefore, must be sensitive to subsequent meanings that may require

## TABLE 2.24

### The Procedure

The procedure is actually quite simple. First you arrange things into different groups. Of course, one pile may be sufficient depending on how much there is to do. If you have to go somewhere else due to a lack of facilities, that is the next step, otherwise, you are pretty well set. It is important not to overdo things. That is, it is better to do too few things at once than too many. In the short run this may not seem important, but complications can easily arise. A mistake can be expensive as well. At first, the whole procedure will seem complicated. Soon, however, it will become just another facet of life. It is difficult to foresee any end to the necessity for this task in the immediate future, but then one never can tell. After the procedure is completed, one arranges the materials into different groups again. Then they can be put into their appropriate places. Eventually, they will be used once more and the whole cycle will then have to be repeated. However, that is part of life.

modification—accommodation—of this world. Readers must be flexible in their interpretations and allow new information to impact their tentative understandings.

Steffensen, Joag-Dev, and Anderson (1979) have investigated the impact of such cultural experiences on comprehension. Individuals from the United States and India read and recalled two passages, one about an American wedding, the other about an Indian wedding. According to the authors, there are significant differences between American and Indian matrimonial costumes. Traditionally, American weddings provide the occasion for an elaborate ritual and highlight the bride's family. In contrast, Indian weddings involve issues of social status and financial interests and the groom's family is dominant. The researchers discovered that when a cultural congruence existed between the individual and the text, readers read more rapidly, recalled greater amounts of information, produced more culturally appropriate elaborations, and generated fewer culturally based distortions.

In the Pat demonstration, the content of background knowledge has been the primary focus. However, there are additional dimensions of knowledge, such as organization, that also impact comprehension. Anderson, Spiro, and Anderson (1978) investigated the effect of organization in a study in which individuals were given two stories to read. One story was about dining at a restaurant, the second concerned grocery shopping. When asked to give an unaided recall after each story was read, readers did far better in the restaurant story. Not only did they remember more of the content, but they also maintained the order of what was eaten and drunk. Interestingly, the same food and drink was mentioned in both stories. However, because most individuals have what the researchers term a "more articulated"—that is, more organized—script for restaurants than grocery stores, they were better able to recall the restaurant story.

Now that you have discovered a number of principles that govern comprehension, read the story contained in Table 2.24 (Bransford & Johnson, 1973). When you finish reading, write a one- or two-sentence interpretation as to what the story is about.

Most readers finish the text knowing little more than when they started. Not only do they have difficulty remembering all of the steps in what is perceived as a rather complicated procedure, they also fail to recognize the procedure itself. In the previous demonstration, the nature of the reader's background played a critical role in how Pat was understood. In this demonstration, many readers initially believe it is a lack of background knowledge similar to that of the writer that is causing them difficulty. However, this is actually an example of the reader having the appropriate background—for example, clothes washing—but being incapable of using it. The author fails to provide the necessary cues for the reader to access the suitable knowledge. Therefore, if comprehension is to occur, writers must help readers link their prior experiences and the ideas in the text.

Although only a demonstration, the difficulty you may have experienced in comprehending the procedure story is all too common for our students (Rumelhart, 1984). This is especially true when they read in the content areas. Writers of social science and science texts may fail to help students build a relationship between what they know and the information being presented. Dewey (1938) believed this occurred because schools taught information in an isolated manner, which made it difficult for students to connect ideas to one another and to what they already knew.

## Writers Writing

As illustrated in Fig. 2.2, the process of writing is also impacted by the relationship between the writer and the reader. The writer operates within a context of situation that influences the individual's purpose for writing. The author's purpose and the audience for whom the text is written are ultimately reflected in both the author's use of language and the content presented. The more that the author and reader share the same purpose, language, and background knowledge, the smoother the process of writing.

Based on the writer's purpose and audience, composing is initiated. The writer searches his or her background knowledge for information relevant to the communicative context. This search is not a one-time event, but rather continues throughout the entire process of writing. Through the use of the various strategies represented in Table 2.25, this information is transformed into an evolving cognitive text as well as evolving written text. The cognitive text represents those mental meanings that the writer has constructed from his or her background knowledge. The written text, as the name suggests, is the set of cognitive meanings that the writer has attempted to make visible through print, the marks on the page.

As indicated in the reading/writing model shown in Fig. 2.2, there is an interplay between cognitive and written texts. As the writer attempts to find the appropriate language for his or her meanings, new ideas or insights may be discovered. This in turn may result in modifications to the mental text and ultimately in the expressed written text. Similarly, as the writer ponders the meanings that have been made visible in language, the need for revisions may be discovered. Therefore, a dynamic two-way relationship exists between visible and mental texts. Writing is not simply a think it → say it process.

Throughout the entire process of constructing a mental and written text, the writer monitors and evaluates the meanings being generated. The writer asks: "Does what I am writing make sense?" "Does it sound like language?" "Does it meet my purpose for writing this text in the first place?" When the answer to such questions is "no," the writer engages in revision strategies. These revisions may be to the mental text, the written text, or both. Similar to the reader, the writer also has a number of options from which to select (Kucer, 1995, p. 23). The writer can:

brainstorm possible ideas or alternatives,

reread what has been written so far,

skip to a part of the text where the writer knows what is to be written and return later,

write it as best as possible and return later,

write it several different ways and select the best one,

write whatever comes to mind,

talk about it with a friend,

read other texts to get some ideas, or

stop writing for a while and come back later.

**TABLE 2.25**

Writing Strategies and Processes

1. **Generates and organizes generalizations and concepts.** Writers give attention to the major ideas that they want to convey. Generalizations and concepts are developed and organized. This does not mean that the major ideas are necessarily known before writing is initiated, just that the writer is constantly attempting to discover a larger framework into which meanings can be arranged.

2. **Expands, extends, and elaborates generalizations and concepts.** Writers fully develop their major ideas through supporting details. Generalizations and concepts are elaborated upon and extended so that they are understandable to the reader.

3. **Organizes or integrates meanings across the text into a logical and coherent whole.** Writers pull ideas together so that they form a unified and noncontradictory whole. Facts and details are linked to major ideas, concepts, or generalizations. Major ideas are related to supporting evidence and supporting evidence is related to major ideas.

4. **Uses a variety of linguistic cues.** Writers use a variety of systems of language through which to express their ideas. They know that their texts must conform to the established rules for the various systems: pragmatic, text type, text structure, genre, semantic, syntax, morphology, orthography, graphophonemic, grapheme.

5. **Uses a variety of text aids—for example, pictures, charts, graphs, subheadings—to mark their meanings.** In addition to the use of linguistic cues, writers utilize text aids to facilitate, extend, and organize text meanings.

6. **Uses relevant linguistic and conceptual background knowledge.** In order to generate meaning, writers make use of relevant linguistic and conceptual background knowledge. Writers bring their knowledge of their world and language to the text in order to make meaning through print. It is through the use of this knowledge that writers are able to determine whether or not what they have written sounds like language, makes sense, and meets their purpose.

7. **Predicts/plans future meanings based on what has been written.** Writers anticipate upcoming meanings based on their purpose, what has been written, and their background knowledge. Previous meanings both support and constrain future meanings.

8. **Monitors and evaluates the meanings generated.** Writers continually assess the meanings generated. They ask themselves: "Does this sound like language?" "Does this make sense?" "Does this meet my purpose or intention?"

9. **Revises when meaning is lost or purposes are not realized.** Writers change their predictions or meanings when they answer "no" to the questions: "Does this sound like language?" "Does this make sense?" "Does this meet my purpose or intention?"

10. **Utilizes a variety of strategies when revising.** When revision is initiated, the writer utilizes a variety of strategies that are appropriate to what is being written. Information may be deleted, added, or substituted. Ideas may be synthesized or reordered. Or, information may be refocused so as to highlight particular ideas over others.

11. **Uses a variety of strategies when encountering "blocks."** Writers utilize various strategies when they do not know what to write next or have difficulty expressing an idea. They may: brainstorm possible ideas and jot them down, reread what has been written, skip to a part that they know what will be written and return later, write it as best they can and return later, write it several different ways, write whatever comes to mind, talk it over with someone, read other texts to get ideas, or stop writing and return later.

12. **Uses writing to explore ideas and to discover new meanings.** Writers explore their ideas and discover new meanings when they interact with print. Rather than simply writing what is already known, they use writing to investigate their thoughts and come to understand what was not previously understood.

13. **Reflects on, and responds and reacts to, what is being written.** Writing is an affective as well as a cognitive process. Meanings generated elicit personal reflections, responses, and reactions from the writer. The writer argues, affirms, talks to, laughs, or cries at the meanings being conveyed.

*(Continued)*

**TABLE 2.25 (*Continued*)**

| | |
|---|---|
| 14. **Varies the manner in which texts are written based on different purposes, intentions, or audiences.** Writers do not process all texts in the same way. Rather, writers vary their writing so as to meet their needs, such as to remember particular information, to update a friend about a personal experience, or to share ideas with an audience that is not personally known. How a shopping list is written varies from that of a friendly letter, and both differ from a newspaper article. | 15. **Revises conventions—spelling, punctuation, capitalization, penmanship—after meanings and purpose are met.** Writers are not unconcerned with the surface structure of their texts. However, they usually wait until meanings and purposes have been met before conventions become the focus. Because revisions to meanings frequently result in the changing of words, sentences, and paragraphs, it usually is not worth the writer's time and energy to be overly concerned with conventions too early in the process. |

Revisions to the mental or written text can result in a number of modifications. Information can be deleted or new information added. Existing meanings can be substituted with other meanings or meanings can be synthesized and combined. Writers may also revise through the reordering of relationships among ideas or give more or less prominence to particular meanings through refocusing.

## THE SOCIOCULTURAL DIMENSION: THE READER AND WRITER AS TEXT USER AND TEXT CRITIC

The sociocultural dimension of literacy shifts our attention from the text and the mind to that of literacy events and literacy practices. A literacy event is any human action that involves the use of print (Harste, Woodward, & Burke, 1984; Heath, 1983). Literacy practices are recurring or patterned literacy events within a particular community or social group (Reder, 1994; Scribner & Cole, 1981). Literacy, therefore, is not simply an individual act of language and cognition; it also represents patterned social acts or behaviors of the group. Literacy occurs not simply because an individual possesses and applies the necessary linguistic and cognitive strategies and processes, but also because group membership requires it (Devine, 1994). The way in which literacy is used by the participants within a particular social configuration—that is, literacy practices—reflects the very nature of the group and the group's position within the society. Our interest, therefore, is to examine (1) the nature of literacy events and practices used by various social groups to mediate their interactions with the world and (2) how various social groups use literacy to produce, consume, maintain, and control knowledge.

### The Nature of Literacy Events and Literacy Practices

By our very nature, we are social beings; or, as Vygotsky (1978) observed, our minds are embedded within society. Inherent in our "beingness" is membership in various social groups. Smith (1988) refers to such membership as belonging to clubs. We all belong, for example, to cultural, socioeconomic, linguistic, gender, and family groups. We may be part of religious organizations and possibly hold membership in various psychological groups, such as being a jock, brain, or even a New Yorker. According to Ferdman (1990), our social identity consists of the totality of the various groups in which we hold membership.

Each social group or community has its own set of guidelines for what is required to be a member in good standing. Put another way, membership has its price as well as its privileges.

The group attempts to socialize—directly or indirectly, consciously or unconsciously—the individual into thinking and behaving in particular ways, ways that are appropriate to the group's view of itself. These guidelines impact the individual's beliefs and behaviors, and frame his or her interpretations of, and interactions with, others. The knowledge, values, and behaviors that an individual comes to reflect, therefore, are not simply the products of his or her own independent psychological interactions with the world. They also are the products of interactions and experiences with the various and significant social groups of which the individual is a member, as well as the groups' interactions and experiences with other groups in the world.

Because the individual belongs to a number of social groups, he or she typically has multiple frameworks for behaving and for constructing and understanding experiences. Madison Avenue advertisers have long known about such group identification. Their various "ad campaigns" oftentimes are focused on selling products and services to particular groups. Similarly, the television corporation Lifetime labels itself as "the station for women" and programs its shows accordingly. Interestingly, it is these very attempts at "selling" to particular groups that can also, in turn, mold the actual identities of these groups. These cultural texts both reflect as well as create cultural norms.

It is important to remember that group ideologies may not be conscious or always explicitly stated to and by its members. In fact, it is just this lack of explicitness that makes these social frameworks and group norms so powerful; oftentimes the group's members are unaware of the source for their beliefs and behaviors. This is especially the case when the individual belongs to the society's dominant groups. Because the beliefs of dominant groups so permeate the society, and because the individual may so seldom encounter alternate perspectives, he or she may come to view these beliefs as not socially constructed, but rather as normative or universal.

The values of any particular group do not, however, impact the individual's beliefs and behaviors in a straightforward, unilinear manner. Nor are group values necessarily deterministic. The framework(s) employed for transacting with or understanding any event is (are) influenced by the event itself, the context in which the event evolves, and the framework(s) privileged or favored by the individual within a particular setting. For example, an Eastern European–American Catholic woman belongs to at least the following groups: cultural (Slavic American), gender (female), religious (Catholic), and national (United States). Her views on such issues as abortion, state funding of religious schools, or the use of armed interventions by the United States in European conflicts may require her to privilege particular beliefs over others when there is a lack of congruence among group ideologies.

Identity, therefore, is dynamic, oftentimes context-specific in nature, and constituted by numerous "fuzzy borders" between and among the various social groups in which the individual has membership (Hoffman, 1996). As observed by McDermott (1995), identities are hammered out on a daily and ongoing basis as the individual encounters the world. Identities and their corresponding behaviors are not predetermined but rather are actively constructed in social relationships (Buckingham & Sefton-Green, 1994). Similarly, not all individuals within a social group are identical in their beliefs and actions. No community is a monolith and its members will differ to varying degrees in beliefs and actions. And, because no community is an island unto itself, any individual may hold membership in numerous clubs; at times there will be competition among the beliefs of these various social configurations.

Finally, social groups themselves are dynamic and evolving in nature. As any group's experiences with the world changes, so too may the group's understanding of itself and the world. In fact, the way any nondominant group is perceived and acted on by the dominant group, and the way the nondominant group has come to deal with such perceptions and behaviors, becomes part of the understandings of both groups (Reder, 1994). In most cases, therefore,

TABLE 2.26

Types and Uses of Literacy

| Type | Definition | Examples |
|------|-----------|----------|
| Daily Living | Literacy activities that relate to ordinary family life, including obtaining food, maintaining shelter and health, finances, shopping, paying bills, care of the children. | Shopping lists, bills and checks, budgets |
| Entertainment or Recreational | Literacy activities that relate to passing the time in an enjoyable or interesting manner. | Television guides, theater listings and reviews, magazines, newspapers, books |
| Spiritual | Literacy activities related to worship or metaphysical endeavors. | Hymnals, bulletins and newsletters, scripture reading, order of the service guidelines |
| Work related | Literacy activities related to one's place of employment. | Office memorandums, order forms, applications |
| Social-interactional | Literacy activities related to written communication with friends or relatives; literacy used to build and maintain social relationships. | Friendly letters, e-mail, greeting cards |
| Educational | Literacy activities related to increasing one's knowledge. | Textbooks, reports and papers, "how to" materials, school forms |
| News related | Literacy activities to gain information about local, state, regional, national, or world events or third parties. | Newspapers and news magazines, flyers and bulletins |
| Archival related | Literacy activities related to materials that are saved and referred to when necessary. | Report cards, birth certificates, paid bills, insurance policies, telephone numbers, leases |

group identification provides an orienting framework for the individual's beliefs and behaviors, not a straitjacket.

Literacy practices are one expression of the knowledge, values, and behaviors of any group. Each group "has rules for socially interacting and sharing knowledge in literacy events" (Heath, 1982b, p. 50). The literacy practices of any individual may reflect group norms and values. That is, the literacy behaviors of the individual express the literacy practices of the various social groups to which the individual is a member. Luke (1995, 1998), in fact, argued that there are no private acts of literacy, only social ones. Literacy, therefore, becomes a vehicle to learn about group characteristics.

Literacy as a social practice has received increased attention during the last decade. This attention has focused on both the function (purposes) and form (linguistic characteristics) of group literacy activity. Table 2.26 contains a list of typical reoccurring literacy practices that have been found in a number of studies (e.g., Anderson & Stokes, 1984; Heath, 1983; Taylor & Dorsey-Gaines, 1988). Although the literacy practices of a number of different social configurations have been explored, cultural groups have received special attention. Culture is a particularly powerful social framework and can significantly impact the nature of other social groups, such as gender and religious. Educational groups or institutions—for example, schools—have received attention as well. Schools are a primary site for literacy sponsorship in American society. Both adults and children expect that literacy will be formally taught and sustained throughout the students' academic careers. As a primary sponsor of literacy within society, the relationship between the function and form of school literacy events to the function and form of nonschool literacy events, especially in the home, has been of special interest. It is an understanding of this intersection between home and school that holds the most promise for those of us interested in promoting literacy development among all students.

Like any institution, schools have specific rules or norms for how language is to be used and how texts are to be formed. These rules and forms may affirm, build on, and extend the way in which language is used in the child's home, may require adaptation in language rules and forms, or may directly contradict home language patterns (Heath, 1983; Scollon & Scollon, 1981). A common as well as privileged school literacy form is that of the essay. Like all texts, there are specific characteristics that this type of discourse must fulfill and display. In school-based essays meanings are stated in a direct, overt, and unambiguous manner. Typically, these texts are constructed as if there is no shared knowledge between reader and writer. This is the case even when the writer is fully aware that the reader is knowledgeable. In other contexts, such explicitness would, at best, be considered insensitive and rude and, at worst, condescending and arrogant (Gee, 1996).

The explicitness of meanings within essays reflects the fixed boundary between the reader and the writer often found in school-based literacy events. The writer is expected to construct a coherent text that exists as an entity independent from the reader. In the monologic structure of such essays, meanings are decontextualized in that they are to stand on their own, without support from the immediate environment. In what Moss (1994) termed radical individualism, essay texts are processed individually and independently; that is, the reader is expected to construct text meanings without assistance.

Finally, there is oftentimes the belief that essays by their very nature transcend social and cultural differences. Essays are to present their claims in a logical, rational, and dispassionate manner. This separation of text from culture is thought to require as well as promote abstract, logical, and decontextualized thinking. Those cultures without literacy or those communities who value other discourse forms may be perceived as having less civilized thinking. Once again, the form and function of literacy of dominant groups becomes linked with superior forms of thinking.

School-based discourse has not only a particular structure and content, but also rules for how students are to interact with such discourse. This is especially true in the early grades when the classroom is highly focused on initial literacy teaching and learning. A central feature in classroom lessons is the initiation-reply-evaluation (IRE) sequence. As documented by Cazden (1988) and Heath (1983), the teacher initiates the IRE sequence by asking a question. In contrast to authentic questions, it is clear to all involved that the teacher knows the answers to the questions being asked. A student is then identified to respond or reply to the question and the teacher explicitly evaluates the adequacy of the response. Again, in contexts other than the classroom, it would be considered inappropriate for a questioner to openly evaluate the acceptability of a provided answer.

As well as norms for school texts and lessons, there are also rules for what text meanings are to be the focus of attention within the IRE lesson sequence. In the early grades, much attention is given to the asking and answering of what questions, for example, What did the boy do after he planted the seed? Selective attention is given to the segmentation of items and meanings in the text as they are discussed and analyzed. Students are expected to listen as an audience to the questions and answers and then to respond and display what they know when called on. This display of knowledge, however, may be limited to the factual meanings in the text that the teacher has solicited; the incorporation of nonschool experiences into the answers is oftentimes discouraged.

Regardless of their cultural identity or socioeconomic status, most children in the United States enter school having encountered numerous literacy events within the home. Few children are initiated into the schooling experience without some knowledge of literacy. The nature of these events and the degree to which the children have directly participated in them, however, may vary. That is, there may not be a one-to-one correspondence between the form and function of literacy used in the home and that found in the classroom setting. Heath (1982, 1983) examined language use in three different settings in the southeastern United States: Maintown, Roadville, and Trackton. Maintown was a mainstream, middle-class, school-oriented community. Both African Americans and European Americans resided in Maintown. Roadville was a European American, working-class mill community and Trackton an African American, working-class mill community.

In terms of school literacy development and school success, there were distinct differences among these three groups. The Maintown children were the most successful, whereas the Roadville children performed well in the primary grades and then began to fall behind during the intermediate years. The Trackton children experienced failure almost from the very beginning.

The reason for the differential impact of school instruction on literacy growth can be found, according to Heath (1982, 1983), in the "ways with words" in the home settings. To a large extent, the manner in which literacy was used in Maintown homes paralleled that found in the school. In this case, school literacy lessons built directly on the home literacy events experienced by the child. For example, in Maintown homes, the mother and child book-reading episodes displayed the initiation-reply-evaluation sequence found in school lessons. The adult typically asked "what" questions, focused on and labeled individual items in the illustrations with attention to particular features, and insisted that the child display the facts known about the text. Throughout the reading, the adult engaged in a running commentary on past and current meanings. Given these experiences, the children from Maintown came to school already knowing how to interact with print in a way that the school would value. In effect, the children had been socialized at home to interact with language in a manner that paralleled that of the school.

Many of the home literacy events encountered by the Roadville children were similar to those of Maintown. This was particularly the case with the frequent use of "what" questions. Parents in this community saw their role as teaching their children to talk, and during initial book-reading experiences focused on such conventions as letters, numbers, and the names of items pictured in the book. Children were encouraged to engage with the books through questions that focused on these conventions and items and to display their knowledge by "doing it right." The adults did not, however, as was done in Maintown, provide a running commentary of responses as they read to the children. At around $3\frac{1}{2}$ years of age, the orientation changed. At this point, the children were restrained from responding. Instead, adults insisted that the children sit and listen quietly as the adults read the story to them. It was not expected that the child was able to contribute knowledge to the literacy event or to link the event to other aspects of the environment.

For the Trackton children, home literacy events were the most distant from literacy events within the school. In general, there was a lack of books or book-based items or games within the home. The adults tended not to read to or with their children. The children in these homes learned to tell stories by creating a context and inviting the audience to participate. The structure of these stories were vastly different from those found in schools. There was an absence of formulaic beginnings—once upon a time—and endings were open ended. Stories did not conclude until the audience shifted its attention to something or someone else. Consequently, the teller of the story was required to be assertive in gaining the floor and then, in order to maintain their attention and involvement, required to invite the audience to respond and evaluate the unfolding story.

As Trackton adults interacted with their children, they also tended not to segment or high-light aspects of the environment through such behaviors as pointing, labeling, or asking "what" questions. Adults did not request or demonstrate the features that were used or shared when comparing one item or event to another. This resulted in children who were able to make comparisons, but who were not capable of specifying the features on which such compar-isons were grounded. And, rather than requesting the child to decontextualize meanings, the meanings were heavily contextualized.

On entering school, the Trackton children immediately encountered unfamiliar types of questions and demands on their behaviors. They were requested to respond to "what" ques-tions, to isolate and identify items, to label features, and in general to respond to an array of questions about what has been read. Without explicit instruction for how these new linguis-tic and content demands were to be met, the children failed to learn the social interactional rules and the content under consideration. It was not uncommon for the Trackton students to link book events with their personal experiences and to provide affective responses. However, these links and responses were not always requested nor valued during early literacy instruc-tion. Such responses were viewed as being "off track." The Trackton students were, there-fore, out of sync from the first day as school language use directly contradicted that of their homes.

In their work with Athabaskans, Native Americans living in Northern Canada and Alaska, Scollon and Scollon (1981) found similar conflicts between home and school discourse patterns. Athabaskans tend not to express their views on a topic unless they first are aware of the views of their audience. Children are not to display knowledge to adults but rather to observe and learn from their superiors. In typical school literacy lessons, however, children are frequently requested and expected to display their knowledge and views. This expectation runs counter to cultural and discourse rules of Athabaskan children. Their response in such situations of-tentimes is to remain silent. In a sense, these children cannot successfully participate in such lessons unless they take on norms and values that are in direct conflict with their own and their families' culture. Learning school literacy becomes possible only by unlearning the home culture.

It is important to note that the forms and functions of the written discourse in these various communities are not deficient in nature. Rather, they simply reflect different rules and norms for the use of written texts in particular contexts by particular discourse communities. It is critical that teachers are sensitive to the ways of knowing about literacy that children do bring with them into the classroom. Ultimately, it is on these ways that teachers will build new literacy learnings and understandings. Rather than valuing middle-class literacy norms as cultural capital and all other norms as insufficient or even as barriers to literacy development, teachers must value and extend literacy forms and functions in all of the children.

Additionally, care should be taken not to automatically assume that children of color or from low-income communities will automatically reflect nonschool literacy norms. This may or may not be the case. In an interesting examination of literacy use among 20 poor, inner-city families, Purcell-Gates et al. (1995, 1996) found great variation. The families represented a range of ethnicities—European American, African American, Latin American, Asian American—as well as a range of literacy use and frequency. In the homes that Purcell-Gates labeled high-literacy families, literacy use permeated the lives of the participants. Print material, such as storybooks, religious materials, and newspapers, abounded. Literacy was not only used for entertainment, but also involved storybook reading between parent and child and the direct teaching of literacy conventions. In contrast, there was a tendency among low-literacy families to use literacy for entertainment—usually related to television viewing—and daily living—such as reading ingredients for a recipe. When storybooks and writing materials were available, they were seldom utilized. On average, the low-literacy families engaged in literacy once every

3 hours. This is in contrast to $2\frac{1}{2}$ literacy events per hour for the high-literacy families. In total, the high-literacy families engaged in literacy nearly eight times more often than the low-literacy families. In conclusion, Purcell-Gates et al. (1995) argued that socioeconomics is not a very reliable variable on which to predict home literacy use or preschooler literacy preparation.

As clearly documented, literacy is intimately woven into the very fabric of daily life in most communities within the United States. The relationship between home and community literacy use, however, may vary. These literacy learning examples also serve as a much needed reminder that there are many paths to becoming literate in our society. Middle-class norms for reading and writing may, in fact, reflect the literacy norms found in many schools. They are not, however, the only route to becoming a reader and writer. Teachers must be cognizant of this fact when they are tempted to lament the "poor preparation" for school that they perceive in certain of their students. Most parents and children, regardless of their backgrounds, expect that schools will build on and extend student abilities. Teachers must be willing to seek out and affirm the aptitudes of their children if such continuity is to occur.

### Literacy, Power, and Knowledge

The reader may be wondering what an exploration of power and knowledge has to do with literacy instruction. Literacy curricula, it might be argued, are focused on helping students learn to generate meanings from written discourse. This involves the development of various linguistic and cognitive strategies for successfully interacting with text. In this view, educational methods or techniques become the key to helping students unlock the meanings underlying the printed page. However, from a critical and sociocultural perspective, the very nature of the texts encountered, and the understandings that children construct through interacting with the texts made available, significantly impact both literacy and concept development. As will be discovered, the texts used in classrooms are the product of power relationships within the society. Texts and their use are sponsored by particular groups representing particular ideologies (Bigelow & Peterson, 1998; Brandt, 1990, 1998; Buckingham & Sefton-Green, 1994; Pennycook, 2001).

Additionally, the background knowledge applied to the text by the reader not only represents idiosyncratic, particularistic experiences. Rather, background knowledge also reflects the beliefs, ideologies, and experiences of groups to which the individual is a member. Gender, ethnicity, and socioeconomic status, for example, all influence the reader's interpretation of any piece of written discourse. Finally, the interpretation of the text is directly and explicitly taught by the sponsors—other groups—of literacy learning. In the classroom, significant literacy sponsors are teachers, publishers, state standards, evaluative instruments such as standardized tests, and administrators who hire and fire teachers.

This is not to say that the participants in literacy teaching and learning are always or even usually aware of the ways in which knowledge is conceived and texts interpreted. Rarely, in fact, is the positioning of reader, text, and writer made explicit in the classroom setting. This, of course, makes the entire enterprise all the more problematic because participants are largely not cognizant of their contributions to the construction of stance, interpretation, and knowledge. Our purpose here is to uncover the ideologies that undergird texts and literacy sponsorship and the knowledge that results from sponsorship.

***The Nature of Knowledge.*** Recently, much media attention has been given to the so called culture wars that are emerging around particular issues. These "wars" are centered on sites where there is a struggle for dominance among conflicting ideologies. Participants, as members of specific groups, vie over whose views and meanings are to find representation and therefore validation in the marketplace of ideas. On a national level, the skirmish over whose voices are to be heard within the setting of the classroom was recently played out with the development of Standards for U.S. History. Commissioned by Congress, the history standards guide was to set parameters for both what was to be taught and how in Grades 5 through 12. The initial guide was especially sensitive of the role of women and people of color in the development of the United States. Additionally, rather than a focus on facts and figures, there was the attempt to help students develop historical knowledge of larger themes, generalizations, and concepts. The development of this knowledge was to move beyond teacher and text "telling" to the use of original sources and inquiry techniques. Students not only were to encounter a wider range of historical content but also learn how to think and behave like a historian.

The response to the initial guide was immediate and divided. Many educators, politicians, and social critics praised the document as a much-needed attempt to include seldom-heard voices in the history of the nation. Others, such as Lynne Cheney, former head of the National Endowment for the Humanities, were quick to assert that the guide represented "just the sad and the bad" and painted a "gloomy" picture of the nation (Hancock with Biddle, 1994). Cheney noted that national heroes of distinction were not mentioned or were given slight attention. Christopher Columbus became the "poster boy" for all that was shameful about the nation's historical roots. In response to the critics and the forces they represented, the standards were revised.

Similarly, various ideologies have come into conflict over the most appropriate ways to teach young children how to read. University researchers, teachers, parents, and school boards have struggled over this issue. These struggles, however, are not just disagreements over "methods." They also represent very different worldviews. The response of Evangelical Christians to whole language curricula perhaps best demonstrates this phenomenon. Putting aside for the moment the overtly political agenda of such groups as the Christian Coalition, Evangelical Christians came into conflict with whole language curricula because of their basic beliefs concerning texts and how they are to be interpreted—hermeneutics. In this case, the text in question is the Bible and the conflict concerns what it represents and how it is to be read.

For Evangelical Christians, the Bible contains the revealed truth of God. Epistemologically speaking, it is the authoritative and controlling text in the life of the believing community. Becoming literate, therefore, is crucial because it allows the individual direct access to God's Word. Given the nature of the text, becoming literate necessarily involves learning to read closely and carefully the written discourse. Each word must be correctly understood for not to do so results in a misunderstanding of God's plans and intentions for humankind. Predicting, guessing, or skipping words simply will not do. The very idea of encouraging various responses or interpretations is anathema because it may lead to the spiritual downfall of the individual (Brinkley, 1998; Goodman, 1998; Weaver & Brinkley, 1998). Evangelical Christians, therefore, are sympathetic and predisposed to the use of phonics and literal comprehension questions as primary tools for literacy learning. They see such instruction as supporting the kind of reading the Bible requires. Given such beliefs, and a concern for the spiritual growth of their children, it was perhaps inevitable that Evangelical Christians would become increasingly vocal about curricula they perceived as threatening their world view.

Debates of this kind are of no small consequence as to what knowledge children ultimately encounter and develop in the classroom. There are various sponsors of literacy learning (Brandt, 1998) who play significant roles in knowledge construction. Literacy is a primary avenue through which this knowledge is developed and conveyed. Sponsorship, therefore, ultimately serves as a gatekeeper for the generation, promotion, and maintenance of knowledge in our society. Sponsorship impacts what knowledge is to be privileged or deemed "official" and what is to be ignored. As demonstrated with the history standards and whole language debates, patronage is not limited to the classroom teachers. Publishers, test developers, and teacher educators all play a role. Political leaders and activists, researchers, and the media are also involved.

Because meanings are seldom if ever neutral—they always assert a particular perspective related to a particular individual as a member of a particular group—meanings reflect particular worldviews of particular groups. However, the impact of group meanings on knowledge—that is, "truth"—is only a potential one. Not all meanings or truths are created equal. Just as important, meanings have the ability to cover up other meanings, to suppress other stories, other voices. Meanings reveal as well as illuminate. The Eurocentric knowledge that many Americans have about colonial explorations of the Western Hemisphere, for example, covers or hides meanings that represent an indigenous perspective (Bigelow et al., 1991). Use of the words "discover," "New World," "savage Indians," and "America" position both Europeans and native peoples. Alternate positions and perspectives are reflected in such words as "steal," "homeland," "one with nature," and "civilized." However, these words and the views they represent are oftentimes not encountered in school and other institutional discourse.

When the origin and nature of knowledge are viewed from this perspective, the "socialness" of knowing is made visible. Knowledge is understood to be socially constructed and promoted by like-minded individuals. As such, knowledge reflects a particular view, a particular position of writer and reader, at a particular point in time, and within a particular context. There is no neutral position from which claims to truth can be made. Whether the knowledge of a particular community receives a "hearing" by the broader society and ultimately finds acceptance is influenced by those in a position of power. Dominant groups have less difficulty finding forums for their ideas because they have ready access to and control over these forums. Less-dominant or disenfranchised groups, on the other hand, may find it difficult to create forums for themselves. Their views may challenge positions of privilege and entitlement and therefore may come under attack by mainstream groups.

Rather than there being only a single kind of knowledge, various forms of knowledge exist. According to Banks (1993), there is knowledge that is personal/cultural, popular, mainstream, academic, transformative, and school based. Table 2.27 elaborates on these various types of

**TABLE 2.27**

Types of Socially Constructed Knowledge

| Type | Definition |
| --- | --- |
| Personal and Cultural: | Knowledge that individuals construct from personal experiences in their homes, families, and community cultures. For example, doing well in school means violating kinship norms and "acting white." |
| Popular: | Knowledge that is institutionalized within the mass media and other institutions that are part of the popular culture. For example, you can realize your dreams in the United States if you are willing to work hard and pull yourself up by the bootstraps. |
| Mainstream Academic: | Traditional Westerncentric knowledge in history and the behavioral and social sciences. Based on a foundationist view of knowledge. For example, Europeans discovered America. |
| Transformative Academic: | Knowledge that challenges mainstream academic knowledge and expands and substantially revises established canons, paradigms, theories, explanations, and research methods. Based on a social constructionist view of knowledge. For example, the history of the United States has not been one of continuous progress toward democratic ideas. |
| School: | Knowledge presented in textbooks, curricular and instructional guides, and other media forms and lectures by teachers. |

knowledge. Because these "knowledges" are social constructs, more than an author is involved, regardless of whose name is on the text. Colleagues, editors, publishers, advocacy groups—all contribute to, that is, sponsor, the production of text.

*The Nature of Texts and Text Interpretation.* In our previous cognitive discussion on comprehension, we found that readers construct meanings from their transactions with written discourse. This transaction is conceived as being among reader, text, and author. As part of this transaction, the reader's own particular background knowledge impacts in a very direct way how any text is comprehended. However, we have also seen that readers and writers have multiple social identities. These identifies reflect and are formed by the particular experiences that members of the group have had with one another and with other groups in the wider society. Therefore, the background a reader brings to the page represents not only his or her own unique experiences, but also the experiences of the various groups in which the individual holds membership. These groups identities impact how the individual both interprets as well as writes any piece of written discourse. In general, shared experiences lead to shared understandings. The cognitive transaction, therefore, is widened beyond the individual and conceives of reader, writer, and text as reflections and products of relevant interpretive communities. Additionally, just as individuals have a number of identities, texts have many layers of meaning. Texts display a multitude of ideas both directly as well as indirectly.

In developing literacy in young children, it is important that students be helped to understand not only explicit meanings, but also the more subtle messages, positions, and stances that the discourse presents or assumes. Teachers also need to be cognizant of the values and norms that children bring to the learning experience. This recognition moves beyond a simple affirmation of the diversity of experiences children have had. Too often, these experiences reflect dominant norms of our society, which continues to struggle with such "isms" as racism, sexism, and classism and homophobia. Simply to affirm childhood learnings risks missing the opportunity to take a more critical look at societal values in terms of justice and equity.

That children themselves bring ideologies and positional frameworks to the classroom that are reflected in what they read and write has been demonstrated by a number of researchers. Kamler (1993) analyzed the self-selected writing of two young children—a girl and a boy— just learning how to write. Almost from the first text written, gendered patterns emerged. Although both children tended to write about personal experiences, their positions in these experiences varied. The stories authored by the boy tended to focus on behaviors within events that positioned him as an actor and doer. He depicted himself as an agent acting in and on his world. Use of description was uncommon in the boy's texts as was the use of commentary. In contrast, the girl situated herself as a describer and commentator. Her role was more passive and reflective in nature and she frequently expressed her feelings and emotions about an event. As noted by Kamler, these positions are not idiosyncratic or by happenstance. Rather, they are aligned with gender stereotypes: males as active and females as passive.

Positioning also was reflected in the very language the children used to convey their experiences. The boy tended to <take, put, play, destroy, get> whereas the girl <slept, gave, left, finished, and came>. When both children described receiving a gift, the boy positioned himself as the focus of the event. His <getting> is emphasized. In contrast, the girl focused on the giver of the gift rather than herself as the recipient. Thus, the very language used by the boy places the focus on himself whereas the language employed by the girl places the focus on others. Other researchers have found similar gendered patterns in student writing (e.g., Gilbert, 1989; Orellana, 1995; Poynton, 1985; Solsken, 1992). Still other researchers have noted the existence of similar gendered patterns in children's books as well as in the types of stories boy and girls select to read (e.g., Adler, 1993; Barrs & Pidgeon, 1994; Bender-Peterson & Lach, 1990).

Although many progressive educators have advocated the use of student-selected writing topics as a mainstay of literacy instruction, studies such as Kamler's (1993) should give us pause. The work of Henkin (1995) only highlights this concern. Henkin investigated the organizational practices of writing workshops within a first-grade classroom. In particular, she focused on issues of participation and equity. Because writing conferences are intended to impart knowledge about the writing process, and because knowledge can be viewed as a form of currency, it is critical that all children have opportunities to encounter such knowledge.

Henkin (1995) found that access to writing conferences was skewed along ethnic and gender lines. There were, in effect, two literacy clubs in the classroom—girls and boys—and the boy's club dominated. The boys refused to conference with the girls, explaining that their interests were too different. Even when the girls wrote about such topics as sports, the boys continued to insist that they were not adequate conference partners. Additionally, boys that did not fit the norm—European American, cooperative—were also excluded from the boys' conferences. The club was hierarchical in nature and a single child—Bart—dominated, conferring membership and status on those boys who cooperated with him. Bart invented many of the literacy club rules and resisted participating in conferences in ways the teacher had demonstrated.

Societal norms that have been constructed by dominant groups also find their way into reader-response conferences. Similar to self-selected writing topics and conferences, the use of response groups has been advocated by progressive educators as a way in which to affirm the multitude of experiences that children bring to the classroom setting. Most educators would agree that this is a worthy instructional goal. However, as documented by Enciso (1994), interwoven with many of these experiences are dominant views on such issues as race and culture. That is, the experiences children bring to the classroom are not solely individualistic or particularistic; they also are grounded in the various social groups of which the students are members.

Enciso investigated the responses of an ethnically diverse group of intermediate elementary students to the book *Maniac Magee* (Spinelli, 1990). The book's main character, Jeffrey Lionel Magee, is a 12-year-old boy who is involved with two racially divided communities—African American and European American. The plot focuses on the boy's attempts to negotiate his way through these two groups. As expected, students responded to the text and interpreted the characters and events based on their personal experiences. However, as Enciso quickly discovered, these responses and experiences also reflected numerous cultural references related to race and ethnicity. Such references framed both the identity of the children and the identity of the characters within the story.

Initially, the use of racial and ethnic ideologies in student responses was implicit. However, when Enciso highlighted race and ethnicity within the story, the children began to make explicit their underlying beliefs. In one response session, for example, students were discussing the physical divide between the African American and European American communities. Based on Enciso's explicit marking of this divide, students began to discuss the concept of segregation. One European American boy, Mark, presented what he knew about the civil rights era in a stand-up, comiclike routine. In his presentation, he made reference to a song from the musical "West Side Story." Although a popular play, the Puerto Rican community is depicted in stereotyped ways. Additionally, Mark appeared to believe that African Americans were unaware that certain kinds of exclusions were occurring within society. Although his responses were certainly based on his background, his background represented the dominant groups to which he belonged. According to Enciso, to allow such views to go unchallenged is to implicitly affirm a distorted view of history and reality.

We should not be surprised at the fact that our children read, write, and think in ways that reflect their social identities. Gender, ethnicity, and class support as well as constrain student work. And, because engagement with print requires the use of background knowledge, teachers will want to encourage their students to draw on their experiential resources. Active teacher intervention, however, is also required when such experiences run counter to the promotion of a more equitable and just society. Not to actively intervene runs the risk that process classrooms, which are intended to affirm diversity, will in the end legitimize existing cultural norms and power relationships (Orellana, 1995).

Bigelow (1989), a public school teacher, has documented his attempts to help students understand the "discovery" of the "new world" from a Native American perspective. As previously noted, the very use of such terms places both the "discovers" and "discovered" in particular positions. In this case, the placement represents the views of the group most dominant. That is, the history told represents the victor's understanding. Bigelow quickly discovered that students frequently resisted his attempts to "deconstruct" the Eurocentric view represented in their history book. The alternate view presented by Bigelow ran counter not only to the books the students had read, but also the representations found in such popular culture texts as movies, television programs, songs, and holidays. In many respects, Bigelow was the big bad wolf trying to tell the "true story," and some students viewed his attempts at presenting alternate perspectives with skepticism.

## CONCLUSION AND SUMMARY

In this chapter, we have explored three dimensions of literacy and literacy use: linguistic (code breaker and code maker), cognitive (meaning maker), and sociocultural (text user and critic). The final dimension, developmental (scientist and construction worker) is addressed in chapter 3. We have given the developmental nature its own chapter because it has the most direct implications for instruction, which is the ultimate focus of this book. Additionally, as indicated in Fig. 1.1, the linguistic, cognitive, and sociocultural dimensions are embedded within the developmental. Therefore, development is always related to the child's becoming more proficient as a code breaker and code maker, meaning maker, and text user and critic.

# 3

# The Developmental Dimension and Instruction

The developmental dimension concerns both the processes as well as the participants involved in the child's learning of the linguistic, cognitive, and sociocultural dimensions of literacy. This relationship between the developmental dimension and the linguistic, cognitive, and sociocultural is why in Fig. 1.1 the developmental engulfs or is wrapped around the other dimensions. Development explains how the child learns to become a code breaker and code maker, meaning maker, and text user and critic.

As we shall see, learners are actively involved in the developmental process, building an understanding for themselves of the way written language operates linguistically, cognitively, and socioculturally. Adults and more capable literacy users play a mediational role in this process, supporting and scaffolding the learners' development. Finally, teachers, as a very special type of adult, promote development through the various types of instructional frameworks they provide the students in their classroom.

## THE LEARNER AS SCIENTIST AND CONSTRUCTION WORKER

The child goes about learning language knowledge much as a scientist goes about developing scientific knowledge: through data collection, rule generation, rule testing, and rule modification. The dimensions of language are actually constructed or built by the child through a process of induction. The child discovers the abstract regularities of the language based on the language data available and the mediation provided. Actively involved in the developmental process, the learner is anything but a passive recipient of the language. Rather, the child experiences or encounters language data expressed by others. In an attempt to make sense of this data, the learner generates hypotheses or rules for how a particular aspect of the language might operate. Using these hypotheses as a guide, the child engages in language use and receives feedback from others. Based on the feedback provided, the hypotheses are modified as warranted.

In the past, it was thought that proficient language users—that is, parents, caregivers, teachers—were largely responsible for or determined language learning. The child was conceived as a passive and empty recipient, filled with language by those who already knew it. However, as illustrated later, research conducted during the last three decades has clearly demonstrated that language development involves a transaction between the child and the environment (e.g., Bruner, 1974; Clay, 1975; DeFord, 1981; Dyson, 2003; Harste et al., 1984; Teale, 1984; Wells, 1986). Both the learner and environment act and are acted on.

Not only is language development an inductive process, the rules governing the various dimensions of language—for example, systems of language, cognitive processes, cultural

**49**

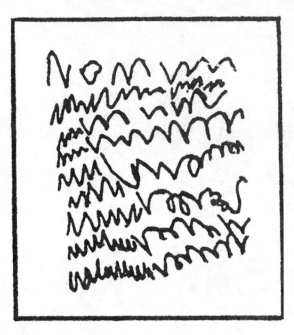

FIG. 3.1.   Dawn's initial writing sample.

norms—are learned tacitly. Initially, the child's focus is on trying to understand the intentions and meanings that undergird the language being used. In the process of attempting to understand, the rules governing the language are constructed. Because of this indirect learning, the child's knowledge is largely implicit. That is, the child is capable of using the rules to generate language, yet is unable to verbalize them. For many children, schools are the first context in which what is known implicitly must be made explicit to be counted as knowledge.

Just as we discovered that miscues reveal the underlying rules and processes used by proficient readers, the "errors" in language use reveal the rules and processes used by developing readers and writers. Unconventional writings, for instance, display the thought processes and rule systems of the young child. In order to demonstrate the rule revealing nature of errors, we examine a number of initial writing samples from preschool children. Many of these samples come from the seminal emergent literacy research of Harste and Colleagues (1984).

In the first examples (Figs. 3.1, 3.2, and 3.3), three 4-year-olds—Dawn, Najeeba, and Ofer respectively—were asked to write anything they knew on a piece of unlined paper (Harste et al., 1984, p. 82). At this point in their lives, the three children had not yet received any form of direct literacy instruction. In fact, their parents were surprised and delighted at what their children actually knew about print. Look closely at these three samples and jot down what each child appears to know about the writing process and concepts of print (Cunningham, 2005). Keep in mind that this "knowing" may be different from the "knowing" of more proficient language users. Nevertheless, consider what hypotheses the child has generated about how the written language system operates.

Although not formally introduced to the written language system, it is clear that all three children had encountered written language in their environments. Dawn, an American child, did her "writing" from top-to-bottom and from left-to-right. Najeeba, a child from Saudi Arabia, first drew lines across the blank paper and then produced a script that contained curlicue formations and numerous dots. His understanding of written language differed from Dawn's

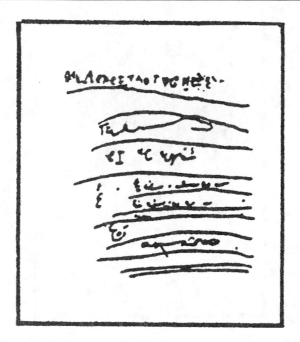

FIG. 3.2.    Najeeba's initial writing sample.

FIG. 3.3.    Ofer's initial writing sample.

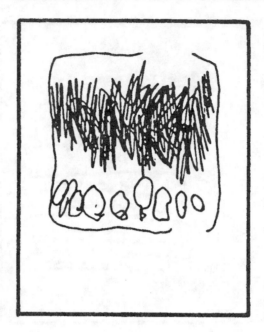

FIG. 3.4.   Shannon's writing and illustration sample.

because the language data to which he was exposed differed. Although difficult to see in Najeeba's sample, the top line contains letters of the English alphabet. Najeeba had recently come to the United States with his parents who were attending a local university. Finally, Fig. 3.3 was produced by Ofer, an Israeli preschooler. His parents were also in the United States attending college. As is the convention in Hebrew, she wrote from right-to-left and then, as is the convention in English, from left-to-right.

These emergent literacy samples clearly demonstrate that the three children were all actively engaged in generating hypothesis from the written language data that had been encountered in their environments. Najeeba, in fact, demonstrates developing knowledge of two written systems—Arabic and English. Although not conventional, the children's very different representations of their language reflect very active attempts to understand how their respective language systems operate.

Beginning around the age of 3, young children also begin to understand the difference between the symbolic system of writing and the iconic system of drawing. Shannon, a 3-year-old in the Harste, Woodward, and Burke study (1984, p. 94), was asked to draw a picture of his family and then to write his name underneath the picture. Figure 3.4 represents the child's response. Never explicitly taught to write and draw, Shannon nonetheless has already begun to tease out the differences between the two communication systems. It should be noted at this point in our discussion that young children use various forms to represent both their knowledge of written language and of drawing. As Shannon's writing sample demonstrates, scribbling is not the only way to represent writing; the use of circles will work just as well.

Until recently, the notion of the learner generating rules for understanding written language was largely ignored. Written language development was thought to come about through direct, skill-by-skill instruction. However, we now know that children also attempt to make sense of the print that surrounds them (Teale & Sulzby, 1991). In the next series of examples, we look more closely at the various hypotheses the young child has generated about particular writing conventions.

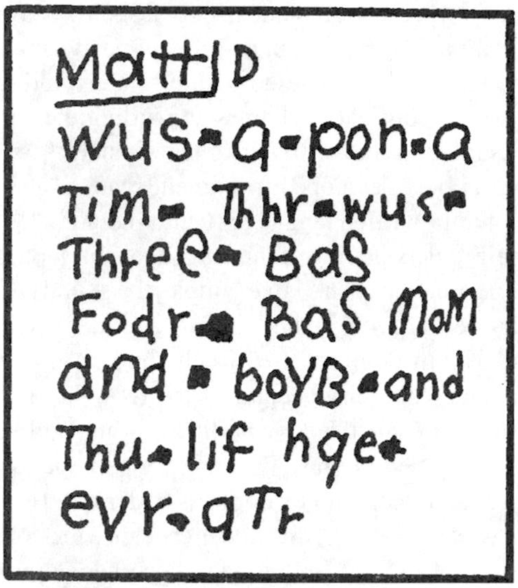

FIG. 3.5.   Using dots to demarcate word boundaries.

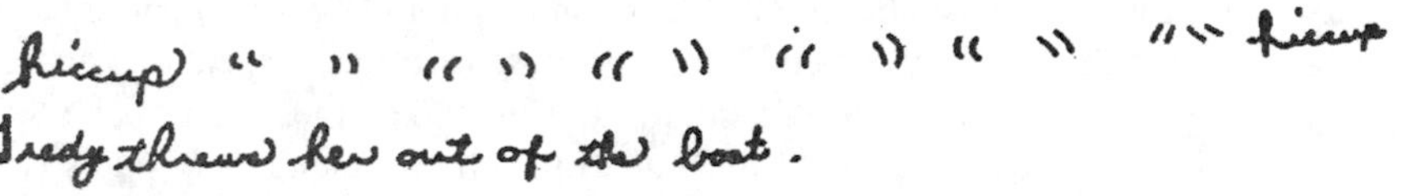

FIG. 3.6.   Using quotation marks to repeat sounds.

In the first example shown in Fig. 3.5 (Harste et al., 1984, p. 87), Matt, 9 years of age, demonstrates his constructed understanding of word boundaries. Rather than the traditional use of space between words, he employs another convention—dots—to mark such boundaries. Matt has previously encountered the use of space to mark word boundaries and has certainly seen the use of dots—periods—to mark sentence boundaries. However, his hypothesis is not a mere imitation or copy of what he has observed. The stance of the child is to understand the rule system through the generation and testing of hypothesis, not to simply reproduce what is seen.

Hypothesis generating and testing does not necessarily end in the early grades. I asked a child entering the fifth grade to write a story to accompany the pictures in the wordless picture book "*Ah-choo*," by Mercer Mayer (1976). When he read his writing shown in Fig. 3.6, the child read <hiccup> for each pair of quotations. The child had essentially combined the use of quotation marks with ditto marks and created a new convention for repeated words.

Even learning to spell, which was largely thought to be a process of memorization and application of phonic rules, reflects the activity of a constructive mind. In his investigation of the spelling of young children, Read (1971, 1975) discovered rule-governed, systematic orthographic patterns that were not necessarily based on adult logic. In their spelling attempts, children tended to use the sounds contained in the letter names—both vowels and consonants—as opposed to letter sounds. For example, <cherry> was represented as <hare>, <museum> as <muzm>, and <day> as <da>. To represent short vowels, the children used the position of the mouth and tongue. The vowel's name and the sound to be represented in print were matched when the position of the mouth and tongue were similar. <Bed> was spelled as <bad>, <fish> as <fes>, and <fell> as <fall>.

Of course, the children's ability to systematically spell such words reflects a growing under-standing of the phonemic nature of oral language (phonemic awareness) and the link between sounds and letters in written language. These children understand, although most likely not consciously, that spoken words consist of syllables and individual sounds and that these sylla-bles and sounds are represented in the written language system. Even if there is some debate as to how this knowledge is best developed, proficient readers and writers understand how sounds and letters are related in written language (Cunningham, 2005; Ehri & Nunes, 2002).

Children also apply their understanding of the language's phonological system in determin-ing how a word is to be represented in print. For example, the sounds of affricatives (e.g., /tr/ and /dr/) are more often the property of /ch/ and /g/ than /t/ and /d/. Therefore, children frequently represent these sounds in print through the use of <ch> and <g>. <Truck> becomes <chruk>, <drive> becomes <griv>, and <dragon> becomes <jragin>. There also are circumstances in which children are unaware as to which letter a particular sound belongs. Preconsonant nasals, such as /n/ and /m/ may be omitted because they are not perceptually salient. The difference between such words as /pat/ and /pant/, for example, is understood as a difference in the vowel. Or, children may omit the vowel before /l/, /m/, and /n/ because the consonant tends to "swallow up" the vowel. <From> becomes <frm> and <open> becomes <opn> (Wilde, 1992).

This constructive stance toward language learning is also evident in bilingual children learning to read and write in English. In a study examining the interaction between Spanish and English orthographies, Fashola, Drum, Mayer, and Kang (1996) compared the English spelling patterns of Spanish-speaking children with those of English-speaking students. The Spanish-speaking students were in the second, third, fifth, and sixth grades, spoke Spanish at home, and were classified by the schools as limited English proficient. The English-speaking students were native speakers and nonproficient in Spanish.

All students were given a list of 40 common English words to spell. In an examination of the spelling errors of Spanish-speaking students, two patterns were discovered. First, students produced misspellings by actively adjusting their perceptions of English phonology to fit within the Spanish phonological system. Sounds that exist in English but not in Spanish, such as the sound of /oo/ in /look/ and the /b/ in /cable/, were mapped onto the closest Spanish sounds, such as /o/ and /v/. Second, with sounds that exist in both English and Spanish, students frequently applied Spanish phonological and orthographic rules rather than English. For example, the English word /hero/ was spelled /jero/, because the sound represented by /h/ in English corresponds to the sound that is marked by /j/ in Spanish. In both cases, the children were not slavishly attempting to memorize the English orthographic system. Rather, they were drawing upon their Spanish linguistic resources so as to make sense of a new English written language system.

As you may have guessed by now, there is little evidence to suggest that language is learned through imitation to any great extent. The child's stance is not to replicate or copy the language that is encountered. Rather, the child attempts to understand the meanings being expressed and the systems of language that serve as the avenue for their expression. Through such attempts at understanding, the language is constructed. As the previous examples indicate, we know that imitations play a minor role in language learning because children generate language forms and conventions that they have never before encountered. Most children have not seen their parents use lines or dots to demarcate word boundaries. Such behaviors are the reflection of an active, constructing mind, the mind of a learner who is generating and testing hypothesis for the data encountered.

Second, even if the child wanted to imitate the language, most rules for the linguistic, cognitive, and sociocultural dimensions of language are not directly displayed. For example, the rules of the syntax that underlie every sentence are not explicitly evident. Nor, given the great variability of letter–sound relationships, are the rules for graphophonemics readily apparent. They are not directly articulated or made visible in the surface structure. In fact, if most adult language users were asked to make explicit their knowledge of the various dimensions of literacy, they would be unable to do so. Such knowledge is implicit and has been learned tacitly.

Finally, as documented by Keenan (1977), in oral language much of what appears to be imitation in fact is repetition. The repeating of what has been heard is used by both parent and child as a strategy for communication. For example, the parent or child may repeat what they heard as a communicative check, to verify that she or he has heard—that is, understood—correctly. Repetition may also serve as a vehicle for topic extension. Even among adults, there is a concept known as the given–new contract. The responder repeats part of what has been said (given) and then builds on additional information (new). Children engage in the same kind of behavior. Finally, information may be repeated to signal agreement or to make counterclaims.

## FROM COLLABORATIVE TO INDEPENDENT ABILITIES

Teachers' behaviors and the materials they use are the primary mediational vehicles within most classrooms. Mediations represent the support structures, or scaffolds, that are built around a learner (Bruner 1986; Vygotsky, 1962, 1978). These configurations, similar to those surrounding a building under construction, provide the social assistance necessary for the learner to meaningfully engage in the particular undertaking at hand, such as in reading a book or writing about a frightening experience. The power of such scaffolds is that the learner encounters the entire activity within a meaningful, purposeful context. And, although the learner may be capable of engaging in only portions of the activity, he or she is aware of the entire scope of the unfolding literacy event.

With time, experience, and growing competency on the part of the learner, the teacher begins to lessen the support provided—deconstructs the scaffold. The learner is encouraged to take on responsibility for certain aspects of the activity that were once performed solely by the teacher or by the teacher and learner working collaboratively. As the scaffold is dismantled, what the teacher once did is now the responsibility of the learner.

The role of mediation becomes even more critical when considering English Language Learners (ELLs). Key to the development of a second language is what Krashen (1985) referred to as "comprehensible input." Krashen argued that for learners to learn a second language they must receive messages that they can understand. Furthermore, these messages must contain language that is slightly ahead of the learner's grammatical knowledge. Referring to the learner's current knowledge as $i$, he defines the input that is slightly ahead as $i + 1$. Going back to our discussion on scaffolding, for second language learners it is then essential that teachers provide the support needed for students to be able to encounter language that is meaningful, yet, just beyond their current ability level.

Furthermore, the use of scaffolds to support language-minority students has been well documented by Tharp and Gallimore (1988). Focusing on the reading development of Hawaiian children involved in the Kamehameha Elementary Education Program (KEEP), these authors document how teachers successfully scaffold literacy instruction for children. Moving beyond modes of traditional classroom discourse where the teacher dominates the linguistic exchange, KEEP teachers used modeling and questioning, as well as features of native Hawaiian storytelling, to help readers construct new understandings. Within these "instructional conversations" (Goldenberg, 1992/1993; Saunders & Goldenberg, 1999), teachers bridge the students' schema, elicit and extend their language and thinking while assisting them in participating in literacy lessons and discussions.

In Fig. 3.7, the major factors involved in mediation and development are depicted. Potential abilities represent those dimensions of literacy that the child has the capability or capacity to develop. As described by Vygotsky (1978), potential abilities are like buds on a tree that with time and nourishment will bloom into flowers and ultimately bear fruit. The nourishment provided by the teacher is the social and collaborative support structure built around the learner—the scaffold. Independent abilities, in contrast, are those literacy behaviors that the child is able to employ without the support or assistance of others. These strategies and processes, once social and external in nature, are now internal, autonomous, and self-governing. The distance between potential and independent abilities is what Vygotsky termed the zone of proximal development (ZOPD). It is within this zone that the teacher and student collaboratively operate.

As represented in Fig. 3.7, the darker portions in the upper-left-hand corner indicate significant degrees of teacher support. At this point in development, the teacher has primary responsibility in the activity. In a book-reading activity, for example, the teacher would be doing most of the reading, with the child contributing whenever possible. As the developmental arrow moves toward the lower-right-hand corner of the figure—toward independence—the background becomes lighter. The support provided by the teacher progressively decreases and the student assumes more accountability. In a book-reading activity, the student would be doing more and more of the reading with the teacher providing assistance only at those points where the child encounters difficulty.

Two primary forces encourage the internalization of the dimensions of literacy: student interest and teacher scaffold deconstruction. Most children are driven toward self-sufficiency; they strive to become independent from the adults around them. The line from the old commercial, "Please, I'd rather do it myself!" is an apt description of most children. This drive, however, only exists when the event or process engages the interest of the learner. As we saw in the previous chapter, children initiate language learning because of the communicative and social currency that language affords them. Therefore, it is the inherent qualities of the activity itself that must motivate students to assume increased responsibility. Students may resist these responsibilities if the task does not speak to them in meaningful and authentic ways.

As has already been noted, the second force encouraging internalization of literacy processes is the lessening of support on the part of the teacher. Too often, however, teachers tell students how something is done and then expect them to take over. There is no gradual teacher release and corresponding student increase of responsibility. A number of researchers have set forth various procedures that teachers can employ to move students through the ZOPD toward independence (e.g., Cazden, 1992, 1988; Pressley, 1998; Pressley, Goodchild, Fleet, Zajchowski, & Evans, 1989). What follows is a general instructional framework that can be applied to a variety of literacy activities. The learning of two strategies to read unrecognized words—reread and read on—is used to illustrate the various degrees of mediation that are provided in this developmental sequence. (See the strategy lesson Selected Deletion/Multiple Known Concepts in chapter 5 for a fuller description.)

1. Initially, the teacher assumes total responsibility for the activity by demonstrating how the two strategies—rereading and reading on—are accomplished. Frank Smith (1981) defined demonstrations as telling or showing the students that "this is how something is done." Demonstrations allow students to vicariously engage in the activity through observations. Through these demonstrations and vicarious engagements, students grow in their sensitivity to, and knowledge of, the various processes involved in the activity.

In teaching strategies for the identification of unknown or unrecognized words, the teacher shows a short, predictable text on the overhead projector. Several words throughout the text

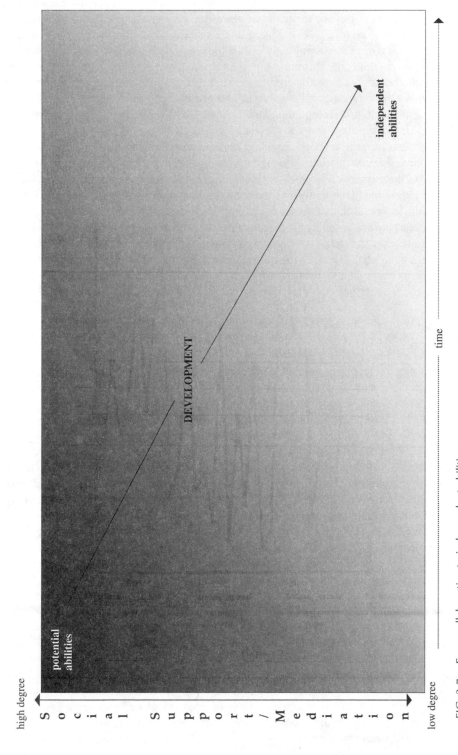

FIG. 3.7.   From collaborative to independent abilities.

57

have been deleted and replaced with a line. These blanks represent words that are not recognized when reading. The teacher orally reads the text up to the first blank. Verbally, the teacher shares several strategies that can be used to predict what word(s) might be appropriate for the blank, in this case reading on and returning to the blank and rereading what came before the blank. The teacher demonstrates or makes cognitively visible the use of both strategies and "thinks aloud" as both strategies are tried out. This think-aloud would include summarizing the meanings that came before the blank as a base for predicting what followed the blank. Various predictions are shared and evaluated based on the previous and subsequent context.

2. As students begin to develop an understanding of, and sensitivity to, the two strategies through such demonstrations and engagements, the teacher encourages participation when possible. This involves the teacher providing partial information and asking the student to provide the remaining information. Although the teacher is still the primary reader, the children take on more of the responsibility. For each blank, the teacher and students might chorally read the sentence before the blank as well as the sentence containing the blank. The teacher then summarizes the information that comes before the blank and asks the student for predictions. These predictions are evaluated by the teacher and students in light of the meanings preceding the blank. The teacher and students then read the sentence containing the blank and the following sentence. The teacher discusses the information that follows the blank, elicits predictions from the students, and evaluates the predictions. Based on information preceding and following each blank, the teacher and students discuss which predictions make the most sense and why.

Another way in which student participation might be encouraged is to reverse the responsibilities in the previous scenario. In this case, the students discuss the ideas that precede the blank and the teacher generates possible predictions. These predictions are evaluated by the students based on the previous context. Similarly, the students summarize the ideas that follow the blank, the teacher generates predictions, and asks for student evaluation. Finally, the predictions are evaluated in terms of the ideas that preceded and followed the blank.

3. At this point in strategy internalization, the teacher cues the specific strategy that she or he wants the student to use. First, the teacher provides the students with a story containing various blanks. As a group, the students chorally read the entire text, inserting words into the blanks as they are encountered. Following the reading, the various predictions for each blank are listed on the board. Each student who provides a prediction is asked to justify it based on the meanings that precede and follow the blank. Other students and the teacher provide feedback as to the meaningfulness of the prediction.

4. Next, students independently read a short story that contains no blanks. This independent reading can be handled in several different ways. For example, individual students might be asked to orally read a text that contains words the student most likely will not recognize. When the student encounters such words, the teacher either tells the student to reread, predict, and evaluate or to read on, return and predict, evaluate. Another possibility is to have students read silently and to record all words unknown. (See Reader-Selected Miscues in chapter 5 for a fuller description of this strategy lesson.) Students assemble as a group and each shares one word on his or her list. The teacher then cues the student to reread or read on, to predict, and to evaluate.

5. Once students are able to effectively use the two strategies, rereading and reading on, the teacher begins to cue only general strategy use. When the student encounters an unknown word, the teacher says, "What can you do when you come to a word that you do not know?" The student discusses the strategies available and the teacher prompts the student to select one, try it out, and to evaluate the results.

6. At this point in the mediation process, the teacher begins to buttress student independent use of the strategies. During or after individual students read aloud, the teacher discusses the student's reading behaviors. Using the text read, the teacher refers to specific strategy use at specific points in the text and discusses its effectiveness.

7. As the students internalize the strategies and begin to effectively apply them independently, the teacher helps the students to build metacognitive understandings of their own behaviors. After a text has been read, the students are asked to identify, share, and explain their reading behaviors. Students share words not initially known and discuss how they solved these problems. Reader Selected Miscues, discussed in chapter 5, is another way in which students can become more aware of what they do as readers.

During the time that the teacher introduces students to various reading strategies and helps students use them independently, it can be helpful to document in the classroom the strategies learned. Developing a series of strategy charts on large poster board and/or providing students with their own list of problem-solving strategies serves to remind students what they can do when encountering difficulties (Kucer, 1995). (See the various Wall Chart strategy lessons in chapter 5 for fuller descriptions.)

The preceding scenario of the lessening of mediation to encourage strategy internalization is not intended to be used as a template for all instruction. Rather, it attempts to illustrate in concrete and specific ways how such internalization can be accomplished. Teachers, as the classroom instructional experts, should adapt their mediational structures to meet the needs of those they teach. As teachers select to implement various instructional strategies found in the subsequent chapters, they will want to consider how the strategies can be modified to provide the support as well as responsibility necessary for their students.

## ORGANIZING STRATEGY LESSONS FOR INTERNALIZATION

Not only can mediation be increased and lessened as necessary within a particular strategy lesson as previously demonstrated, various strategy lessons can also be arranged so that they move students toward independence. Table 3.1 illustrates how this might be accomplished. We discovered the usefulness of the explicit ordering of instructional strategies through a preservice university student that one of us taught. In the literacy methods class in which the student was enrolled, the students were introduced to the six reading and writing lessons listed: teacher reading/writing, shared reading/writing, choral reading/writing, guided reading/writing, paired reading/writing, and independent reading/writing. Each lesson was demonstrated to the students and they were encouraged to use the lessons with the young child being tutored as part of the class.

The following year, the student in the class shared an experience she had encountered during a job interview. When asked about her knowledge of reading instruction, the student confidently shared some of the strategies she had learned in her university methods class. The interviewer—a principal in this case—then asked how she would order the activities in terms of their support for young children. A great question, but one that the prospective teacher had difficulty answering. She had never been asked in her university course to explicitly consider the mediational differences across these lessons. Because of this experience, we have realized that such explicitness can be helpful in selecting and arranging the appropriate strategy lessons for our students.

The reading and writing strategies in Table 3.1 are grouped and ordered by the degree of support provided by the teacher, from most to least. Paralleling Fig. 3.1, those strategy

TABLE 3.1

Strategy Lessons and Mediation

*Most Support*

### *Reading and Writing To*

| | |
|---|---|
| *Teacher Reading*: The teacher reads aloud a text to the children, responding at various places and encouraging the children to respond as well. | *Teacher Writing*: The teacher demonstrates the writing of a text, discussing his/her thinking as s/he writes. |
| *Shared Reading*: The teacher reads aloud a text to the children, asking them to predict upcoming meanings when appropriate or to chorally read with her/him particular parts. | *Shared Writing*: The teacher records a text that the children dictate; the teacher supports student generation of ideas by asking questions and reflecting on text content, development, organization, conventions, etc. |

### *Reading and Writing With*

| | |
|---|---|
| *Choral Reading*: The teacher and the children orally read a text together. | *Choral Writing*: The teacher and the children write a text together; the teacher and individual students take turns generating and recording new ideas. |
| *Guided Reading*: Individual children read a text aloud with support provided by the teacher as necessary. | *Guided Writing*: Individual children write a text with support provided by the teacher as necessary. |

### *Reading and Writing By*

| | |
|---|---|
| *Paired Reading*: Two children orally read a text aloud together. | *Paired Writing*: Two children write a text together. |
| *Independent Reading*: Each child silently reads a text independently. | *Independent Writing*: Each child silently writes a text independently. |

*Least Support*

lessons with the darkest background require the most support; those lessons with the lightest background require the least. Stated somewhat differently, the strategy lessons at the top of the table represent collaborative abilities that progressively become internalized and independent as we move to the lessons at the bottom. Throughout any literacy program, students should encounter such strategy lessons on a regular basis. The strategy lesson selected for use at any particular instructional moment is determined by the degree of difficulty of the text to be read or written as well as the ability of the students who will be experiencing the literacy activity. What follows is a general overview of these strategies so as to demonstrate the decreasing mediational support from lesson to lesson. For a fuller discussion of these strategies, see chapter 5.

Teacher Reading and Writing provide students with the most support in the sense that the teacher is largely responsible for the processing of print. The teacher reads or writes aloud, with the students observing the demonstration and responding when appropriate. Throughout the process, the teacher makes visible his or her thinking by verbally reflecting on the interaction with print. Teacher Reading and Writing frequently occurs with texts that students would have difficulty processing, even with teacher mediation.

In Shared Reading and Writing, the students are more actively engaged and can actually see the print, such as in a big book. As the teacher reads a text aloud, the students are asked to predict meanings or even to chorally read predictable portions of the text. When writing, the teacher promotes active student engagement through asking for their ideas and judgments as to what is being written.

Choral Reading and Writing involve the teacher and students in a fairly equal relationship. A book that is chorally read has both the students and teacher reading aloud and in unison. Texts that are written chorally have the teacher and students taking turns adding ideas to an evolving story that is being collaboratively constructed. In contrast to Shared Reading and Writing, all participants assume the same degree of responsibility.

During Guided Reading and Writing, students assume the primary responsibility for meaning making. As students read or write, the teacher's role is to provide support when difficulties are encountered. The teacher may prompt particular strategy use, ask students to look at the pictures to help identify an unrecognized word or to reread what has been written when writer's block is encountered. The teacher acts as a guide, but the students largely drive the process.

Students who have developed some independence can be paired to collaboratively read or write. In such cases, each student assists and supports the other when difficulties are encountered. In most cases, the students have developed the necessary abilities to read or write, but may on occasion experience difficulty and need help in working through the problem.

Texts that are intended for independent reading and writing are those that students can basically handle on their own. Little if any assistance is necessary as students apply what they have learned to difficulties they may experience during the reading or writing.

## VARIABILITY AND LITERACY DEVELOPMENT

As teachers encourage, and students move toward, independence, it is important to keep in mind the inherent variability of literacy development. Traditionally, "mastery" has been the goal of much classroom instruction. Through mastery, the child was able to consistently and effectively apply the learned skill across space, time, and contexts. When problems with this application were experienced by the child, "reinforcement" or "remediation" of the skills was the typical instructional response. Previously introduced skills were revisited and practiced so as to ensure or maintain their mastery.

Development, however, is not the same as mastery. Rather, development represents the learner's growth in the ability to effectively and efficiently apply the literacy strategies across an ever widening range of contexts. As represented at the bottom of Fig. 3.8, the learner initially has limited knowledge of the literacy strategies and is able to apply them to only a narrow range of contexts. A young child, for example, may be able to proficiently and independently read a number of predictable books, such as *The Great Big Enormous Turnip* (Tolstoy, 1976) or the well-known British folktale *The Three Little Pigs*. However, the child may demonstrate little of this literacy knowledge and ability when given less predictable and supportive texts to read.

This disparity in the child's interaction with various types of texts is not an indication that the child is unable to "really read" that is, has not mastered the process—as is frequently asserted. Rather, it demonstrates the child's narrow range of literacy development and the limited settings in which he or she can independently apply various literacy strategies. With time, experience, and mediational support, these strategies will become more fully developed and differentiated. The child comes to apply these strategies to texts that are less supportive in nature, as indicated by the progressive widening of the spiral in Fig. 3.8. However, there will still exist texts with which the child will encounter difficulty.

Of course, this developmental spiral can be applied to most of us. Development typically continues throughout the course of one's life as long as literacy is encountered and used in

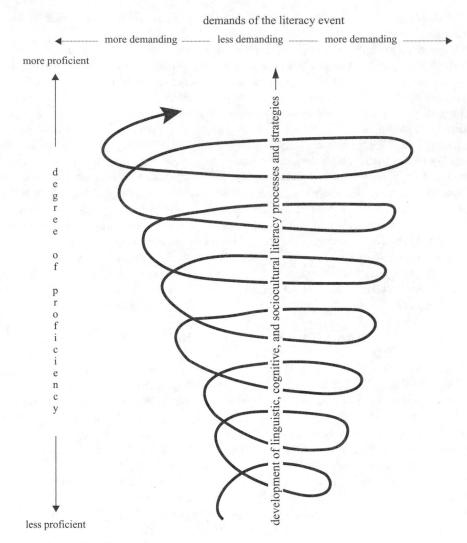

FIG. 3.8.   Profile of literacy development.

new or novel ways. Additionally, there always exist literacy contexts in which we are less than proficient, if only because we lack experience or interest in these situations. At times, we may even seek to avoid such contexts, hiring others to read for us. The authors of this book, for example, avoid reading the tax codes and forms sent to us from the Internal Revenue Service. Rather, we employ accountants to read them for us—and, hopefully, to take responsibility for any misreadings that may have occurred during an audit! Before the invention of the printing press and the wider distribution of literacy, it was common for scribes to be employed to read and write for those who were unable to do so. As indicated in the IRS example, this tradition continues today in a somewhat modified form.

There is a second and related reason why literacy behaviors that are evident and controlled in one context may suddenly appear to be absent in other situations. As we found in our analysis of the cognitive nature of language, there are always limits to the cognitive resources available to any language user. When new learnings are developing, energy and attention must be allocated to these learnings. This results in less energy being available for other aspects of language and thought. When such situations occur, it is not uncommon for the more recent learnings to become unstable because energy is not available to control them. Donald Graves (1983), for example, has proposed that the last aspect of writing learned is the first aspect to be lost when the demands of the writing task overload the writer. Over a 2-year period, Graves documented the writing development of 6- to 10-year old elementary students. Each piece of writing produced by the students was holistically evaluated in terms of the use of information, organization, and language. Although the general quality of the writing improved over the 2 years, not every piece was better than the one before. As illustrated by the writing of Andrea shown in Fig. 3.9, such factors as the topic, text structure, and audience impacted the quality of the piece and which aspects of the writing process the writer was able to control. Writing ability was not monolithic, a process that the child was able to uniformly control across texts, contexts, and contents.

Not limited to young children, the to-and-fro nature of development is found in more proficient language users as well. For example, the ability of a group university students to control coherence—that is, the overall organization of a text—during the course of a semester-long composition course was examined (Kucer, 1983a, 1983b). Regardless of any student's overall writing ability in general, and command of coherence in particular, control of coherence

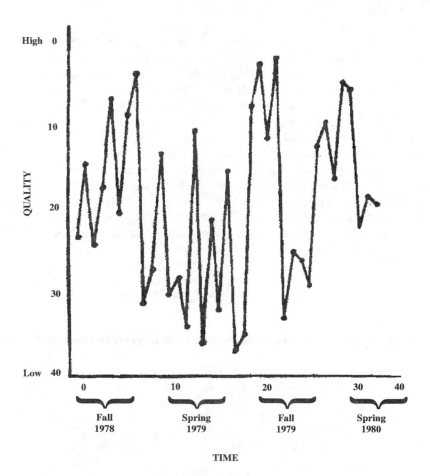

FIG. 3.9.   The recursive nature of writing development.

within one writing activity was not predictive of control within another. Even the most proficient writers in the class did not demonstrate consistent proficiency on all writing assignments. Nor did those writers having the least control over coherence always produce highly incoherent texts. There existed conditions under which both groups of writers displayed a high degree as well as a low degree of control over the process. Furthermore, different writers were impacted differently by different tasks. Throughout the course of the semester, it was not uncommon for a writer to produce one of the most coherent texts in the class under one writing condition and then produce one of the most incoherent texts under another condition.

## THE PHONICS QUESTION

Because of the ongoing and increasingly acrimonious debate over the teaching and learning of phonics as a foundation for literacy development, we end this chapter with a closer examination of the issue. In Table 3.2, we pose a number of issues that need to be considered when the "phonics question" is explored. These issues relate to the linguistic, cognitive, and developmental dimensions of literacy. Linguistically, we have seen that the relationship between letters and sounds in English is a tenuous one. (See Tables 2.12, 2.13, and 2.14.) That is, although English is an alphabetic language, the letters and are sounds are only loosely related. Spelling is as much related to what the words mean as to how the words are actually spoken. (See Table 2.15.) Because English consists of many variations—that is, dialects—even the way letters are ultimately pronounced will vary by language groups. Therefore, in general and at best, the use of phonics during reading can provide an approximate identification of a word. The use of phonics when writing—spelling—provides a similar approximation.

Cognitively, we have found that reading, as a perceptual process, involves the selective picking up of information from a text. What is ultimately selected is influenced by the usefulness of the information. Consonants are more useful than vowels and the beginnings and to a lesser extent endings of words provide more information than the middles. Readers fill in these "perceptual gaps" through the employment of background knowledge and the use of the other systems of language—that is, context. In contrast, during writing the selective process does not operate and writers must represent the spelling of each word in full.

Developmentally, we have seen how literacy abilities become internalized over time through the construction and gradual deconstruction of scaffolds that the teacher provides the students. These scaffolds are built around authentic texts and contexts. Although a particular language

**TABLE 3.2**

The Phonics Question

| Dimension | Question |
| --- | --- |
| Linguistic | What is the relationship between letters and sounds in written language? |
| Cognitive | What is the role of letters and sounds in the reading and writing processes? |
| Sociocultural | What value do various social groups and sponsors of literacy use place on letter–sound knowledge? |
| Developmental | What knowledge of letter–sound relationships is necessary to learn in order to become a proficient reader and writer? |
| | How are letter–sound relationships learned in beginning reading and writing development? |

or cue system of the text or a particular strategy may be highlighted, students have an understanding of the "big picture" within which this highlighting unfolds. Students comprehend the whole before their attention is shifted to the parts.

In promoting the development of graphophonemic knowledge, the teacher will also want to be cognizant of the place of letters and sounds in the linguistic and cognitive dimensions of literacy. Students certainly will and do benefit from an understanding how letters and sounds relate linguistically. However, students will also benefit from understanding that letter–sound relationship is a loose one and be taught those relationships that are the most consistent and encountered in what is read and written.

Cognitively, it is also important to recognize that knowledge of graphophonemics is more critical in writing than reading. As we have seen, readers are selective in what print is processed. In writing, however, students cannot be selective in what letters they represent. Words must be fully spelled. Therefore, it might be argued that students come to more fully understand and appreciate letter–sound relationships through having to represent their ideas in writing. Writing comes to serve as a primary mediational vehicle through which students learn about graphophonemics and how to apply these learnings to the reading process.

## CONCLUSION AND SUMMARY

In many respects, this chapter completes the discussion of the dimensions of literacy begun in the previous chapter. Student development and teacher instruction were linked and various ways in which teachers can move students toward independence addressed. The importance of the teacher's role in mediation cannot be overemphasized. All too frequently, teachers reject instructional strategies as failures or unworkable when students do not respond as they had hoped. The problem, however, may not be with the basic outlines of the activity, but with the degree or type of support structures provided the students. A modification of the scaffolds may be all that is required to make an ineffectual activity successful.

In the chapters that follow, various linguistic, cognitive, and sociocultural literacy strategies are presented. By necessity, each activity is addressed in a general manner, followed by a discussion of possible variations. However, it is impossible to fully address all instructional contexts in which teachers will find themselves. The teacher will therefore need to adapt the strategies—reconfigure the mediation—for particular groups of students. This chapter has provided a number of ways in which such modifications can be accomplished.

# II

# Strategy Lessons

Chapters 4, 5, and 6 present strategy lessons to support classroom teachers as they plan ways of engaging students in developing knowledge about the linguistic, cognitive, and sociocultural dimensions of literacy. In these lessons we draw from chapter 3, where we discussed factors involved in the mediation and development of literacy and conceptualized the reader or writer as scientist and construction worker. We view the developmental dimension of literacy as engulfing all other dimensions. This dimension focuses not only on the learner's active participation in developing the linguistic, cognitive, and sociocultural dimensions, but on the role of the teacher—or other more capable literacy user—in mediating the developmental process. Undergirding the development of any literacy strategy is the understanding that this mediation must occur within the zone of proximal development (ZOPD) (see Fig. 3.7).

As teachers develop literacy strategies to scaffold instruction, it is also important to revisit the notion that variability is an inherent characteristic of literacy development. Rather than ignoring student differences and relying on the one-size-fits-all approach toward instruction, teachers use a variety of literacy instructional strategies and materials to meet the learning needs of all students. Teachers' behaviors and the materials they use become not only the primary mediational vehicles within the classrooms but also the primary avenue to differentiate instruction. In place of using the same lesson and the same materials with all learners, teachers base strategy presentations on the linguistic, cognitive, and sociocultural needs of the learners. Furthermore, learning activities and materials not only vary to respond to students' needs, but should also vary in response to students' interests.

The strategy lessons that follow are grouped around key literacy themes within each of the dimensions. Chapter 4 focuses on the linguistic dimension, chapter 5 on the cognitive dimension, and chapter 6 on the sociocultural one. Each strategy lesson is composed of the following elements: concept, materials, procedures, and if appropriate, variations and sample materials. Links to other strategy lessons are noted when relevant, and can be located in the table of contents or subject index.

## CONCEPT

The strategy lessons begin by highlighting key literacy concepts related to each of the dimensions presented in chapter 2. The concepts describe literacy understandings proficient readers and writers draw on to comprehend and compose text. Though each strategy lesson focuses on a particular concept, overlap across concepts and dimensions is inevitable and even desirable when teachers present strategy lessons within a meaningful, purposeful context.

In selecting concepts, teachers keep in mind that development represents the learner's growth in the ability to effectively and efficiently apply literacy strategies across a wide range of contexts (see Fig. 3.8). Information gained from observing students over time, in a variety of situations, and with a variety of texts, is used to select concepts for demonstration. As teachers observe students engage in reading and writing, they "kid watch" to detect patterns in the ways students integrate literacy strategies into their own reading and writing behaviors. These observations then guide teachers in the selection of concepts to present in strategy lessons. As a result, not all students will need to experience the same lesson.

The selection of concepts must be based on the linguistic, cognitive and sociocultural needs of each student. This is a key factor when considering ways of differentiating instruction to meet the diverse needs of the students in the classroom. Consequently, effective strategy lessons that differentiate instruction initially focus on concepts that students need in order to further develop their own strategy use across all three dimensions of literacy. As students become more proficient with any given concept, the teacher can plan other lessons where students encounter the same concept while using more difficult texts or in a new context. The tables outlining reading and writing strategies and processes (Tables 2.22 and 2.25) presented in chapter 2 might be particularly useful for teachers as they identify new concepts when developing their own strategy lessons for classroom use.

## MATERIALS

Each lesson contains a description of the materials necessary for its implementation. In order to make the strategy lessons easily adaptable, we highlight the general characteristics of the reading material the teacher must select to implement the lesson. In the cases where we need to better illustrate the concepts presented in the lesson, we make use of specific materials and conclude the discussion of the lesson by providing the reader with a copy of the sample materials.

The process of selecting materials is closely linked to the concept selection process. In chapter 3, when discussing issues of variability in literacy development, we examined the difference between development and mastery. We discussed how students, rather than "mastering" a strategy, learn to apply the strategy to a broader set of contexts. Consequently, when selecting materials, teachers need to consider the level of proficiency of the students with a particular literacy concept in relation to a particular set of materials. Whereas less-proficient students will require the use of more supportive texts, more-proficient students will benefit from applying their knowledge in new contexts or with less predictable texts.

Similar to the previous discussion on concept selection, differentiation is key in meeting the needs of diverse student in the classroom. For example, English language learners who are literate in their first language can transfer their previous knowledge of the reading and writing processes to their new language. They do not need to relearn how to read and write. These students, however, benefit from instruction that allows them to apply and expand their literacy understandings to a new context using more predictable materials in English. Students' background knowledge and familiarity with different text types (see Table 2.2), text genres (see Table 2.3), and text structures (see Table 2.4) are particularly important when making decisions regarding the predictability of the materials.

## PROCEDURES

Each strategy uses the Into-Through-Beyond framework for lesson procedures. This framework allows us to more closely mirror the ZOPD model depicted in Fig. 3.7 and addresses the factors involved in mediation and development presented in the model. Such scaffolding enables classroom teachers to provide the support needed for students at various points of development to engage in the strategy lessons. This type of differentiation is again key to meeting the needs of diverse students in the classroom. Initially, less-proficient students will require extensive support. Teachers gradually withdraw such support as student take on more responsibility and move toward independence.

In the Into phase of the strategy, the teacher assumes the most responsibility for the lesson. The Into phase provides the teacher with the opportunity to activate or build students' background or elicit the students' interest in the context of the lesson. During the Through phase of the lesson, the teacher gradually releases responsibility of the lesson to the students. In this phase the students are engaged in giving demonstrations, problem solving, discussions, making new discoveries, and asking and answering questions. The Through phase of the lesson allows students to interact with the teacher, with each other, and with a set of supportive materials.

The Beyond phase of the lesson serves to move students to the independent use of the strategies demonstrated in the lesson. As students apply strategies independently, the teacher helps students build metacognitive understandings of their own literacy behaviors. Students are encouraged to reflect on their own understanding of the strategies they have learned and identify other applications.

## VARIATIONS

The variations section of the lesson provides the reader with other ways of presenting the lesson, depending on the needs of the students.

## SAMPLE MATERIALS

These are specific materials needed for lesson implementation.

# 4

# Teaching the Linguistic Dimension of Literacy

The linguistic dimension of literacy is concerned with the reader and the writer as code breaker and code maker. Linguistic strategies support learners in understanding how the various systems of language interact in order to make meaning. Although the developmental, cognitive, and sociocultural dimensions are always present in all strategy instruction, linguistic strategy lessons highlight the language dimension of literacy.

The linguistic strategy lessons are organized around the following themes:

- Using Conventions of Written Language Strategies: strategy lessons that help students develop written language conventions in order to improve communication
- Exploring Letters and Sounds Strategies: strategy lessons that help students develop and apply knowledge of letter–sound patterns when making meaning
- Spelling Strategies: strategy lessons that help learners develop and understand the English spelling system
- Features of Text Strategies: strategy lessons that help students to understand how text features aid in comprehending and composing written language.

# Using Conventions of Written Language Strategies

# Editing Own Writing

(Adapted from Atwell, 2002)

## CONCEPT

Writers revise conventions—spelling, punctuation, capitalization, penmanship, grammar—after meanings and purposes of the writing have been met.

## MATERIALS

A draft of student writing that has been revised for meaning and is in need of editing before it
  is published
Editing Checklist (see Sample Materials)
Colored pencils and highlighters

## PROCEDURES

### Into

1. Discuss with students that when authors are going to publish a piece of writing, they typically tidy up the piece. The author reviews the text, checking such things as spelling, punctuation, capitalization, and grammar.
2. After students have selected and revised a draft for publication (see Revision Circle strategy lesson), they can begin to edit their own work.

### Through

3. Using an Editing Checklist, students edit their own writing.
4. Although the Editing Checklist will vary from student to student, most students can begin by focusing on spelling. For example, after being introduced to the Crazy Spelling strategy lesson, students can be asked to circle all of the words that they think might be misspelled. The student then selects some of the words—the number dependent on the ability of the student—and generates a number of ways in which the words might be spelled. After editing for spelling using the Crazy Spelling strategy lesson, the student places a check mark on the Editing Checklist.

5. As other conventions are introduced during minilinguistic writing strategy lessons or Editing Conference strategy lessons, students can be asked to gradually increase their own editing responsibilities.

**Beyond**

6. After editing and checking their own work, students can meet with peers (see Editors' Table strategy lesson) and/or submit their draft to the teacher for a final editing conference (see Editing Conference strategy lesson).

7. Once texts have been revised and edited, the students can be engaged in the Authors' Chair strategy lesson to celebrate what they have written.

## SAMPLE MATERIALS

Editing Checklist

Name: _____

Date: _____

Title of Piece: _____

| Convention | Author ✓ | Editors ✓ | Teacher Comments |
|---|---|---|---|
| Correct spelling | | | |
| Capitalize letters at the beginning of sentences | | | |
| | | | |
| | | | |
| | | | |
| | | | |
| | | | |
| | | | |
| | | | |
| | | | |
| | | | |
| | | | |
| | | | |
| | | | |
| | | | |
| | | | |
| | | | |
| | | | |
| | | | |
| | | | |
| | | | |
| | | | |

# Editing Conference

(Adapted from Atwell, 1998)

## CONCEPT

Editors support authors in preparing a text for publication. Editors reread drafts for conventions such as spelling, punctuation, and capitalization. Editing for conventions occurs after the meaning and purposes of the writing have been met.

## MATERIALS

Draft of a piece that has been previously edited by the author (see Editing Own Writing strategy lesson) that includes an Editing Checklist
Colored pencils and highlighters
Individual Proofreading List (see Sample Materials)

## PROCEDURES

### Into

1. After students have edited their own drafts (see Editing Own Writing strategy lesson) they submit their text to the teacher for final copyedit.

### Through

2. The teacher edits the text and checks off the Editing Checklist submitted by the author with the original draft.
3. As the teacher edits the piece, he or she makes note of one to three conventions that the writer is not yet using. Notes are added to the Teacher Comments column of the Editing Checklist originally submitted by the student. All marks are done on the draft first edited by the student using a different colored pen or highlighter.
4. The teacher meets with the student and conducts a focused editing conference. Conferences, particularly with emergent writers, can begin by highlighting a convention that the writer has been successful at using.
5. The teacher then conducts a minilesson that focuses on one of the conventions that the writer is not utilizing. Using the student's text, the teacher demonstrates the use of the convention.

**Beyond**

6. The student records the convention(s) taught on his or her Individual Proofreading List.

7. Students select relevant conventions from the Individual Proofreading List when editing their own work the next time they engage in a self-editing conference.

8. Once texts have been revised and edited, the students can be engaged in the Author's Chair strategy lesson to celebrate what they have written.

## VARIATIONS

Common topics for ministrategy lessons on conventions include:

- How to capitalize for beginning of sentences, words in title, proper nouns
- How to use common punctuation marks (periods, commas, quotation marks, questions marks, exclamation points)
- How to use proofreading symbols
- How to proofread for spelling
- How to eliminate sentence fragments
- How to watch out for homonyms
- When to use I or me
- How to use paragraphs

## SAMPLE MATERIALS

Individual Proofreading List

Name: _____

| |
|---|
| 1. Circle all of the words that you think are misspelled. Choose five of the words and do a "Crazy Spelling." |
| 2. Capitalize letters to begin a sentence. |
| 3. |
| 4. |
| 5. |
| 6. |
| 7. |
| 8. |
| 9. |
| 10. |
| 11. |
| 12. |
| 13. |
| 14. |

# Editors' Table

(Adapted from Short, Harste, & Burke, 1996)

**CONCEPT**

Writers employ a number of strategies to revise conventions. Editing for conventions occurs after the meaning and purposes of the writing have been met.

**MATERIALS**

A rough draft that has been previously edited by the author and includes an Editing Checklist
   (see Editing Own Writing strategy lesson)
Colored pencils and highlighters
Dictionary, thesaurus, stylebooks, and other reference books
Visors or buttons to identify the editors

**PROCEDURES**

**Into**

1. Introduce students to the role of an editorial board. Discuss with students how editors support authors in getting their work ready for an audience.
2. Discuss the role of the editorial board in rereading for meaning and conventions:
   - Semantic editing: Editors look for ideas in the text that need clarification. When questions of meaning arise, the editors meet with the author. If agreed to by the author, the author makes the necessary changes.
   - Editing for conventions: The editors reread the draft for conventions, check off the Editing Checklist submitted by the author and mark any necessary changes directly on the draft.
3. Have students examine a variety of published materials, such as trade books and newspapers, and discuss what editors do in preparing these materials for publication.

**Through**

4. Ask for volunteers to serve as editors for class publications. Students can use visors or buttons to identify themselves as editors.

5. Help the editors establish rules and editing symbols to begin editing.
6. Have writers interested in publishing their texts submit their pieces to the editors.

**Beyond**

7. After the editors complete their job, they return the draft to the author who then types and illustrates the piece.
8. Repeat the process of selecting an editorial board so that other students can serve in this role.
9. Once texts have been revised and edited, the students can be engaged in the Author's Chair strategy lesson to celebrate what they have written.

# Minilinguistic Writing Strategies

(Adapted from Atwell, 2002; Dorn & Soffos, 2001; Weaver, 1996)

## CONCEPT

Writers employ a number of conventions to construct and revise meaning. These conventions can occur at any point in time during the drafting and revising process.

## MATERIALS

Sample of student writing or published writing that demonstrates the use of the convention to be demonstrated.

## PROCEDURES

### Into

1. The teacher decides on a particular convention of writing with which the students need additional support. Ministrategy lessons to support strategy development can focus on a variety of conventions and problem-solving strategies:
   - How to use a variety of systems of language—pragmatic, text type, genre, text structure, semantic, syntactic, morphemic, orthographic, graphophonemic, graphemic —to facilitate, extend, and organize text meaning
   - How to use a variety of text aids—headings, subheadings, pictures/illustrations, charts, graphs, color—to facilitate, extend, and organize text meaning
   - How to use punctuation—periods, commas, question marks, exclamation points, capitalizations—to help readers understand the meanings being expressed

   (See the Minicognitive Writing strategy lessons for a focus on meaning.)

### Through

2. Demonstrate the strategy to the students. Strategies can be demonstrated in various ways:
   - Conduct a think-aloud to help students see how the teacher uses this particular convention as a writer.
   - Use a piece produced by a student to show how a peer has successfully used the convention.
   - Read a text to illustrate how a published author has used the convention.

When conducting a think-aloud or using student examples, it is best to use overhead transparencies or chart paper so that all students can see the materials used in the demonstration.

### Beyond

3. The teacher then coaches the students into applying the convention used during the demonstration. Students can:
   - Apply the convention to their own writing.
   - Look for additional examples of the convention in other published works.

## VARIATIONS

1. When working with more-proficient writers, the students can use a spiral notebook to take notes of the points presented in the minilesson.
2. Students can use the Investigating Spelling Patterns strategy lesson to find common patterns and make generalizations regarding the use of any particular convention.
3. The Word Walls strategy lesson can be used to support students with the spelling of frequently used words, including homonyms.

# Exploring Letters and Sounds Strategies

# Alliteration

## CONCEPT

Readers make use of linguistic cues and apply their knowledge of letter–sound patterns to make meaning from text. Predictable books that include alliteration support emergent readers in learning about the alphabetic system as they associate consonant letters and sounds and learn to identify consonant letter names.

## MATERIALS

A predictable text that includes alliteration—the repetition of initial consonant sounds in neighboring words. Although big books are ideal for this strategy, individual books also work well. For example:

Base, G. (1986). *Animalia*. New York: Harry Abrams.
Gordon, J. R. (1991). *Six sleepy sheep*. New York: Puffin.
Seuss, D. (1963). *Dr. Seuss's ABC*. New York: Random House.

## PROCEDURES

### Into

1. Introduce the text to the student and conduct a picture walk. (See Predictable Books strategy lesson for more information on picture walks.)
2. Read the book and encourage the students to read along.

### Through

3. Reread the book and, when appropriate, stop to discuss the examples of alliteration that occur in the book. Help the students recognize the repeated sound by exaggerating the initial sounds in the neighboring words.
4. The teacher may use a window tag with a hole in the middle to frame the examples of alliteration that occur in the book.
5. The teacher discusses the sounds and letters of the initial consonants being highlighted. Have students identify other words that they know that begin with the same sound.

**Beyond**

6. Reread the book aloud with the students.

## VARIATIONS

After reading the book, students can engage in writing their own books using alliteration.

# Alphabet Books

(Adapted from Freeman & Freeman, 2004)

## CONCEPT

Readers use a variety of linguistic cues to make meaning from what they are reading. Emergent readers begin to learn about the alphabetic system as they associate letters and sounds and learn to identify alphabet letter names.

## MATERIALS

A collection of alphabet books. Initially, teachers might want to select alphabet books in which the illustrations clearly relate to the letters of the alphabet, such as:

Martin, B. (1989). *Chicka chicka boom boom*. New York: Simon & Schuster.

Wildsmith, B. (1996). *Brian Wildsmith's ABC*. Long Island City, New York: Star Bright Books.

## PROCEDURES

### Into

1. Conduct a shared reading (see Shared Reading strategy lesson) to introduce the alphabet book to the students.
2. After discussing the book, reread it and encourage students to discuss other words they have seen that also begin with each of the letters presented in the book.

### Through

3. Over a period of time, introduce students to a variety of alphabet books. Have the students compare how different authors use different objects to illustrate each letter of the alphabet. Help the students notice salient characteristics of each letter by comparing size and fonts.
4. After reading several alphabet books, the students can create their own alphabet book. Brainstorm possible themes for the book. Identify potential words to be included in the book. Students may draw their own illustrations or cut out pictures from newspapers and magazines to illustrate their words.

**Beyond**

5. Read the student-authored alphabet book to the class. Be sure to place the book in a location where the students can reread it on their own.

## VARIATIONS

1. Emergent readers can write their own alphabet book using their classmates' names.
2. Older students can also engage in alphabet books as part of a thematic unit of study, such as:

   Pallota, J. (1986). *The icky bug alphabet book*. New York: Scholastic.

   Pallota, J. (1993). *The extinct alphabet book*. New York: Scholastic.

# Phonics Generalizations

(Adapted from Clymer, 1996)

## CONCEPT

Readers make use of linguistic cues and apply their knowledge of letter–sound patterns to make meaning from text. Phonics generalizations vary in terms of their utility in supporting readers in pronouncing unknown words. (See chapter 2, Table 2.14.) Not all generalizations account for a variety of languages and dialects. Consequently, readers can fail to recognize words even if pronounced correctly because of limited experiences with English or because of dialectical differences.

## MATERIALS

A reading selection that the students will find interesting and in which they can encounter
  unknown or unrecognized consonant or vowel letter–sound patterns
Small sticky notes or removable highlighter tape to cover up the part of the words that do not
  contain the letter–sound pattern the teacher is presenting in the lesson

## PROCEDURES

### Into

1. Introduce the book to the students by discussing the title and author and conduct a picture walk (see Predictable Books strategy lesson) or book talk (see Guided Reading strategy lesson).
2. Discuss with the students the letter–sound pattern being highlighted in the lesson and the way in which the pattern is pronounced. For example, to highlight the generalization that when <c> and <h> appear next to each other, they make only one sound, write the word *chair* on the board and discuss how in English these two consonants are combined to create one sound, called a digraph. Have the students identify other words they know that contain the same letter–sound pattern and write these on the board. Demonstrate how the same digraph also occurs at the end of words (e.g., peach).
3. Draw the students' attention to the text. Using small sticky notes or removable highlighter tape, cover up the part of the words that do not contain the letter–sound pattern

being presented in the lesson. Encourage the students to focus on the letter–sound being highlighted in the lesson as they read those words.

**Through**

4. Have the students begin reading. Encourage them to use the letter–sound strategy previously discussed as they read. As the students read to themselves, the teacher listens and provides individual instruction.

**Beyond**

5. Discuss the text. Guide students to share their favorite parts, main ideas, and personal responses to the text. Support learners by allowing them to reread text passage and point to the illustrations.
6. Discuss reading strategies by validating students' use of successful strategies observed during the lesson.

## VARIATIONS

1. Variations can focus on the following high-utility letter–sound generalizations (Clymer, 1996):
   - The *r* gives the preceding vowel a sound that is neither long nor short (horn). Percent of utility: 78.
   - Words having double *e* usually have the long *e* sound (seem). Percent of utility: 98.
   - In *ay* the *y* is silent and gives *a* its long sound (play). Percent of utility: 78.
   - When *y* is the final letter in a word, it usually has a vowel sound (dry). Percent of utility: 84.
   - When *c* and *h* are next to each other, they make only one sound (peach). Percent of utility: 100.
   - *Ch* is usually pronounced as it is in *kitchen, catch,* and *chair,* not like *sh*. Percent of utility: 95.
   - When *c* is followed by *e* or *i*, the sound of *s* is likely to be heard (cent). Percent of utility: 96.
   - When the letter *c* is followed by *o* or *a* the sound of *k* is likely to be heard (camp). Percent of utility: 100.
   - When *ght* is seen in a word, *gh* is silent (fight). Percent of utility: 100.
   - When two of the same consonants are side by side, only one is heard (carry). Percent of utility: 99.
   - When a word ends in *ck*, it has the same last sound as *look* (brick). Percent of utility: 100.
   - In most two-syllable words, the first syllable is accented (famous). Percent of utility: 85.
   - If *a, in, re, ex, de,* or *be* is the first syllable in a word, it is usually unaccented (belong). Percent of utility: 87.
   - In most two-syllable words that end in a consonant followed by *y*, the first syllable is accented and the last is unaccented (baby). Percent of utility: 96.
   - If the last syllable of a word ends in *le*, the consonant preceding the *le* usually begins the last syllable (tumble). Percent of utility: 97.

- When the first vowel element in a word is followed by *th, ch,* or *sh,* these symbols are not broken when the word is divided into syllables and may go with either the first of second syllable (dishes). Percent of utility: 100.
- When there is one *e* in a word that ends in a consonant. The *e* usually has a short sound (leg). Percent of utility: 76.
- When the last syllable is the sound *r*, it is unaccented (butter). Percent of utility: 95.

2. To support students in reading and writing high-frequency words that do not follow high-utility letter–sound generalizations, teachers can use the Word Walls strategy lesson.

# Rhyming

## CONCEPT

Proficient readers recognize speech sounds and connect these sounds to written language. Young readers often enjoy reading and rereading rhyming poetry, songs, and books.

## MATERIALS

Any rhyming poetry, song, or book that the students will enjoy. When working with a large group it is best to use poster charts or big books so that all students can see the text from a distance. The use of picture cards or small objects that represent the rhyming words used during the activity will provide learners with additional support for language development and comprehension.

## PROCEDURES

### Into

1. Introduce the text to the students by drawing on their background knowledge.
2. Read and discuss the rhyming poem, song, or book with the students.

### Through

3. Reread the text. This time, stop and identify the rhyming words. Discuss with the students how rhyming words have the same ending sound. Model by pronouncing two rhyming words (e.g., cat and hat). Use picture cards or small objects that correspond to the rhyming words being presented when additional support is necessary.
4. Continue by demonstrating to students how nonrhyming words do not have the same ending sound. Demonstrate by pronouncing words that do not rhyme (e.g., cat and big).

### Beyond

5. Invite the students to reread the text. This time, the teacher stops and has the students guess the rhyming word by allowing them to chime in with the rhyming words.

**VARIATIONS**

1. When rereading the text, use sticky notes to cover up the rhyming words. Ask the students to predict the rhyming word that is covered.

2. Extend the activity by having students produce other words that rhyme with the ones encountered in the text. Make a list of the rhyming words.

3. If appropriate, have students substitute the rhyming words that appear in the text with other rhyming words they know.

4. Have the students clap, stand up, or put their thumbs up when they hear pairs of rhyming words.

5. Have students listen to a group of four or five words. Ask the students to clap every time they hear a word that ends with a particular rhyme. For example, ask the students to clap every time they hear a word that ends like pig. Demonstrate by pronouncing big, dog, rig, wig, and cat. Clap when pronouncing big, rig, and wig.

6. Using a deck of picture cards with pairs of rhyming words, have students play Concentration. Put the rhyming cards face down and have students take turns looking for pairs of pictures that rhyme. If the pictures rhyme, the student keeps the picture cards. Otherwise, picture cards are turned face down again. The student with the most cards wins.

7. Using the small objects or picture cards of rhyming words, students can sort the rhyming words by putting the pictures or objects that are alike in the same group.

8. Challenge students to produce their own rhyming words. Display a picture of hat. Ask children to produce other words that rhyme with hat.

9. Show students that by changing the onset—the consonants preceding the vowel in the syllable—they can make new words. Invite students to add a different initial consonant to create a list of new words (e.g., hop, pop, mop, bop, cop, top).

10. Support students in exploring spelling patterns (see Investigating Spelling Patterns strategy lesson). By relating what they know about onsets and rhymes, they can spell many new words. Select common rhymes (e.g., -op, -at, -en, -ig, etc.) that appear in the various rhyme or poetry books. After reading the text, write the words on the board (e.g., hop and pop). Underline the rhyme (e.g., pop). Have students look for other words that have the same rhyme.

11. Demonstrate how students can also change a word by changing the final consonant (e.g., hop, hot, hog).

# What Is in My Name?

## CONCEPT

Frequently, young readers and writers begin to recognize speech sounds and connect these sounds to written symbols as they explore their own names.

## MATERIALS

Sentence strips to write students' names
Pictures of individual students
Markers
Pocket chart
Word wall

## PROCEDURES

### Into

1. Begin the school year by taking individual pictures of each class member.
2. During the first weeks of school, each day randomly select the names of one or two students to add to the word wall (see Word Walls strategy lesson). If selecting two individuals, introduce each name at separate times (i.e., morning and afternoon). This ensures that each student has the opportunity to be celebrated on an individual basis. Continue adding names until all students in the classroom have their names on the wall. The teacher must be sensitive to students' pronunciation of their own names throughout this activity.

### Through

3. Gather the students at the rug or large sitting area. Call the "special student" to the front.
4. Use the sentence strip to write the student's name. As you write the student's name, spell it aloud. Encourage the students to participate in spelling each name if they are ready to do so.

5. As the students' names are introduced, have the class notice different phonological and graphic features of these words. On separate occasions, demonstrate for the students and have the students engage in any of the following activities:
   • identifying a student's name recognizing the initial sound of each name
   • naming other students who have a name the begins with the same sound
   • identifying two out of three words that start with the same sound (e.g., Lupe, lion, cat)
   • chanting the spelling of each name
   • counting the number of letters in each name
   • counting the number of times a specific letter appears in each name (e.g., How many a's are in Maria?)
   • noticing the differences between lowercase and capital letters
   • arranging the letters of the name (write the name on a separate sentence strip and cut and mix the letters)
   • stretching out the sounds in the name (e.g., /ppppaaaatttt/)
   • identifying a student's after the teacher stretches the sounds in his or her name
   • clapping and counting the number of syllables in each name
   • graphing the number of students whose name begin with the same letter

**Beyond**

6. Clip the student's picture to the strip with the student's name and add it to the word wall.

## VARIATIONS

1. Duplicate the names and pictures and have students match names and pictures.
2. Have the students sort the names by beginning alphabet letter.

# Spelling Strategies

# Crazy Spelling

(Personal Communication, Burke, 1980)

## CONCEPT

Proficient spellers use their visual memory for how words "look" as much as their knowledge of how words "sound" when deciding on the spelling of a word.

## MATERIALS

A list of words that are spelled correctly
Student drafts of something they have written

## PROCEDURES

### Into

1. Discuss with the students that one way to decide whether a word is spelled correctly is how is "looks." Being able to identify misspelled words and to generate alternate spellings is something that good spellers are able to do.
2. Write a word that students know how to spell correctly on the board, chart paper, or overhead transparency. Then say, "If the word was not spelled this way, how might it be spelled?"
3. With the students, brainstorm and list all the ways the word might be spelled. For example, the word "cat" might be spelled "kat," "katt," or "catt." Generate alternatives for several words until students understand the concept.

### Through

4. Ask the students to read through a draft of something they have written and to circle all of the words that they think are misspelled.
5. Ask the students to select several of the words circled, the number selected depending on the ability of the students and the number of words circled. Students then generate several alternatives for each of the words selected.

6. Students look through the alternatives they have generated for each word and circle the one that "looks" the most correct.

**Beyond**

7. As students engage in writing throughout the year, ask them to generate possible spellings when they encounter words that they do not know how to spell.

# Independent Word Study

(Adapted from Atwell, 2002)

## CONCEPT

Proficient spellers use their visual memory for how words "look" as much as their knowledge of how words "sound" when deciding on the spelling of a word.

## MATERIALS

Personal spelling word list where five individual words have been selected by each student because he or she does not know how to spell them and think are important
Overhead transparency of an Independent Word Study Grid (see Sample Materials)

## PROCEDURES

### Into

1. The teacher begins the demonstration by discussing how the list of words selected by each student are personally difficult to spell and that they will be needed for writing.

### Through

2. Write the first word in the first column.
3. Read the word.
4. Look at the word. Examine each of the letters closely and notice visual details.
5. Say the word aloud. Spell the word aloud. With a pencil, touch each letter as it is pronounced.
6. Ask the students to close their eyes and visualize the word. Tell the students to make a picture of the word in their heads and say each letter of the word aloud.
7. Use the rewrite columns to print the word three times. Say each individual letter as it is printed.
8. Take a 5-minute break and then come back to the spelling task.

9. Cover the words and spell each word.

10. Proofread by checking the word, letter by letter.

**Beyond**

11. Put a star by the word if it is spelled correctly. Repeat the process if it is misspelled.

12. Go on to the next word and repeat the process.

**SAMPLE MATERIALS**

Independent Word Study Grid

Name: _____

Date: _____

| COPY | REWRITE | REWRITE | REWRITE | SPELL | SPELL AGAIN OR ★ |
|------|---------|---------|---------|-------|-------------------|
| 1. | | | | | |
| 2. | | | | | |
| 3. | | | | | |
| 4. | | | | | |
| 5. | | | | | |
| 6. | | | | | |
| 7. | | | | | |
| 8. | | | | | |
| 9. | | | | | |
| 10. | | | | | |

# Investigating Spelling Patterns

(Adapted from Freeman & Freeman, 2004)

## CONCEPT

Proficient spellers understand that in English there are common spelling patterns. They approach spelling as a problem-solving activity that involves making generalizations.

## MATERIALS

3 × 5" cards
Chart paper
Reading materials for researching spelling patterns

## PROCEDURES

### Into

1. Inform the students that they will be conducting a spelling pattern investigation. Similar to what linguists do, they will be studying the environments in which the sound being studied occurs in order to make some generalizations about its spelling.

### Through

2. Divide students into pairs and have each pair of students look through books and other print materials for words that contain the specified sound. For example, words that have the /k/ sound. Have the students write each word they find on a 3 × 5" card.
3. Once the students have identified a number of examples, the teacher and the students sort the index cards into different groups according to spelling patterns, for example, c (cot), k (kite), ck (tick), ch (chemistry), q (queen), que (unique).

### Beyond

4. After the students have sorted their words by spelling patterns, the teacher has the students begin to formulate hypotheses to account for the data they collected. Invite students to examine how the words in each group are alike. For example, students might notice that with words that have the /k/ sound, the c spelling is always followed

by a consonant or the vowels *a*, *o*, or *u*. Similarly, they may also notice that when these words are spelled with a k it is because the sound /k/ is followed by *e* or *i*.

5. The students continue to find additional examples and exceptions. The teacher encourages students to identify patterns and make additional generalizations about the different spelling patterns they find.

## VARIATIONS

1. The teacher can identify spelling patterns for investigation by observing if the students are consistently using incorrect spelling patterns in their writing.
2. Students can investigate letter–sound relationships and patterns.
3. Students can investigate commonly misspelled homonyms.
4. Additional investigations can focus on contractions, compound words, synonyms, antonyms, plurals, possessives, and word origins.
5. Add examples of words used in the investigation to the word wall (see Word Wall strategy lesson) for future reference.

# Mnemonics

## CONCEPT

Proficient spellers make use of mnemonic devices to help associate spellings of troublesome words with something already known.

## MATERIALS

Words that are difficult for students to spell because the words do not follow any particular spelling generalization.
Overhead transparency
Writing folders with students' drafts

## PROCEDURES

### Into

1. Share with the students that with words that are difficult to spell, sometimes it helps to use a story or jingle to remember their spelling.

### Through

2. Demonstrate to the students how to develop a mnemonic device to spell a word. For example, discuss with the students how many writers get confused when trying to spell desert and dessert. Discuss how writers develop a mnemonic and that you know dessert has two s's because "you always want a second helping."

### Beyond

3. Invite the students to go back through their writing folders and identify words that they often misspell. Have the students work in pairs to develop mnemonic devices to help them remember the spelling.

# Spelling Wall Chart

(Adapted from Kucer, 1995)

## CONCEPT

Proficient spellers have various strategies for determining how to spell a word.

## MATERIALS

Various writing activities throughout the year
Chart paper or an overhead transparency

## PROCEDURES

### Into

1. Occasionally, as students engage in various writing activities during the year, ask them to keep a list for how they handle words that they do not know how to spell. What do they do to try and spell the word correctly?
2. After a writing activity in which students have been asked to monitor their spelling behavior, ask the students to share their spelling strategies.
3. Record these strategies on the board, chart paper, or overhead transparency.

### Through

4. As the Spelling Strategy Wall Chart develops, encourage students to use it when they encounter words they do not know how to spell. Also, as students discover new spelling strategies, add these to the chart.

### Beyond

5. After the wall chart is developed, it can be photocopied and distributed to the students for use when they write.

## VARIATIONS

Students can be engaged in the Crazy Spelling strategy lesson that shows them how to generate multiple spellings for words that they are trying to spell.

## SAMPLE MATERIALS

### Spelling Strategy Wall Chart

1. Think of "small words" that are in the word and write these first.
2. Write the word several different ways and choose the one that looks the best.
3. Write the letters that you know are in the word.
4. Write the first and last letters of the word. Put a line for the letters that go in the middle of the word.
5. Draw a line for the word.
6. Think of other words that are related to the word you want to spell, such as medical for the word medicine or musician for music.
7. Ask a friend.
8. Look it up in the dictionary or use a computer spell check.
9. Sound it out.

# Word Walls

(Adapted from Cunningham, 2005)

## CONCEPT

As readers interact with meaningful text, they use a variety of linguistic strategies to recognize and spell words.

## MATERIALS

Cardboard strips or 3 × 5" cards
Word Wall consisting of a wall or bulletin board space divided into sections, one section for each letter of the alphabet

## PROCEDURES

### Into

1. Begin by selecting five words with which the students frequently need help when reading or writing. Students can help in the selection process.
2. Write the words on a cardboard strip or 3 × 5" cards. Direct the students' attention to particular features of the word (e.g., letters, sounds, onset, rime, syllables, etc.).
3. Read the words and talk about their meaning. Students can illustrate the meaning of the word on the back of the cards.

### Through

4. Place the word below the alphabet letter with which it begins. Help the students learn to recognize words by having them:
   - clap and chant the spelling of the words,
   - write the spelling of the words on small white boards or pieces of paper,
   - guess the "mystery" word using four or five clues given by the teacher (e.g., begins with, rhymes with, has four letters, etc.),
   - refer to the word wall as they are engaged in writing.

**Beyond**

5. Continue to add words to the word wall. Many teachers add five new words every week. Allow 5 to 10 minutes every day to review the words on the wall.

## VARIATIONS

1. Name Walls: Introduce the word wall using the students' names. (See What Is in My Name? strategy lesson.)

2. Word Sorts: Have students focus on specific features of the words by engaging in word sorts. Select and have the students write 10 to 15 words from the word on small slips of paper. Students then sort the words in different piles according to features shared by the words (e.g., number of letters, begin with the same letter, share the same letter–sound pattern, etc.).

3. Rhyming Words: As words are introduced to the word wall, help students notice common word patterns that are helpful in reading and spelling new words. For example, when introducing "say," model other rhyming words (i.e., pay, day) as you write the words on the board. Place a star or sticker next to the word in order to identify it as one of the "special" words on the word wall.

4. Homophones: Homophones commonly misspelled by students when writing can be added to the word wall (e.g., ant/aunt, to/too/two, there/their). Students can attach clues to these words by adding illustrations or common phrases.

5. Portable Word Walls: Individual students can reproduce the classroom word wall by copying the words onto a file folder that has been divided into sections, one section for each letter of the alphabet. As words are added to the class wall, these can be added to the individual folders. Students can take these portable word walls home or to other classroom settings.

# Features of Text Strategies

# Previewing

## CONCEPT

Authors use a variety of text aids or text features to help organize, highlight, clarify, and extend their ideas: headings and subheadings; illustrations and pictures; charts, tables, and graphs; bold faced, italicized, and enlarged type; and so on. Readers similarly use these text aids to assist in organizing, highlighting, clarifying, and extending the meanings that they construct from the text.

## MATERIALS

A text that contains a variety of text aids. (see Sample Materials) Social science and science books, newspapers, and magazines typically contain text aids. Students should have their own individual copies of the text. It can also be helpful if an overhead transparency is available for showing on an overhead projector.

Text Prediction Grid (see Sample Materials)

## PROCEDURES

### Into

1. Share with the students the text to be read. With the students, identify the various text aids and ask why authors might use these aids. List the reasons on the board, chart paper, or overhead transparency.

### Through

2. Give the students a few minutes to individually examine the text aids in the text. The amount of time provided will vary, depending on the length of the text and the number of text aids used. Students should have enough time to read the text aids but not enough time to begin reading the connected discourse.
3. Ask the students to write down everything they think the text will be about based on their examination of the text aids. Students are to use information only from the text aids and not the connected discourse.

4. As students share their predictions, record them on the board, chart paper, or an overhead transparency using the left-hand column of the Text Prediction Grid.

5. Give the students the opportunity to read the text. As they read, the students should record the major ideas that were actually developed.

**Beyond**

6. After the text has been read, students share the major ideas developed in the text. Record these in the right-hand column of the Text Prediction Grid.

7. Students compare/contrast their predictions from the text aids with what was actually presented in the text.

## VARIATIONS

1. Rather than giving students a text with both the text aids and the connected discourse, provide students only the text aids. Ask students to predict and record what they think will be written about for each text aid (see Sample Materials; the various photographs from the text are not included).

2. Students can also learn about the function of text aids by using them in their own writings. Engage students in the Aiding the Text strategy lesson to help them use text aids as they compose.

**SAMPLE MATERIALS**

Text Prediction Grid

Text Read: _____

| Text Predictions | What the Text Actually Said |
|---|---|
|  |  |

Text Aids Without the Connected Discourse
"Extraordinary Eyes: How Animals See the World"*

---

## Extraordinary EYES
How Animals See the World
By Sandra Sinclair

**Catchers of Light**

**Animals See Colors Differently**

**Predatory and Prey**

**Single-lens and Compound Eyes**

**Thinking Eyes**

**Eye and Brain: How Mammals See**

**Depth of Vision**

---

* Excerpted from: Sinclair, S. (2002, July/August). Extraordinary eyes: How animals see the world. In *Ask: Arts and science for kids, 1* (pp. 6–12). Peru, IL: Carus Publishing Company.

# Aiding the Text

**CONCEPT**

Authors use a variety of text aids or features to help organize, highlight, clarify, and extend their ideas: headings and subheadings; illustrations and pictures; charts, tables, and graphs; bold faced, italicized, and enlarged type; and so on. Readers similarly use these text aids to assist in organizing, highlighting, clarifying, and extending the meanings that they construct from the text.

**MATERIALS**

A short text with a variety of text aids
Drafts of student texts that would benefit from the use of a variety of text aids

**PROCEDURES**

### Into

1. Students should have experienced the Previewing strategy lesson before engaging in Aiding the Text. Review with students the Previewing strategy lesson, discussing the various types of text aids and the various reasons authors use them. To enhance this discussion, share with the students a text with various text aids.

### Through

2. Ask students to reread their written drafts and to consider where the use of text aids might be helpful.
3. Students rewrite their drafts, inserting text aids where appropriate.

### Beyond

4. Give students the opportunity to share their revised drafts, discussing where and why text aids were inserted.

## VARIATIONS

For students in need of more support and mediation, the teacher can share with the students a text without text aids. Working with the class or a small group, the teacher identifies possible text aids and inserts them into the text with student assistance. Throughout this process, the teacher shares the reasons for the text aids generated and the rationale for inserting them at particular points in the text.

# Publishing and Celebrating

(Adapted from Atwell, 2002; Moline, 1995)

## CONCEPT

Authors use a variety of text aids to help organize, highlight, clarify, and extend their ideas: headings and subheadings; illustrations and pictures; charts, tables, and graphs; bold faced, italicized, and enlarged type; and so on.

## MATERIALS

Draft of a piece of student writing that has been edited and is ready for publication
Computer and software students can use for publication
Materials for binding books
Different kinds of paper
Markers, crayons, paints, pencils, pens
Variety of book that integrate graphics and text. Information big books and science textbooks are particularly useful for this strategy.

## PROCEDURES

### Into

1. Invite students to examine how professional designers use graphic design when publishing books. Discuss with the students how designers pay attention to:
   - Layout: Arrangement of written language and visual elements of the page (e.g., columns, white space, color, size)
   - Typography: choice of typefaces and fonts
   - Signposting: layout and typographic features that direct the reader through the text organization (e.g., headings, subheadings, bullets, boxes, etc.).

### Through

2. Using a book with various design features, ask students to focus on the graphic design features.
3. To support students in examining graphic design, the teacher can ask questions such as:

- How does the layout help the reader find information?
- How is the information organized?
- How do the text and the graphics support each other?
- Are graphics just decorative or do they add information to the text?
- Hoes does the typography help the readers know which topics are more important than others?
- How does the use of a font contribute to the meaning of the text?
- How does the reader find his or her way around the page? Is the page cluttered?

**Beyond**

4. Have students examine their own written drafts and consider the use of various design features in publishing their own books.

5. Allow time for students to produce a final draft using various design features.

6. There should be a time for the students to share and celebrate their published pieces. This may be done through "author of the day," book parties, book sharings, and the like. If possible, the published pieces should be available to the students throughout the year for reading and rereading. Student published pieces often become the favorite "books" in the class.

**VARIATIONS**

To support students in the publishing process, they can read:

Christelow, E. (1999). *What do illustrators do*? New York: Clarion Books.

Aliki. (1986). *How a book is made*. New York: Harper & Row.

# Reading Text Signals

## CONCEPT

Authors use special types of words to indicate or signal conceptual relationships or connections among various ideas. Readers use these signals both to predict and construct connections among the ideas that they are reading.

## MATERIALS

Several texts that contain a number of connective words (see Sample Materials)
Connective Word Grid (see Sample Materials)

## PROCEDURES

### Into

1. On an overhead transparency, show the students a text in which various connective words have been underlined. For each underlined word, ask the students what the word means or indicates based on the context in which it is found. Help the students to understand that these words signal to the reader that a particular kind of relationship is being indicated by the author. These words are special because they help the reader to connect ideas within a sentence or across sentences.
2. As each word and indicated relationship is identified, write the word and relationship on the Connective Word Grid, which is shown on the board, chart paper, or an overhead transparency.

### Through

3. Give the students a second text to read independently or in small groups. Students identify all connective words and their relationships. Students record these words and relationships on a Connective Word Grid.
4. As a class, students share the connective words identified and the relationships that are signaled. The teacher can record these on the board, chart paper, or an overhead transparency.

**Beyond**

5. As students read various texts throughout the year, occasionally ask them to identify and share signal words and the relationships indicated. Based on this sharing, construct a Connective Word Wall Chart that lists the various relationships that have been identified and the words that signal each relationship.

## VARIATIONS

1. Students can be encouraged to consider what kinds of connectives or signals authors use in various disciplines, such as in literature, social science, mathematics, and science or in various text structures, such as time order, comparative/contrast, cause/effect, and so on. Connective Word Wall Charts can be constructed for each discipline or text structure in which the students read.

2. As students become comfortable identifying and using connective words in their reading, they can be encouraged to use them in their writing as well. See the Writing Text Signals strategy lesson for teaching procedures.

**SAMPLE MATERIALS**

Text With Text Signals
"Extraordinary Eyes: How Animals See the World"*

Eyes are one of nature's most extraordinary creations. The <u>first</u> living creatures on Earth had no eyes at all—just small clumps of cells that were sensitive to light. We call them eyespots and they are still found in many small, soft-skinned creatures such as earthworms. Eyespots detect light, which helps a creature find warmth and food.

The <u>next step</u> in the evolution of the eye was gaining the ability to detect motion. The <u>third major step</u> was the ability of the eye to form images.

The eyes of all invertebrates—animals without internal skeletons such as worms, clams, crabs, and insects—evolved from a part of the skin. This fact may account for the unusual locations of eyes in some primitive invertebrates. <u>For example</u>, the eyes of the queen conch are found at the ends of its tentacles, and the starfish has eyes on its feet.

<u>However</u>, the eye of the vertebrate animal—mammals such as human beings, as well as fish, birds, reptiles, and amphibians—is a direct outgrowth of its brain. The nerve cells of the eye and the brain are so similar that some vision scientists believe that the brain evolved as a result of primitive eyes trying to make sense of the images they received from the world around them.

---

\* Excerpted from: Sinclair, S. (2002, July/August). Extraordinary eyes: How animals see the world. In *Ask: Arts and science for kids, 1* (pp. 6–12). Peru, IL: Carus Publishing Company.

Connective Word Grid

| Text Signal | Indicated Relationship |
|---|---|
| | |
| | |
| | |
| | |
| | |
| | |
| | |

Connective Word Wall Chart

| Text Signal | Indicated Relationship |
|---|---|
| also, again, another, finally, furthermore, likewise, moreover, similarly, too | another item in the same series |
| afterwards, finally, later on, next, after | another item in a time series |
| for instance, for example, specifically | another example or illustration of what has been said |
| accordingly, as a result, therefore, thus, so | a consequence of what has been |
| in other words, that is to say, to put it differently | a restatement of what has been said |
| all in all, altogether, finally, in conclusion, the point is | a concluding item or summary |
| but, however, on the other hand, on the contrary | a statement opposing what has been said |
| granted, of course, to be sure, undoubtedly | a concession to an opposing view |
| all the same, even though, nevertheless, nonetheless, still | the original line of argument is resuming after a concession |

Connectives and Text Structures

| Text Signal | Typical Connective/Signal |
|---|---|
| time order | time, not long after, now, as, before, after, when |
| compare/contrast | however, but, as well as, on the other hand, not only . . . but also, either . . . or, while, although, unless, similarly, yet |
| problem/solution | because, since, therefore, so that, consequently, as a result, this led |
| cause/effect | to, so that, nevertheless, thus, accordingly, if . . . then |
| idea development | to begin with, first, second next, then, finally, most important, also, in fact, for instance, for example |

# Writing Text Signals

## CONCEPT

Authors use special types of words to indicate or signal conceptual relationships or connections among various ideas. Readers use these signals both to predict and construct connections among the ideas that they are reading.

## MATERIALS

A text that would be improved with the use of connective words
Student drafts that would be improved with the use of connective words
Connective Word Wall Chart (see Reading Text Signals strategy lesson)

## PROCEDURES

### Into

1. This Writing Text Signals strategy lesson is most effective when students have experienced the Reading Text Signals strategy lesson and when a Connective Word Wall Chart has been developed.

2. Review the Connective Word Wall Chart with the students and discuss the purpose of connective or signal words.

3. On the board, a wall chart, or an overhead transparency, show the students a text that lacks the use of connective words. Ask students to suggest where connective words might help the author to more clearly mark or signal relationships or connections among ideas. Discuss what connective words would be the most appropriate to use at the various locations identified.

4. As various locations and connective words are decided on, the teacher inserts the words into the text.

5. After all connective words have been added, the teacher and/or students orally read the text to "get a feel" for the impact of the added words.

**Through**

6. Students identify a text they have written that would be improved with the use of connective words. Give students the time to insert such words where appropriate.
7. Allow various students to share their revised texts, noting where and why connective words were added.

**Beyond**

8. Throughout the year, review with students the usefulness of connective words and ask students to consider using them in their writing.

# 5

# Teaching the Cognitive Dimension of Literacy

The cognitive dimension of literacy is concerned with the reader and writer as meaning maker. Cognitive strategy instruction introduces children to various avenues through which they can more effectively and efficiently construct ideas in written language. Although the linguistic, sociocultural, and developmental dimensions are always present in all strategy instruction, cognitive strategy lessons highlight the meaning making dimension of literacy.

The cognitive strategy lessons are organized around the following themes:

- Audiences and Purposes Strategies: strategy lessons that help student engage in writing for a variety of purposes and audiences.
- Idea Generation Strategies: strategy lessons that help students to develop ideas when reading and writing.
- Learning from and through Others Strategies: strategy lessons that help students to gradually internalize literacy processes through the support of more proficient readers and writers.
- Organizing Meaning Strategies: strategy lessons that help students to structure or organize their ideas when reading and writing.
- Reader Response Strategies: strategy lessons that help students to interact with what is being read or written.
- Reading and Writing Block Strategies: strategy lessons that help students to overcome problems when reading and writing.
- Using Context Strategies: strategy lessons that help students to use context when reading.
- Writing Revision Strategies: strategy lessons that help students to reconsider and change what they have written.

# Audiences and Purposes Strategies

# Classroom Newspapers

**CONCEPT**

Classroom newspaper provides authors the opportunity to engage in writing for a variety of purposes and audiences.

**MATERIALS**

Various newspapers
Recommended: Publishing hardware, software and a digital camera

**PROCEDURES**

### Into

1. Begin by exploring how students and their families read newspapers at home. Who reads the newspaper at home? Do families read newspapers in languages other than English? What part of the newspapers does each family member like best? Have students bring copies of newspapers their families read to school.

2. Give students an opportunity to examine the various newspapers brought to class. In small groups, ask students to identify the main sections of the newspaper (e.g., front page, editorials, sports, etc.). Have one of the group members record the information.

3. Once small groups have had the opportunity to examine their newspapers, using chart paper, record the students' observations. As students identify each major section, discuss the general nature of the articles a reader might expect to find in that particular section of the paper.

### Through

4. Discuss with the students the type of newspaper they would like to publish for the classroom. Students need to consider:
   - What types of articles will be included in the classroom newspaper?
     Examples: class news, special features, announcements, opinion pieces, interviews, editorials, letters to the editor, advice column, jokes, cartoons, puzzles, book reviews, movie reviews, want ads, and so on.

- What jobs need to be created in order to publish a newspaper? How will these positions be filled?

  Examples: editor, assistant editors, reporters, photographers, cartoonists, artists, layout designers, and typists.

  Keep track of their ideas by writing them on different pieces of chart paper. Once students have decided on the types of articles and positions they need, have the students decide on a name for the newspaper and on a publication date.

5. As articles for the newspaper are drafted, revised and edited, engage the students in various ministrategy lessons that highlight particular features of newspaper writing and publishing:

   - Writing leads, using quotes, developing headlines
   - Conducting interviews, generating questions, taking notes
   - Layout, variety of text aides, captions and headlines, photography (publishing hardware and software as well as the use of digital cameras will facilitate the layout and publishing of the newspaper)

**Beyond**

6. Distribute the newspapers to class members and families as well as other classes in the school.

7. Decide on the date of publication for the next edition of the newspaper.

## VARIATIONS

Students can produce class magazines as an avenue to publish the pieces they produce in the classroom.

# Creating Narratives

(Adapted from Atwell, 2002; Graves, 1994; Piazza, 2003)

**CONCEPT**

Authors vary the manner in which texts are written based on different purposes, intentions, or audiences. Through narrative writing authors create imaginary stories to entertain their audience.

**MATERIALS**

Text Sets (see Text Sets strategy lesson) that support students in developing as fiction writers. Text Sets will vary depending on the particular elements of fiction that the teacher has identified as the focus of the writing.

**PROCEDURES**

**Into**

1. Tell the students that they will be reading stories and identifying elements of fiction that authors use to write good stories.
2. Gather a text set of stories for students to read and discuss. After responding to the stories, use a Grid (see Text Sets strategy lesson for sample materials) to help students identify similarities across texts in terms of
   - Plot
   - Character
   - Setting
   - Problem
   - Solution

**Through**

3. Tell the students that they will be writing their own stories using these story elements.
4. Have students engage in drafting and revising their own stories. During revision conferences (see Revision Circle strategy lesson), students focus on ways their drafts reflect the story element(s) they had identified earlier. The number of elements considered will depend on the needs and abilities of the students.

5. While writing their own stories, students engage in ministrategy lessons that will support them in further developing as fiction writers. Again, it is important that students have an opportunity to both examine how published writers use the various elements introduced in the ministrategy lessons and to have students incorporate these elements into their own writing. Ministrategy lessons topics can focus on:

   • Character development: How does the author describe the character? What does the character look like? What does the character like? What does the character want? What does the character think? What does the character say? Does the dialogue sound real?

   • Plot: How is the problem introduced? What obstacles does the character encounter in solving the problem? How does the story build to a culminating event? How quickly—or slowly—does the plot move? How does the author move the plot (e.g., foreshadowing, flashbacks)?

   • Setting: How does the setting support the characters? How does the setting add to the mood of the story? How does the setting influence events in the story?

   • Point of view: From which point of view is the story told? First person? Single character? Omniscient view? Multiple characters views? Why does the author use a particular point of view?

   • Beginnings: How does the author begin the story? How does the author set the tone for the story? How does the author establish the direction of the writing?

   • Endings: How does the author end the story? How does the author give the reader a sense of completion?

### Beyond

6. Once students have edited their final draft, have the students publish and celebrate their story.

# Independent Reading

## CONCEPT

Proficient readers use reading not only to increase their knowledge of their worlds—efferent reading—but also for enjoyment, for leaving the here and now and traveling to new worlds—aesthetic reading. Reading for interest and enjoyment further increases proficient readers' ability to more effectively transact with print.

## MATERIALS

A range of different types and lengths of reading materials—picture books, chapter books, short stories, magazines, newspapers—and text types—narratives, expositions, poems, dramas—at various reading levels. It is helpful if books are arranged by topic and/or type. One efficient way to manage this arrangement is to put related books into plastic containers—dishwashing tubs work well. During Independent Reading, individual tubs can be distributed around the room for easy student access. This arrangement limits student crowding when all of the reading materials are kept in a single location.

Independent Reading Logs (see Sample Materials)

## PROCEDURES

### Into

1. Independent Reading is most effective when it is scheduled on a regular and ongoing basis—days and times should be specified and adhered to when possible.
2. Introduce students to the concept of Independent Reading Time and the Independent Reading Logs. The arrangement and location of the reading materials should be specified so that students can easily access materials of interest.
3. Students should be informed that the Independent Reading Log is not a book report. Rather, it is a way for students to keep track of what they are reading, how much, and what they think of what has been read. At the beginning of each Independent Reading Time, students should fill in the date, the name of the text and author, and what page they are beginning to read.
4. At the beginning of every Independent Reading Time, provide students time to return and select new material. Students should be encouraged to select several pieces to

read in case they find one text too difficult, too easy, or not of interest. This will limit students sitting and reading nothing because what they have selected is inappropriate for whatever the reason.

5. The teacher should also have something to read during this time. As with the students, the material should be something of genuine interest, not material that must be read for an "assignment."

6. Allow students time to locate a suitable place to read.

**Through**

7. During the reading time, it is advisable to limit student movement. Students should not be returning or selecting reading materials. Rather, the class, including the teacher, should be reading.

**Beyond**

8. After the reading time is over, students complete their Independent Reading Logs, specifying the page on which they stopped reading, whether they plan to continue reading the text, have finished reading, or have decided to select another text during the next Independent Reading Time, and any comments or reactions to what was read.

9. With a partner, in small groups, or with the entire class, give students the opportunity to informally share what they have read or the comments they have written in their Reading Logs. This sharing will introduce other students in the class to possible texts of interest and validates the reading that students have done during Independent Reading Time.

10. If students are frequently not finishing texts that have been selected for Independent Reading, the teacher will want to help them select more appropriate texts. Selecting appropriate texts is particularly difficult for struggling readers who oftentimes pick reading materials that are too difficult for them, but may contain numerous pictures, diagrams, and so on.

## VARIATIONS

Occasionally, the teacher may want to use the time set aside for Independent Reading to informally assess the students' reading and material selection. During this time, the teacher asks different students to sit by him or her and read aloud and discuss the material being read for Independent Reading.

**SAMPLE MATERIALS**

Independent Reading Log

Student Name: _____

| Date | Name and Author of Text | Pages Read | Continued Finished Quit | Comments |
|------|-------------------------|------------|-------------------------|----------|
|      |                         |            |                         |          |
|      |                         |            |                         |          |
|      |                         |            |                         |          |
|      |                         |            |                         |          |
|      |                         |            |                         |          |
|      |                         |            |                         |          |
|      |                         |            |                         |          |

# Independent Writing

## CONCEPT

Proficient writers use writing not only to express their knowledge of their worlds—efferent writing—but also for enjoyment, for leaving the here and now and traveling to new worlds—aesthetic writing. Writing for interest and enjoyment further increases proficient writers' ability to more effectively transact with print.

## MATERIALS

Bound notebooks
Independent Writing Logs (see Sample Materials)

## PROCEDURES

### Into

1. Independent Writing is most effective when it is scheduled on a regular and ongoing basis—days and times should be specified and adhered to when possible.
2. Introduce students to the concept of Independent Writing, the writing notebooks, and the Independent Writing Logs. Students should be informed that the time set aside for independent writing is intended for students to select their own topics to write about. Students may continue a writing entry across a number of days and/or select different writing topics each day.
3. It can be helpful to occasionally brainstorm with students various topics that they might write about. Inside the front or back cover of the writing logs, or on the first few pages in the log, give students the opportunity to list various topics on which they might write. These topics can be shared with the class to further stimulate possible writing topics. Students can then refer to these topics when they have difficulty thinking of a topic for Independent Writing. See the Writing Topics List strategy lesson for more information about topic generation.
4. It can also be helpful to discuss with students where writers locate their topics. Writing topics frequently emerge from the writer's ongoing personal experiences with the world and need not be based on some "special" event.

5. The teacher should also select a writing topic during this time. As with the students, the topic should be one of genuine interest, not something that must be written for an "assignment."

6. Allow students time to locate a suitable place to write.

**Through**

7. During the writing time, it is advisable to limit student movement. Students should not be sharpening pencils, changing locations for writing, and so on. Rather, the class, including the teacher, should be writing.

**Beyond**

8. After the writing time is over, students complete their Independent Writing Logs, specifying the name of their text; how many pages were written; and whether they plan to continue writing, have finished the text, or will quit and move on to another writing topic. Students can also record any comments or reactions to what they have written.

9. Provide students the opportunity to informally share what has been written. This sharing can be done in small groups or with the entire class. This sharing will introduce other students in the class to possible topics of interest and validates the writing that students have done during Independent Writing Time.

## VARIATIONS

Occasionally, the teacher may want to use the time set aside for Independent Writing to informally assess the students' writing and topic selection. During this time, the teacher asks different students to sit by him or her and read aloud and discuss what is being written during Independent Writing.

**SAMPLE MATERIALS**

Independent Writing Log

Student Name: _____

| Date | Name of Text | Pages Written | Continued Finished Quit | Comments |
|------|--------------|---------------|-------------------------|----------|
|      |              |               |                         |          |
|      |              |               |                         |          |
|      |              |               |                         |          |
|      |              |               |                         |          |
|      |              |               |                         |          |
|      |              |               |                         |          |
|      |              |               |                         |          |

# Patterned Poems

(Adapted from Koch, 1970)

## CONCEPT

Proficient writers make use of organizational patterns to structure their ideas and language.

## MATERIALS

Selected "I wish" poems from:
  Koch, K. (1970). *Wishes, lies, and dreams*. New York: Vintage Books/Chelsea Publishers.

## PROCEDURES

### Into

1. Read aloud to the students several "I Wish" poems from *Wishes, Lies, and Dreams*. Invite the students to collaborate in writing a class "I Wish" poem.
2. Give the students the opportunity to talk about wishes. Encourage students to wish for things normally considered outrageous or silly. List these wishes on the board, chart paper, or an overhead transparency.

### Through

3. Have each student contribute a line to the class poem. Every line must start with "I wish" and the lines do not have to rhyme. List these lines on the board, chart paper, or an overhead transparency.
4. Discuss with the students the order in which the "I wish" sentences should be arranged. Decide which sentence should first, second, and so on. Arrange the sentences in the order decided.
5. Read aloud the poem with the students.

### Beyond

6. Have students write and share their own "I Wish" poems.

## VARIATIONS

Students can experiment by starting their lines with other patterns:

1. Begin every odd line with "I used to be" and every even line with "But now" or every odd line with "I seem to be" and every even line with "But really I am." See the I Seem to be, But Really I Am strategy lesson.
2. Use color in every line. Each line can begin with the same repetition and color (i.e., "Red is . . .") or students use different colors in every line.
3. Use a comparison in every line (i.e., "a . . . is like . . .").

# Persuasive Writing

## CONCEPT

When writing to persuade, authors attempt to convince their audience to agree with their way of thinking. Authors establish their arguments and purposely craft their message to influence their audience into accepting their ideas.

## MATERIALS

A copy of Zolotow, C. (1972). *William's doll*. New York: Harper & Row.

## PROCEDURES

### Into

1. Begin by exploring ways in which persuasion is used in the students' everyday lives. For example, have students discuss a time when they had to convince their parents to let them do something or perhaps buy something special. Let the students know that they will be engaging in persuasive writing or writing a piece to convince someone to agree to something they believe or want.

2. Read *William's Doll*. Have students respond to the book. Discuss why William needed to persuade his dad that he wanted a doll.

### Through

3. Brainstorm possible topics to write about. Elicit different ideas and use the board, chart paper, or an overhead transparency to begin a list of possible topics.

4. Select a topic to use for a class demonstration. Brainstorm arguments that might be used to convince an audience to accept a position related to the chosen topic. Think aloud some of the questions a writer should consider when attempting to identify potential arguments:
   - What do I know about this topic?
   - How do I feel about this topic?
   - What do I need to say?
   - What kind of evidence do I need?

- What might the counterarguments be? What are some possible emotional reactions to this argument?
- Which are the most important arguments?

5. Have students select a topic and use the Card strategy lesson to generate and organize their own ideas for writing.

6. As students draft and revise their papers, conduct ministrategy lessons that will help students to improve their persuasive pieces.

**Beyond**

7. Students publish and share their papers.

## VARIATIONS

In order to further develop student understanding of persuasive writing, they can examine a variety of persuasive texts (e.g., editorials, advertisements, film or book reviews, etc.) and discuss ways the author approaches:

- arguments
- support for the arguments
- use of facts, quotes and statistics
- word choice
- signal words and text structures (see Reading Text Signals and Writing Text Signals strategy lessons)

# Researching Big Questions

(Adapted from Piazza, 2003; Short, Harste, & Burke, 1996; Tomlinson & Lynch-Brown, 2002)

## CONCEPT

Authors engage in writing to share information with their audience. Through informative writing, authors report or explain information on topics with which they are familiar to their readers.

## MATERIALS

Text Sets (see Text Sets strategy lesson) to support students in developing background knowledge about selected research topics and in understanding informational text features and structures

## PROCEDURES

### Into

1. Have the students compare an informational book with a folktale or myth. For example, the class can read a "pourquoi" (e.g., how the zebra got its stripes, why the rabbit has long ears, etc.) and an informational book on the same animal. Have the class create a Venn diagram (see Venn Diagram strategy lesson) to compare the two books.

2. To help students see how authors present information to their audiences, have students study a variety of informational materials. These may include nonfiction trade books, newspapers, reference books, how-to books, photo essays, and the like. Students can examine how informational books vary in terms of:
   - purpose (inform, report, explain)
   - presentation of factual information
   - language use
   - use of text aides to support meaning.

### Through

3. Have students identify topics they might want to explore for their inquiry (see Writting Topic Lists strategy lesson). As students explore various topics, begin an "I wonder . . ." list to record possible questions to guide their inquiry.

4. Once students have identified an inquiry question, support the students in gathering Text Set materials they might need to develop their background on the topic. Use the KWL strategy (see KWL strategy lesson) to organize and record information they gather about their topic as they conduct the research. As students gather materials for their research, ministrategy lessons can focus on evaluating sources of information. (e.g., where to look for information, author credentials, timeliness, accuracy of information, etc.).

5. When students have collected enough information about their topic, they begin the process of drafting and revising their papers. The Card strategy lesson is particularly helpful for students as they generate and organize their ideas for writing.

6. As students draft and revise their papers, students can become acquainted with common text structures authors use to organize their writing. Using Text Sets strategy lesson, help students see how authors use common text structures to organize their writing:
   - description
   - cause/effect
   - problem/solution
   - compare/contrast
   - chronological order.

   Introduce the Reading Text Signals strategy lesson to help students see how authors use signal words within these common expository text structures.

**Beyond**

7. Once students have edited their final draft, have the students publish their writing.

# Idea Generation Strategies

# Brainstorming Writing Ideas

## CONCEPT

As part of the writing process, writers often engage in brainstorming activities. Brainstorming allows writers to generate potential ideas to be used in the drafting process.

## MATERIALS

No special materials are required.

## PROCEDURES

### Into

1. Inform the students that they are going to use a brainstorming strategy to generate ideas for writing. Let them know that the purpose of brainstorming is to come up with as many ideas as possible about a particular topic.
2. Identify a topic on which students might want to write. List this topic on the board, chart paper, or an overhead transparency.
3. For this activity, ask students to withhold judgment as to whether they believe a certain idea is silly or might not work. All ideas are accepted.

### Through

4. Encourage students to make free associations. Create a list as the students quickly call out their ideas about the topic. These ideas should be recorded on the board, chart paper, or an overhead transparency.
5. Continue adding ideas until the students no longer can come up with any new ideas.

### Beyond

6. Review the list and consider the usefulness of the various ideas.
7. Display the chart so that the students can refer to it while beginning to compose their first draft.
8. Allow students to add new ideas to the list as they begin the composing process.

## VARIATIONS

1. A variation of this strategy involves the use of webs (see Web Diagrams strategy lesson). A web allows students not only to brainstorm ideas, but also to begin to link and organize their ideas prior to writing.

2. Using the same structure, students can generate potential writing topics. After potential writing topics have been brainstormed and listed on the board, chart paper, or an overhead transparency, students record those topics that they might be personally interested in writing about. Students attach their lists to their writing folders. Encourage students to add to their topic lists as they find new ideas to write about. New topics can be generated while students are engaged in reading, listening to classmates as they discuss their writing, or after having personal experiences that they might want to record.

3. After brainstorming ideas, students can use the Card strategy lesson to organize the major ideas they wish to include in their writing.

# Card Strategy

(Adapted from Kucer, 1986)

## CONCEPT

A significant part of the writing process involves the generating and organizing of major ideas. As writers put pen to paper, they continually seek to discover their major ideas and how the ideas relate to one another.

## MATERIALS

Index cards or slips of paper (blank of both sides)
A large surface on which to lay the cards

## PROCEDURES

### Into

1. Inform the students that they are going to be writing. This writing may be on an assigned topic related to a theme under study or students may select their own topic. If necessary, brainstorm possible writing topics with the students and record them on the board (see Brainstorming Writing Ideas strategy lesson).
2. Give the students several cards and ask them to write down topics on which they might write.
3. As the generating of topics is taking place, the ideas should be informally shared, allowing for further stimulation of possible writing topics.
4. Once adequate time for generating and sharing has been allowed, the students are to select the topic card on which they would most like to write. All other cards are put into the student's "writing topics" envelope, which can be used at some other time.

### Through

5. After selecting their topics, the students are to think of all of the major or big ideas that are related to their topic. These major ideas are also recorded on individual cards, one idea per card. The students should be encouraged to generate as many major idea cards as possible, more than they might be able to actually use. This brainstorming process will open them to the possibility of discovering new ideas.

152

Because the language on the cards simply serves as a placeholder for meaning, the size of the language should not be restricted or specified. The ideas written in the cards do not need to be complete sentences.

6. As was done with the topic cards, give students the opportunity to share their major ideas.

7. After allowing time for the sharing of major idea cards, the students are to select those cards they predict will be included in their texts. Cards not used should be set aside. The cards chosen should then be laid across a table or desk and put in the order that the students predict they will appear in their texts.

8. Working with a partner, students briefly discuss their ideas cards and explain their reasons for arranging their cards in this particular manner. Partners focus on whether the organization makes sense. Partners can suggest changes to improve the flow of the writing. They can also suggest that new ideas be added or cards be deleted.

9. Using the cards as a guide, students begin writing. Because the cards are only placeholders for predicted meanings, the writers are free to accept or reject these predictions in any way they choose. Cards may be taken out, added, or reordered as required. The teacher should not expect to find a one-to-one correspondence between the cards and the actual text produced.

## Beyond

10. After drafts have been completed, the students share what they have written. If texts are to be published, the students engage in writing conferences and provide time for revision and editing (see Writing Revision Strategies section and Using Conventions of Written Language Strategies section.)

## VARIATIONS

1. Language Experience Strategy (see Language Experience strategy lesson). The Card Strategy can also be used to write a class language experience story. As students generate big ideas, the teacher writes these on 3 × 5" piece of overhead transparency and places them on an overhead projector for all students to see. After the brainstorming of major ideas, students decide which will be used in the text and discuss the order of the ideas. As possible variations for ordering are discussed, the teacher arranges and rearranges the major ideas on the overhead so that students can see the different arrangements. Using the cards as a guide, the students dictate the text and the teacher writes it on the board, chart paper, or an overhead transparency. Or, students can write the text themselves, either individually or in small groups.

2. Shuffle Strategy. The Shuffle Strategy can be used with those students who need support discovering that at times ideas can be arranged in more than one way. After the students have arranged their major idea cards, ask them to shuffle them so that the cards are no longer in order. In pairs, students exchange cards and each student becomes the "reader" and attempts to put the cards in an order that makes sense. Once both students have found a meaningful order, each explains the arrangement to the author. The author then puts the cards in the original order and explains and gives reasons for his or her order. Each author then decides which order works best and begins writing.

3. Expansion Strategy. Sometimes students will experience difficulty expanding and elaborating on their major ideas. One way to help students overcome this difficulty

is to have them generate minor ideas that relate to particular major ideas. This may be done before writing begins or after a draft has been written.

If done before writing begins, ask the students to brainstorm minor ideas that relate to each of their major ideas. These minor ideas can be written on 3 × 5" cards, selected, and ordered. Or, if done after a draft has been written, ideas that are in need of further development are identified. Minor ideas are then generated, written on 3 × 5" cards, selected, and ordered. Students can then revise the texts using their minor idea cards as a guide.

4. Research Strategy. Many students experience difficulty integrating and synthesizing information when they write research papers. Too often, these papers are simply "retellings" of what has been read. The Research Strategy can help students solve this problem.

After students have recorded notes on the topic under investigation, ask them to review their notes, looking for the major ideas to include in their papers. Students write each major idea on a 3 × 5" card. These cards are then arranged in a meaningful order. Students use their cards as a guide to write their reports. To help students move away from "copying" their notes, they may be told that they are first to review their notes that correspond to their first card. Then, without referring back to their notes, they write about their first major idea. They then review their notes related to the second card, put their notes aside, and write about the second card. This procedure continues until all the cards have been written about. After drafts have been completed, students can then return to their notes to expand what has been written.

5. Reading Strategy. In order to highlight the links between reading and writing, the Card strategy lesson can be paired with the Cloning an Author strategy lesson. After reading a text, ask students individually or in groups to generate and order major idea cards that they think the author might have used to write the text that has been read. These cards can then be shared with the class and similarities and differences among the students or groups discussed.

**SAMPLE MATERIALS**

Bandit

smart

gets out of his cage

cute *

brown and white

fat

jogs

bites

when I first
got him

eats

small *

Bandit

My hamster is veBy smart.
He gets out about twice a week.
He has a system, he first
checks the door and sees if
it's lose if it is he tries to lift
it up, But if it's not lose he
goes up to his tower to see
if there is any tape on, if it's
not he unscrews the tower. He has
one more way of getting out he can
get out of the top he climbs up
on his food bowl and pulls hiself up,
but if it's locked he can't.

He loves to jog or
run he runs about 6 to 8miles
a night. He likes to run up and
down the stairs it took him
14.7 to get down a 16 flight
of stairs. he took 17.3 to get
up the stairs. He has to
expand hiself in getting up
the stairs, when he does, he
looks like a smashed hamster.

Sometimes I let him run around the room he can slip under the door and go down the stairs and go into the kitchen. We have holes under the oven were he goes and stays for a while the longest he's ever stayed was two weeks.

When I got him he was in this little box about 10 inches long and 7 inches wide.

He was struggling to get out, and by the time we got home I was holding him in my hands. When I tried to open the car door he bit me right on the thumb it started to bleed pretty bad I couldn't use my thumb very well. He bit me about 9 times from then on but he always would like to bite my brother. He's retired from biting and I'm glad.

# Character Development in Writing

**CONCEPT**

Characters drive the plot in a story. Proficient writers focus on character development as their stories evolve.

**MATERIALS**

Various pictures of possible characters that have been cut out of magazines and newspapers. These characters can be people, animals, insects, reptiles, amphibians, and the like
Blank $8\frac{1}{2} \times 11"$ paper
Glue

**PROCEDURES**

**Into**

1. This strategy lesson is most effective if the students have experienced the Character Development in Reading strategy lesson. Review with the students the Character Development in Reading strategy lesson. Discuss the importance of character development to the plot of a story.
2. Tell the students that they are going to be writing a story. First, however, they are going to consider what characters they might include in their stories.
3. Share with the students the various characters that have been cut out of magazines and newspapers. Students are to select several characters that they might want to include in their stories.

**Through**

4. In the middle of a blank $8\frac{1}{2} \times 11"$ piece of paper, students glue one of their characters. Students then web various characteristics that their character might have. This procedure is repeated for each character.
5. Give students the opportunity to share their character webs.
6. Using their character webs as a guide, students write their stories.

**Beyond**

7. Students share their completed stories along with the pictures of the characters.

## VARIATIONS

Once students have become comfortable with the strategy lesson, they can generate their own pictures of the characters before webbing is initiated.

# Crossing the Communication Systems

**CONCEPT**

Meanings can be generated through various communication systems: language, art, mathematics, music, and movement. Transforming meaning from one communication system to another can lead to new insights and deeper understandings of the meanings being manipulated.

**MATERIALS**

A written text that students will be able to easily understand
Various communication tools, such as colored markers, paint, musical instruments, and so on

**PROCEDURES**

### Into

1. Introduce the students to the text and ask them to read it for the purpose of understanding the basic ideas that the author is conveying. This reading may be done by the teacher or by students reading in small groups or independently.
2. After the text has been read, students share the basic ideas that the text conveyed. The teacher lists these ideas on the board or an overhead transparency.

### Through

3. Discuss with the students that meanings can be conveyed in a number or ways besides language: art, mathematics, music, and movement.
4. Students are to convey the meanings from the text in another communication system. The teacher may select the system, such as art, or allow students to select their own.
5. Working in small groups or independently, the students create an "alternate text" based on the text that was read.

### Beyond

6. Students share their alternate texts and discuss any new insight they gained from engaging in the process of crossing the communication systems.

## VARIATIONS

1. Rather than beginning with a written text and moving the meanings to another communication system, a nonlanguage text may be used as the starting point. Students begin by listening to a song, analyzing a painting, or viewing a dance. This nonlanguage text is then conveyed through the writing of a text.

2. Students can be given a key concept from an expository text, such as the water cycle, and be asked to communicate the idea through a nonlanguage communication system, such as movement.

# Help Me

## CONCEPT

Readers frequently encounter ideas or meanings that they have difficulty understanding. Seeking assistance from others is one strategy to clarify what has been read.

## MATERIALS

Any reading material that might contain ideas that students will have difficulty comprehending

## PROCEDURES

### Into

1. The Help Me strategy lesson can be used any time students are engaged in reading. The reading material can be selected by the teacher or be material that the students have selected for the Independent Reading strategy lesson. When introducing the strategy lesson, however, it is helpful if all students are reading the same text.
2. Before the students begin reading, discuss with them that not understanding a particular idea when reading is common for most readers. As they begin reading, the students should keep a list of anything that they have difficulty comprehending. The page on which the difficulty was located should also be recorded.

### Through

3. Students are paired with a partner or placed in small groups. Taking turns, each student shares a difficulty encountered, the location in the text, and receives help from the other student(s).

### Beyond

4. If there remain difficulties that the students have not been able to comprehend, these can be shared with the entire class. Other students and the teacher can then help clarify these difficulties.

# Immigration Autobiography Interviews

(Adapted from Brisk & Harrington, 2000)

## CONCEPT

Writers draw from their personal experiences when developing text. Interviews can provide writers with ideas for further developing their own writing.

## MATERIALS

Immigration Text Set (see Text Sets strategy lesson) that students have previously read:
> Cohen, B. (1995). *Molly's pilgrim*. New York: A Yearling Book.
> Knight, M., & O'Brien, A. (1993). *Who belongs here?* Gardiner, ME: Tilbury House.
> Levitin, S. (1987). *Journey to America*. New York: Aladdin Paperbacks.
> Say, A. (1993). *Grandfather's journey*. Boston: Houghton Mifflin.
> Surat, M., & Mai, V. (1983). *Angel child, dragon child*. New York: Scholastic.

## PROCEDURES

### Into

1. Review with the students the similarities they encountered when reading the immigration text set.
2. Explain to the students that they will be writing their own immigration autobiographies.
3. Discuss with the students that they will be interviewing their parents, grandparents, and other family members regarding their immigration experiences. Brainstorm potential questions to ask during the interviews. List these questions on the board, chart paper, or an overhead transparency.
4. Demonstrate for students how to take notes during the interviews.

### Through

5. Have students conduct the immigration interviews.
6. Students develop a draft of their autobiographies using their interview notes.

**Beyond**

7. After the draft is revised and edited, students can publish their autobiography (see Revision strategy lesson and Using Conventions of Written Language section).

# KWL

(Adapted from Ogle, 1986)

## CONCEPT

Learning in general, and inquiry specifically, involves being aware of and monitoring what one already knows, what one wants to know, and what one is learning.

## MATERIALS

A variety of materials and resources—for example, books, magazines, videos, CDs—that focus on a particular topic under investigation

KWL Grid (see Sample Materials)

## PROCEDURES

### Into

1. A topic for investigation is decided on. This topic may be selected by the children or by the teacher, or may be a topic that is addressed in one of the textbooks—for example, social science or science—that is being used in the classroom. When a topic is decided on for the children, the teacher will want to consider giving the students the opportunity to select subtopics within the general topic under study.

2. Introduce the students to the KWL Grid. Inform the students that the $K$ stands for what is already known about the topic; the $W$ represents questions that they have, and the $L$ reflects what is learned as they progress through their inquiry.

3. Ask the students to share what they already know about the topic. This can first be done in small groups if time allows. As students share what they know, list these under the "What We Know" column.

4. As the "knowns" are identified and listed, there will be times when students will challenge particular ideas that have been shared. The teacher acknowledges the challenge and records a question mark by the idea that is in dispute. As students explore the topic, they will want to look for confirmation or disconfirmation of the ideas that have been challenged. Additionally, students may discover that other

ideas are also in need of modification, even if they have not been disputed during the original listing.

5. The teacher then asks the students what they want to learn about the topic and list these in the middle column of the grid. It is important to remember that asking good questions comes with time and experience. Initially, students may ask questions that are only factual in nature, such as, "Why are plants green?" This is an important and meaningful question. However, the teacher will also want to help students develop questions that will lead them to the development of broader meanings and generalizations, such as "What impact do plants have on the development of a community?"

## Through

7. Before students begin their investigations, the teacher will need to decide how the research will be organized. Individual students or groups of students may select a single or several questions to investigate. Or, individual students or groups of students may investigate all of the questions listed.

8. It can also be helpful to briefly introduce the materials that have been gathered for the inquiry and to identify additional sources, such as the school or community library, individuals to interview, and so on that the students may want to explore. Such an introduction provides students with an overview of what is available to them.

9. It is often the case that as students begin their research, additional questions arise. These questions should be listed on the KWL Grid, either at the time that they arise or at designated times during the inquiry.

10. As students locate answers to their questions, they can either record them on the KWL Grid or in an inquiry notebook that is then shared with the class at designated times.

## Beyond

11. Throughout the inquiry as well as at the end, the teacher will want to periodically review the KWL Grid, the questions that are being asked and the various answers to the questions recorded. Particular attention should be paid to learnings that are contradictory in nature. Rather than being problematic, conflicting learnings can serve as points for meaningful and important discussions among and students as well as a search for additional information.

12. To highlight the conflicting nature of knowledge, students can be involved in the Inquiry Chart strategy lesson.

**SAMPLE MATERIALS**

KWL Grid

Name: _____     Topic: _____

| What We Know K | What We Want To Know W | What We Have Learned L |
|---|---|---|
|  |  |  |

# Personal Journal

## CONCEPT

Journals provide writers with opportunities to explore ideas and discover new meanings. Journals can serve to record memories, events, feelings, ideas, and daily life experiences. Journal entries often provide writers with ideas for further writing.

## MATERIALS

Notebook

## PROCEDURES

### Into

1. Introduce the journal by discussing its purpose. Discuss with students how journals can be used to record different kinds of writing.
2. Before having the students engage in journal writing, the teacher must decide whether or not the students are going to share their journal entries with other members of the class.

### Through

3. Allow students to journal on a topic of their choice.

### Beyond

4. If journal entries are going to be shared with the class, the teacher models response strategies for the students.
5. Have the students periodically reread previous journal entries and note topics that they could use when engaged in other writing activities.

# Quickwrites

## CONCEPT

Writers frequently use the process of writing itself to discover ideas on which they might further write and develop.

## MATERIALS

No special materials are required.

## PROCEDURES

### Into

1. Discuss with the students the purpose of a Quickwrite as a strategy to help them discover ideas for writing. Emphasize that Quickwrites allow the writer to explore a particular topic or idea by focusing on meaning without concern for spelling or the quality of the piece. The point here is to keep the pen or pencil moving and the ideas flowing. Encourage the students to cover the page with as much writing as possible.

### Through

2. Ask the students to start writing about any topic that comes to their mind. Tell them how much time they will have for the Quickwrite strategy lesson.
3. If students have a difficult time thinking of something to write, ask them to write "I cannot think of anything to write" until an idea comes to mind.

### Beyond

4. Allow the students the opportunity to share the ideas they have explored in their Quickwrites.

## VARIATIONS

1. Quickwrites are effective in helping students to explore a variety of class subjects. After reading about a social studies or science topic, for example, the teacher can have

students engage in a Quickwrite. Students are asked to focus on a particular topic or idea and write everything "that comes into their heads." Again, the purpose here is to keep ideas flowing.

2. The Quickwrite strategy lesson can be added to the Writing Wall Chart strategy lesson and used by students if they are "stuck" and do not know what to write next when drafting a piece.

# Setting a Story

(Adapted from Bell, 2003)

## CONCEPT

Writers expand and elaborate on their major ideas through the use of supporting details.

## MATERIALS

No special materials are required.

## PROCEDURES

### Into

1. Inform the students that they will be discussing ways to use details so that readers can visualize the settings that they describe. Explain to the students that authors use details to provide readers with a sense of setting in a story.

2. Have the students close their eyes and visualize their favorite room in their house or apartment. Encourage the students to use their senses as they explore the room: What do they see? Hear? How do things feel in the room when they are touched? Are there special smells? Perhaps even some special tastes?

3. Ask the student to make a list of every detail they can recall, even if it does not seem important at the moment.

4. Have the students take the list home and add other details. Try to have the students include at least 15 items on the list.

### Through

5. Review the lists in class. Have the students circle three items that evoke a strong reaction. Have the students use those words to begin to develop a piece that shows something special about their room. They can use their lists to add other details as they write.

### Beyond

6. Have students work in partners. As the writer reads his or her draft, the partner visualizes the room being described. The partners can also be asked to illustrate the

room being described. Have the partners identify ways in which the writer showed his or her room in the writing.

**VARIATIONS**

1. Have students look through magazines and identify settings that are significant to them.
2. Read and discuss how published authors create believable places for their characters. Discuss the relationship between setting and characters in the story.
3. Have the students reread drafts of other pieces they are currently working on. Have them examine how they are using details to provide vivid descriptions of their settings.

# Sketching Character

(Adapted from Atwell, 1998, 2002; Bell, 2003; Graves, 1994)

## CONCEPT

Proficient fiction writers expand, extend, and elaborate on their story characters. Authors know much more about their characters than what they are able to develop in a story.

## MATERIALS

Character Questionnaire (see Sample Materials)
Personal writing journals

## PROCEDURES

### Into

1. This strategy lesson is most effective if the students have experienced the Character Development in Reading strategy lesson.
2. Tell the students that they will be looking at ways they can develop strong characters within their stories.
3. Conduct a think-aloud to demonstrate ways students can more fully develop characters for their own stories. Reproduce the following Character Questionnaire on the board, chart paper, or an overhead transparency:
   - What is the character's name?
   - What is the character's age?
   - What does the character look like?
   - Where does the character live?
   - What problem is the character facing?
   - What does the character like to do?
   - What is different about the character?
   - What does the character care about?
   - What does the character fear?
   - What are the character's dreams?
   - What does the character think is important?
   - What does the character want?
   - How will the character change?

4. Identify a potential character for a story. Use the Questionnaire to more fully develop details regarding this character. Encourage the students to participate and contribute to the discussion. Record the discussion on the board, chart paper, or an overhead transparency.

5. Have the students go through their Personal Journals (see Personal Journal strategy lesson) to choose a character that they would like to know and more fully understand. Students can answer questions individually or they can interview each other regarding their characters of choice.

### Through

6. During the following class session, review the Character Questionnaire and develop a sketch profile of the character. Conduct a think-aloud, using the board, chart paper, or an overhead transparency to record thoughts. Begin by establishing that there is something that the character wants. Take about 10 minutes to sketch the character.

7. Have students sketch their own characters.

### Beyond

8. Have students work in small groups and read their character sketches to each other. As each author reads the sketch, the group members look for ways in which the character was revealed. Students provide feedback by discussing what they have learned about the character from the sketch. Students also ask each other questions about the character that they would like to know more about.

9. Revise the character sketches.

### VARIATIONS

Have students bring three objects from their home in a paper bag. Place bags in a large container and have students randomly select a bag, they cannot select their own. Using the items in the bag, have students sketch a character. Have students do a Quickwrite (see Quickwrite strategy lesson) and then share their piece with others.

## SAMPLE MATERIALS

### Character Questionnaire

- What is the character's name?
- What is the character's age?
- What does the character look like?
- Where does the character live?
- What problem is the character facing?
- What does the character like to do?
- What is different about the character?
- What does the character care about?
- What does the character fear?
- What are the character's dreams?
- What does the character think is important?
- What does the character want?
- How will the character change?

# Storyboard

(Adapted from Short, Harste, & Burke, 1996; Tomlinson & Lynch-Brown, 2002)

## CONCEPT

In addition to using language, authors use a variety of text aids to facilitate, extend, and generate meaning. When creating picture books, authors sketch out the actions of a story using art as a medium.

## MATERIALS

Small pieces of paper or large sticky notes
Crayons, markers, pencils, and pens
Text set of picture books

## PROCEDURES

### Into

1. Read a variety of picture books to the students. Discuss with the students ways in which pictures and text work together in these books. Help students notice how:
   - Illustrations extend the text by adding information regarding the characters, plot, or setting
   - Illustrations contribute to the theme and mood
   - Text and illustration are both responsible for telling the story.

### Through

2. Let the students know that they will be using storyboards to create their own picture books. Storyboards will allow them to visually plan how the story will be told.
3. Provide students with the small pieces of paper or large sticky notes.
4. Have the students begin sketching and writing the story. Remind them that the objective of this strategy is to visually plan how the story unfolds and that they only need to sketch and write down key points. They will have an opportunity to elaborate at a later point in time.
5. Students can move and reorder their small pieces of paper as necessary.

**Beyond**

6. Have students share their storyboards with other authors. As they listen and respond to each other, have the students discuss how art and writing was used in the story. Focus on ways in which illustrations extend the text.

## VARIATIONS

Rather than using small pieces of paper or large sticky notes, students can use presentations software such as PowerPoint, HyperStudio, Inspiration, or KidsInspiration.

# Wordless Picture Books

## CONCEPT

Meanings can be generated in a variety of ways, such as through language, art, music, mathematics, and movement.

## MATERIALS

Various wordless picture books, such as:
    dePaola, T. (1983). *Sing, Pierrot, sing*. New York: Harcourt Brace Jovanovich.
    Mayer, M. (l983). *I was so mad*. Racine, WI: Western Publishing.
    Ormerod, J. (1981). *Sunshine*. New York: Puffin.
    Winter, P. (1976). *The bear and the fly*. New York: Scholastic.
Slips of paper, index cards, or sticky notes

## PROCEDURES

### Into

1. Discuss with students that "authors" can express their ideas and meanings in various ways, such as through language, pictures, and music.
2. Share with the students a wordless picture book, telling them that this author used illustrations to tell his or her story.
3. Give each student or small groups of students the wordless picture book. Students look through the book, telling themselves the story the pictures convey.
4. Discuss with the students the stories they have "read" in their wordless picture books.

### Through

5. Distribute slips of paper, index cards, or notes. For each picture in the wordless picture book, students write the words that might accompany the picture. Each written slip of paper, index card, or note can then be paper clipped or attached onto the page from which the words were generated.

**Beyond**

6. After all texts have been written, provide students the opportunity to share their stories.

## VARIATIONS

1. Students can select a story they have previously written and be asked to illustrate pictures to accompany their texts. These texts and pictures can then be compiled into a book to be shared with the class.
2. Divide the class into groups and give each group a different wordless picture book. Have each group create a new story.

# Writing Topics List

(Adapted from Atwell, 1998)

**CONCEPT**

Proficient writers frequently keep a "writer's notebook" in which they record possible ideas and topics on which they might write about in the future.

**MATERIALS**

Writer's Notebooks or blank sheets of paper that can be attached to the students' writing folder

**PROCEDURES**

**Into**

1. Explain to the students that they will be generating a topic list of writing ideas that can be used when they are struggling with finding something to write about.
2. Discuss where writers frequently "find" their ideas. These ideas frequently come not only from "special" experiences and events in the writer's life, but from everyday, ordinary experiences and events. Walking to school, a friend's house, or the grocery store can lead to thoughts worth writing about. Ideas from books, movies, and television programs also can provide topics for writing.

**Through**

3. As a class, generate a list of topics that the students might be interested in writing about. Discuss where these ideas came from as the ideas are shared.
4. Record all topics on chart paper titled "Writing Ideas."

**Beyond**

5. Using the list generated by the class, have students record the topics that they might be personally interested in writing about. These ideas can be recorded in the front or back of the students' Writing Notebooks or recorded on blank sheets of paper that are attached to the inside of the students' writing folders.
6. Post the chart where it is easy for students to see.

7. Periodically, generate additional topic ideas and list them on the Writing Ideas chart.

8. Encourage students to add to their own personal topic lists as they find new ideas to write about. New ideas can be generated while the students are engaged in reading or while then are listening to classmates discuss their writing, or after having personal experiences that they might want to record.

# Written Conversation

(Adapted from Short, Harste, & Burke, 1996)

## CONCEPT

Informal writing provides authors opportunities to generate and explore potential ideas prior to engaging in drafting a piece of writing.

## MATERIALS

No special materials are required.

## PROCEDURES

### Into

1. Introduce the strategy by discussing with the students how similar to oral conversations, writers can engage in written conversation.

### Through

2. Using the board, chart paper, or an overhead transparency, begin by writing a question.
3. Ask for a volunteer to continue the conversation and hand him or her the pen. The student responds to the question and returns the pen to the teacher.
4. The teacher and student continue to change roles until they decide to terminate the conversation

### Beyond

5. Invite the class to engage in a written conversation. Students, in pairs, take turns writing and responding to each other.

## VARIATIONS

1. Students can respond to a reading through the use of Written Conversations.
2. Have students use Written Conversations to discuss problems and solve conflicts that might emerge in the classroom.

# Learning From and Through Others' Strategies

# Teacher Reading

## CONCEPT

Readers draw on their previous linguistic, cognitive, and affective experiences with written language when they encounter a new piece of writing. The more experiences the reader has with written material, the more predictable new experiences with written language become. Adults play a critical role in helping young readers value reading.

## MATERIALS

Any well-structured text that the students will find of interest and comprehensible. The material may be related to a thematic topic under study or a recent classroom, school, cultural event that has engaged the students. The material may be short enough to read in one sitting or require several readings to complete.

## PROCEDURES

### Into

1. Introduce the material to the students. Connect the content of the material to any experiences that the students may have had. If appropriate, the teacher may ask students to predict the content of the text based on the title.

### Through

2. Begin reading the text to the students, showing the pictures if they are present. Throughout the reading, when and where appropriate, stop and ask students to react, respond, and/or discuss what has been read. The teacher should share his or her own responses as well. The teacher can also consider asking some of the questions found in the Literature Response Groups strategy lesson.
3. At each stopping point, after students have responded to what has been read, they can be asked to predict what might happen in the next portion of the text to be read.

**Beyond**

4. If the text is to be read over several days or weeks, at the conclusion of each reading, ask the students to briefly summarize what has been read.

5. At the beginning of the next teacher reading of the same text, once again ask students to briefly share what had been read the previous day. This summarizing and reviewing helps students maintain a coherent understanding of the entire text as it is read over time.

6. When reading chapter books and longer texts, it is helpful if the text is read each day. Allowing too much time to occur between readings makes it difficult for students to remember what has transpired during previous readings.

## VARIATIONS

If the students are listening to a fairly long chapter book, groups of students can be asked to illustrate a summary picture at the end of each chapter. These pictures can be put in chronological order on a bulletin board and reviewed each day before a new chapter is read.

# Shared Reading

(Adapted from Holdaway, 1979)

## CONCEPT

Readers draw on their previous linguistic, cognitive, and affective experiences with written language when they encounter a new piece of writing. The more experiences the reader has with written material, the more predictable new experiences with written language become. Emergent readers gradually internalize various reading processes through learning what other, more-proficient readers do when they read.

## MATERIALS

Any well-structured text that the students will find of interest and comprehensible. Predictable texts are particularly useful when doing Shared Reading with beginning and/or struggling readers. The material may be related to a thematic topic under study or a recent classroom, school, or cultural event that has engaged the students. The material should be short enough to read in one sitting. The material can be presented in a big book format or students can have individual copies of the text. The text may be new to the students or be one they have encountered through the Teacher Reading strategy lesson.

## PROCEDURES

### Into

1. Introduce the text to the student, making any connections to topics under study or recent classroom, school, cultural, or similar events that have engaged the students. If appropriate, the teacher may ask students to predict the content of the text based on the title.

### Through

2. Before reading the text to the students, have the students examine the cover and the illustrations and make predictions about the text.
3. The teacher will want to read slowly enough so that students can follow along. When portions of the text are predictable, the teacher can encourage students to orally read them with him or her. In contrast to the Teacher Reading strategy lesson, in Shared

Reading the students are to begin tracking the print and making attempts to read when possible.

4. Throughout the reading, when and where appropriate, stop and ask students to react, respond, and/or discuss what has been read. The teacher should share his or her own responses as well. The teacher can also consider asking some of the questions found in the Literature Response Groups strategy lesson.

5. Discussion can also focus on:
   • Expanding on key concepts of vocabulary
   • Story elements (e.g., plot, characters, setting, problem, solution)
   • Word features
   • Letter–sound patterns
   • Language patterns

   When highlighting letter–sound patterns or word features, the teacher may use sticky notes to cover the particular component he or she wishes the students to focus on during the reading (e.g., individual letters, diagraphs, blends, word families). An alternative to using sticky notes is to use a window tag with a hole in the middle to frame the text feature.

6. At each stopping point, after students have responded to what has been read, they can be asked to predict what will come next in the next portion of the text to be read.

**Beyond**

7. After the text has been read, ask if any of the students can independently read predictable portions of the text. If a student needs help once she or he begins reading, the teacher and/or the class can orally read along.

8. Students can dramatize different parts of the text or extend their understanding of the text through their own writing or illustrations.

# Choral Reading

## CONCEPT

Readers increase their proficiency with the reading process not only by engaging in the process, but also through learning what other, more-proficient readers do when they read.

## MATERIALS

Any well-structured text that the students will find of interest and comprehensible. Predictable texts are particularly useful when doing the Choral Reading strategy lesson with beginning and/or struggling readers. The material may be related to a thematic topic under study or a recent classroom, school, cultural, or similar event that has engaged the students. The material should be short enough to read in one sitting and students should have individual copies of the text to be read. The text may be new to the students or be one they have encountered through the Teacher Reading and/or Shared Reading strategy lessons.

## PROCEDURES

### Into

1. Introduce the text to the student, making any connections to topics under study or recent classroom, school, cultural, or similar events that have engaged the students. If appropriate, the teacher may ask students to predict the content of the text based on the title.
2. Engage the students in a picture walk. As pictures on each page are discussed, the teacher should informally use some of the language from the text.

### Through

3. Begin reading the text aloud, telling the students that they should follow along in their books and read aloud when comfortable. Students can be encouraged to read aloud by the teacher raising his or her voice toward the end of a sentence and then pausing. Students will frequently finish reading the sentence when they experience this teacher behavior.

4. Discuss with the students how, when reading aloud, readers use a variety of strategies to read with expression and capture their audience's attention (e.g., stopping at commas; pausing at periods; varying reading in response to exclamation points, question marks, quotation marks, etc.). Have the students examine the text and discuss strategies they could use to enhance their fluency and expression.

**Beyond**

5. As students become comfortable reading aloud in unison, the teacher begins to stop reading when possible. Students then assume as much of the reading as they are able, with the teacher reading only at those points at which the students need support.

## VARIATIONS

Texts that have dialogue can be divided into parts and each part assigned to a different group of students. In unison, each group reads the dialogue assigned to the narrator or their particular character. Students may select to add actions while reading the lines of each character (e.g., Goldilocks eating porridge, sitting on a chair, etc.).

# Guided Reading

(Adapted from Fountas & Pinnell, 1996)

**CONCEPT**

Proficient readers apply various strategies when they encounter "unknowns" when reading a text.

**MATERIALS**

Any well-structured text that the students will find of interest and comprehensible. Predictable texts are particularly useful when doing the Guided Reading Strategy lesson with beginning readers. The material may be related to a thematic topic under study or a recent classroom, school, cultural, or similar event that has engaged the students. The material should be short enough to read in one sitting and students should have individual copies of the text. The text may be new to the students or be one they have encountered through the Teacher Reading, Shared Reading, and/or Choral Reading strategy lessons. Finally, the text should be one in which the teacher believes the students will encounter unknown, unrecognized, or not readily understood words or ideas.

**PROCEDURES**

### Into

1. Before engaging in Guided Reading, the students should have been introduced to various strategies to help them work their way through unknown words or ideas in a text. The use of the Reading Wall Chart, Selected Deletion/Multiple Known Concepts, Reader-Selected Miscues, and Predicting Word Meanings strategy lessons all provide students with such an introduction.
2. If students have previously encountered the text, review the content with the students. If the text is new to the students and additional support is necessary, students can be engaged in a picture walk. As the teacher walks the students through the book, the following might be highlighted:
   - Letter–sound patterns
   - Key concepts (draw from the students' background and experiences that relate to the text)
   - Story elements (e.g., plot, characters, setting, problem, solution)

- Illustrations (highlight illustrations to make content more comprehensible)
- New vocabulary (support learners by pronouncing difficult words)
- Language patterns (read language patterns that might be new for the learners as they appear in the text)

Before reading begins, it can also be helpful to review the various strategies the students have learned for handling unknown words or ideas in a text.

## Through

3. Ask the students to begin reading the text individually.
4. The teacher listens to each member of the group read individually. The student can "whisper read" or simply read aloud as the teacher listens.
5. The teacher prompts the use of particular strategies that have been previously taught when the student encounters a difficulty in what is being read. Students are encouraged to use the strategies they had discussed and added to the Reading Wall Chart (see Reading Wall Chart strategy lesson).

## Beyond

6. After the text has been read, the teacher brings together the group of students to discuss the text. Students can share their favorite parts, main ideas, and personal responses to the text.
7. The teacher discusses reading strategies by validating the students' use of successful strategies observed during the lesson. The students are asked to share problems they encountered in their reading and the strategies they used to overcome the problems.
8. The teacher lists problems and solutions on the blackboard, chart paper, or an overhead transparency. These can focus on a number of topics (e.g., comprehension, fluency, word analysis, vocabulary), depending on the aspects of text that presented difficulties to the students during the reading. For many learners, problem–solution discussions provide opportunities to focus on unfamiliar words and link these to their personal experiences. Letter–sound patterns and word learning strategies are much more meaningful when presented as part of a problem-solving strategy within the context of the text being read.

## VARIATIONS

The teacher can emphasize the use of a particular strategy, rather than prompting general strategy use, and direct students to focus on its use. For example, if the teacher has been teaching students to use a "read on and return" strategy when an unknown word is encountered, the teacher encourages the use of this strategy.

# Paired Reading

## CONCEPT

Readers increase their proficiency with the reading process not only by engaging in the process, but also through learning what other, more-proficient readers do when they read.

## MATERIALS

Any well-structured text that the students will find of interest and comprehensible. Predictable texts are particularly useful when doing the Paired Reading Strategy lesson with beginning readers. The material may be related to a thematic topic under study or a recent classroom, school, or cultural event that has engaged the students. The material should be short enough to read in one sitting and each pair of students should have one copy of the text. The text may be new to the students or be one they have encountered through the Teacher Reading, Shared Reading, Choral Reading, and/or Guided Reading strategy lessons.

## PROCEDURES

### Into

1. Introduce the text to the student, making any connections to topics under study or recent classroom, school, cultural, or similar events that have engaged the students. If appropriate, the teacher may ask students to predict the content of the text based on the title.
2. If the students have not previously encountered the text and they need additional support, engage the students in a picture walk. As pictures on each page are discussed, the teacher should informally use some of the language from the text.
3. If students have encountered the Reading Wall Chart strategy lesson, briefly review the strategies on the chart.

### Through

4. Students are paired with a "buddy" and given time to read the text chorally. Each student helps the other when unknown words or ideas are encountered.

**Beyond**

5. After the text has been read, the teacher brings together the students. The students are then asked to share the problems they encountered with their buddy and the strategies used to overcome the problem. These problems and solutions can be listed on the blackboard, chart paper, or an overhead transparency by the teacher, or added to the Reading Wall Chart from the Reading Wall Chart strategy lesson.

6. Engage the student in paired reading activities until he or she begins feeling more confident with the reading.

## VARIATIONS

1. Teacher and student can pair for reading. Tell the student that you will be choral reading together. Begin reading together. When the student feels comfortable reading alone, fade out and signal to the student to continue reading alone. If the reader struggles with parts of the text, allow him or her a few second to try to figure it out before helping out. If the reader begins to struggle with the text, chime back in and continue reading together.

2. Pair students with other classmates, upper-grade students, tutors, parents, volunteers, and so on.

3. Allow the students to select materials they want to read during paired reading.

# Tape-Assisted Reading

**CONCEPT**

Proficient readers focus on meaning while reading text fluently and with expression.

**MATERIALS**

Any reading selection will work. For this strategy it is best to use material that is easily predictable by the students.
Tape recording of the reading selection

**PROCEDURES**

### Into

1. Make an audiotape of the reading selection. Make sure that a proficient reader tapes the selection and that the text is read slowly enough for students to follow. Young children often enjoy listening to audiotapes recorded by school personnel or members of the community (e.g., secretary, principal, parents, even older students).

### Through

2. Have the students listen to the tape and follow along by pointing to the text as they read.
3. As students become more comfortable with the text, they can follow along orally.

### Beyond

4. Students can read the selection back to the teacher when they feel they can read it without the assistance of the tape.

# Language Experience Approach

(Adapted from Peregoy & Boyle, 2005)

## CONCEPT

Readers and writers draw from their personal experiences to compose written text.

## MATERIALS

No special materials are necessary.

## PROCEDURES

### Into

1. Provide the students with an experience they can discuss and write about. The experience needs to be tailored to the students and take into consideration their interests, background knowledge, and language proficiency. Language experiences can focus around field trips (e.g., trip to the zoo or a farm), special school events (e.g., special guests or presentations), cooking or art activities, science experiments, or the retelling of stories students have read.

2. Begin the strategy lesson by engaging the students in a general discussion about the experience. During the discussion, the teacher records on the board, chart paper, or an overhead transparency the main ideas that the students discussed.

### Through

3. Discuss with the students that the class is going to write about the experience that was discussed. Review the ideas that were recorded and decide which to include in the writing. These ideas can be marked with a check.

4. Ask the students to consider which ideas should be written about first, second, third, and so on. Number each idea as to when it is to be addressed in the text.

5. Ask various students to provide sentences for the first idea to be discussed. Record these sentences on the board, chart paper, or an overhead transparency. As each statement is transcribed, repeat it one word at a time (e.g., if Maria said "First, you measure the flour," the teacher slowly repeats each word—"Maria, said, first, you, measure, the, flour"—as each word is transcribed).

6. Draw attention to concepts of print as each word is written (i.e., letter names, letter sounds, capitals, sentence structure, etc.).

7. After writing individual statements, read the statement back to the students.

8. Have the students reread the statement by themselves. Point to each word at it is being read.

**Beyond**

9. After the students are done dictating their experiences, have them reread the entire text in unison. Individual students can then be asked to take turns reading the entire text or parts of the text.

10. Return to the text and highlight a particular feature of the text. For example, the teacher might help the students see that several words begin with the same letter or that the same word appears several time. These words can then be underlined with the marker.

11. Give students the opportunity to illustrate the text.

## VARIATIONS

1. Working with individuals: Teachers can record individual language experiences based on the experiences each child wants to share.

2. Pocket Charts: Rather than using the board, chart paper, or an overhead transparency, record the language experience on sentence strips. When the students are comfortable with the reading the strips, they can be cut apart into individual words. The students can re-create the text or use the words to create a new story.

3. Photographs: Use a camera to record the experience. Have the students use the pictures when developing the language experience. This is particularly useful if the students do not have an opportunity to discuss and dictate the story immediately after the experiences.

# Teacher Writing

## CONCEPT

Writers increase their proficiency with the writing process not only by engaging in the process, but also through learning what other, more-proficient writers do when they write.

## MATERIALS

Any writing topic that the students might find of interest

## PROCEDURES

### Into

1. Once a topic has been selected, the teacher begins to engage in the writing process. On the blackboard, chart paper, or an overhead transparency, the teacher demonstrates how she or he begins writing a text. The teacher, for example, might first brainstorm ideas for the text and record these on a "jot list." The teacher then decides which idea is to addressed first in the writing.

2. Regardless of how the writing is initiated, it is important that the teacher make visible his or her thinking processes by verbally sharing them with the students. Students need to see the process being demonstrated as fully as possible (see Think-Aloud strategy lesson).

### Through

3. As the written text evolves on the blackboard, chart paper, or an overhead transparency, the teacher continues to share what she or he is thinking. Considerations and decisions about content, organization, word choice, spelling, punctuation, and so on are shared with the students.

4. The teacher will want to take care to share revisions that are made to the text and why the changes were made. This will demonstrate to the students that writing involves thinking, writing, reflection, and revision. Too often students only encounter finished, published texts and have no idea how the product came to look as it does.

5. As well as sharing revisions, the teacher will also want to share points of "writer's block." These are places where the teacher is unsure as to what to write next or how to express an idea. How the teacher works his or her way through these blocks are to be communicated to the students.

**Beyond**

6. After the text has been completed, discuss with the students the various writing behaviors in which the teacher was engaged. List these processes on the blackboard, chart paper, or an overhead transparency where they can be referred to during other writing activities.

## VARIATIONS

As the students become familiar with the writing process, the teacher can engage them in the Writing Wall Chart strategy lesson.

# Shared Writing

## CONCEPT

Writers increase their proficiency with the writing process not only by engaging in the process, but also through learning what other, more-proficient writers do when they write.

## MATERIALS

Any writing topic that the students might find of interest

## PROCEDURES

### Into

1. Once a topic has been selected, the teacher begins to engage in the writing process. On the blackboard, chart paper, or an overhead transparency, the teacher demonstrates how she or he begins writing a text. The teacher, for example, might first brainstorm ideas for the text and record these on a "jot list." The teacher then decides which idea is to be addressed first in the writing.

2. In contrast to the Teacher Writing strategy lesson, the teacher actively encourages students to provide suggestions for all aspects of the writing process. Students, for example, should be involved in the brainstorming of ideas and deciding the order in which the text is to be written.

### Through

3. As the written text evolves on the blackboard, chart paper, or an overhead transparency, the teacher continues to share what she or he is thinking and elicits student ideas. Considerations and decisions about content, organization, word choice, spelling, punctuation, revisions, and so on are considered and decisions made with the students. This step of the process offers the teacher innumerable opportunities to highlight the process. For example, the teacher and students can consider:
   - Generating and organizing ideas: What do we want to say about this topic? How should we say that? What should I write first? Why should I do this?

- Forms: Should we write it with a lowercase or a capital letter? Why? Let's say that words slowly? What sound did you hear first, next? What should I use at the end of the sentence? Why should we use a question mark?
- Revisions: Does this make sense? Does it say what we want it to say?
- Language blocks: If we don't know how to write that word, what might we do?

**Beyond**

4. After the text has been completed, discuss with the students the various writing behaviors in which the teacher was engaged. List these processes on the blackboard, chart paper, or an overhead transparency where they can be referred to during other writing activities.

## VARIATIONS

As the students become familiar with the writing process, the teacher can engage them in the Writing Wall Chart strategy lesson.

# Choral Writing

## CONCEPT

Writers increase their proficiency with the writing process not only be engaging in the process, but also through learning what other, more proficient writers do when they write.

## MATERIALS

Any writing topic that the students might find of interest.

## PROCEDURES

### Into

1. Once a topic has been selected, the teacher begins to engage in the writing process with collaboration of the students. On the blackboard, overhead transparency, or chart paper, the teacher and the students begin writing the text. The teacher and the students, for example, might first brainstorm ideas for the text and record these on a "jot list." The teacher and students then decide together which idea is to addressed first in the writing.

2. In contrast to the Shared Writing Strategy lesson, the students are actively engaged in all aspects of the writing process, from the selection and ordering of ideas, to their development, to their actual transcription, and to their revision.

### Through

3. Taking turns, individual students contribute their ideas by first sharing them with the class and then writing them on the board, chart paper, or overhead transparency.

### Beyond

4. After the text has been drafted, the teacher and students consider where revisions would strengthen the text. Some possible considerations include:
   - Idea development: Are there ideas that are in need of fuller development? Are there ideas that need to be deleted?

- Idea organization: Are there ideas that need to be reordered in the text? Should some ideas come before others?
- Language: Are there ideas that need to be expressed in a different way? Should language be changed to more adequately express the ideas?

5. As revisions are suggested and agreed upon, various students should be selected to make them.

# Guided Writing

## CONCEPT

Writers increase their proficiency with the writing process not only by engaging in the process but also through learning what other, more-proficient writers do when they write.

## MATERIALS

Any writing topic that the students might find of interest

## PROCEDURES

### Into

1. Once a topic has been selected, students begin drafting their texts. Students may all write on the same topic, or individual student topics can be selected.

### Through

2. As the students write, the teacher circulates and provides assistance as necessary. The teacher may prompt particular strategy use, help students clarify their ideas, suggest language for the expression of ideas, or refer students to the Writing or Spelling Wall Charts if students have experienced Writing or Spelling Wall Chart strategy lessons.

### Beyond

3. After the texts have been drafted, the teacher and students consider where revisions would strengthen the text. Some possible considerations include:
   - Idea development: Are there ideas that are in need of fuller development? Are there ideas that need to be deleted?
   - Idea organization: Are there ideas that need to be reordered in the text? Should some ideas come before others?
   - Language: Are there ideas that need to be expressed in a different way? Should language be changed to more adequately express the ideas?
4. As revisions are made, the teacher once again provides assistance as necessary.

# Paired Writing

**CONCEPT**

Writers draw on their previous linguistic, cognitive, and affective experiences with written language when they encounter a new piece of written language. The more experiences the writer has with written material, the more predictable new experiences with written language become.

**MATERIALS**

Any writing topic that the students might find of interest

**PROCEDURES**

### Into

1. Students are paired with a "buddy" and writing topics selected. The entire class may decide the topic, or buddies may select their own topic, depending on the needs of the teacher and the students.
2. Students are told that each buddy is to take turns writing and to help one another when problems are encountered. If students have encountered the Writing Wall Chart or the Spelling Wall Chart strategy lessons, briefly review these charts.

### Through

3. As writing begins, the students should be encouraged to brainstorm ideas, the order in which they are to be presented, and any other writing strategies to which the students have been introduced.

### Beyond

4. After the writing time is over, provide students the opportunity to informally share what has been written. This sharing can be done in small groups or with the entire class.
5. As an entire class, have students discuss various problems and solutions they encountered during writing. If students have encountered the Writing Wall Chart or the Spelling Wall Chart strategy lessons, new solutions can be added as necessary.

# Organizing Meaning Strategies

# Beginning, Middle, End

(Adapted from Fletcher & Portalupi, 1998; Graves, 1989)

## CONCEPT

Fiction writers often have a general idea of where a piece of fiction is going prior to starting their writing. Beginning writers sometimes encounter difficulties planning the general direction of their stories prior to engaging in the writing process.

## MATERIALS

Beginning, Middle, End Grid (see Sample Materials)
Fiction selection with a clear beginning, middle, and end

## PROCEDURES

### Into

1. Inform the students that they will be listening for the beginning, the middle, and the end of a story. Show them the Beginning, Middle, End Grid.
2. After reading the story, ask students to discuss which parts of the story were the beginning, the middle, and the end. Write down the students' suggestions in the appropriate box in the grid.

### Through

3. Discuss how a good story generally has a beginning, a middle, and an end. Use another grid to demonstrate how to brainstorm the general direction a story will take prior to engaging in writing.

### Beyond

4. Invite the students to use a Beginning, Middle, End Grid to plan a new story.

## VARIATIONS

Provide students with three-page stapled blank books. Have students use each page to develop the beginning, the middle, and the end of their stories.

## SAMPLE MATERIALS

Beginning, Middle, End Grid

| Beginning |
| --- |
| |

| Middle |
| --- |
| |

| End |
| --- |
| |

# Cloning an Author

(Adapted from Short, Harste, & Burke, 1996)

## CONCEPT

Readers must be able to take the ideas put forth by the author and re-create these ideas to develop their own understandings of the text. Readers identify key reading ideas and then examine how other ideas presented in the text relate to these main concepts.

## MATERIALS

Any reading material will work with this strategy. Expository text that might be difficult for the students because of the number of concepts that are introduced is particularly well suited for this strategy
Index cards or slips of scrap paper

## PROCEDURES

### Into

1. Distribute eight cards or slips of papers to each student.
2. Have students identify eight key ideas from the reading and write each idea on a separate slip of paper. The number of ideas identified will vary depending on the text and the students. Students can write these key ideas while engaged in the reading selection or after completing the readings.

### Through

3. Of the eight ideas previously selected, have students identify the five ideas that they think are most important. Discard the remaining three slips of paper. This helps students further examine ideas in terms of their significant meanings.
4. Ask the students to review their new stack and identify the idea that they think is central to the reading and place this slip of paper on the table. If a central idea has not been identified, give students the opportunity to identify one and to record this on an additional card.
5. Have students place the remaining slips of papers around the key idea.

**Beyond**

6. Ask the students to engage in the cooperative structure *Think, Pair, Share* (Kagan, 1994):
   - Think: Have students first think how their slips of paper tie to
     ◦ the idea they identified as central to the reading, and
     ◦ to each other.
   - Pair: Students form pairs and take turns discussing their reasons for selecting their key idea and for placing the remaining cards around it.
   - Share: Students share with the group or the entire class commonalties and differences they found as they discussed their ideas.

7. Debrief the strategy by having students evaluate the usefulness of the activity. Focus the discussion on how students went about making their first decision (identifying eight key ideas) and how they then narrowed these to five ideas. Ask students to discuss how they decided which slip of paper to place in the middle. Ask students to note any changes that must take place before they use this strategy again.

## VARIATIONS

1. As with other strategy lessons, although Cloning an Author can be used for large-group discussions, we find this strategy to be most effective when working in small groups.

2. This strategy works when paired with the Card strategy lesson. Both strategies help students see how ideas are organized, one from the reader's perspective and one from the writer's point of view.

3. Students can transfer their ideas to a sheet of paper and then draw connecting lines and arrows to show the relationships among these ideas.

# Flowcharts

(Adapted from Moline, 1995)

**CONCEPT**

Reading requires synthesizing and ordering information.

**MATERIALS**

A text that presents a process (e.g., water cycle, photosynthesis) in a narrative form
Slips of paper or index cards

**PROCEDURES**

**Into**

1. It is a good idea to introduce this strategy by first having students create a flowchart of a common daily event with which they are familiar (e.g., steps involved in playing a game or making a peanut butter sandwich).
2. The students brainstorm all the information that they know about the common daily event selected. The teacher writes the information on the board, chart paper, or an overheard transparency. The events are transcribed in the order that the students mention them.
3. Distribute slips of paper or index cards. Have the students make an individual card for each of the events listed on the board, chart paper, or an overhead transparency.
4. Lay the cards across a table or floor and have the students put them in a sequence that they think makes the most sense. Encourage the students to move the cards and try different ways of organizing the events.
5. Provide students the opportunity to share their various card arrangements.

**Through**

6. Introduce the students to the narrative text that addresses a process. As students read the text individually or in small groups, they list each major step in the process on a slip of paper or index card.
7. After all major steps have been identified and recorded, students arrange the cards in the order addressed in the text.

8. Students paste the cards onto a large piece of paper and add numbers or arrows to show the sequence of events.

**Beyond**

9. Students share and compare and contrast their flow charts with other members of the class.

## VARIATIONS

Instead of writing each event on a slip of paper, students can draw pictures or symbols to represent each event.

# Life Story Time Line

(Adapted from Short, Harste, & Burke, 1996)

## CONCEPT

Reading and writing requires synthesizing and organizing information. When writing, the writer selects and organizes key ideas that later on can be elaborated when writing.

## MATERIALS

No special materials are required.

## PROCEDURES

### Into

1. The teacher introduces this strategy to the students by recalling and, on the board, chart paper, or an overhead transparency, making a time line of events that happened in his or her life the previous day.
2. Once the list is completed, the teacher reviews the list and identifies an event that could be further developed into a piece of writing. Think aloud for the students the reasons this particular event or idea was selected.

### Through

3. Have the students create their own time lines.
4. In pairs, have the students discuss their time lines and identify events that could be developed into a piece of writing

### Beyond

5. Have each student select one of the ideas to develop into a draft.

# Reading Card Sort

## CONCEPT

Comprehension involves a process of building conceptual links among major ideas within the text.

## MATERIALS

A variety of idea cards on a particular topic, issue, or theme that can be related to one another in a number of different ways. The cards should be numbered, with a different number on each card. (see Sample Materials) The number of idea cards will vary depending on the topic and the students.
Envelopes to put each set of idea cards

## PROCEDURES

### Into

1. The Reading Card Sort strategy lesson works best when it is used within a thematic unit or a topic that the class is studying.
2. Introduce the students to the set of ideas cards that have been assembled. Discuss how the cards are related to the topic under study.
3. Form the students into small groups and provide each group with a single envelope containing all of the idea cards.
4. Tell the students that they are to first read all of the cards in the envelope. Then, the cards should be sorted into piles. All cards in each pile should be related to one another in some manner.
5. Before the actual sorting begins, it can be helpful if each group first generates a list of possible sorting categories after all of the cards have been read. Assign one student in each group the task of recording the categories. If students need additional support, these potential categories can be shared with the entire class before the sorting within groups begins.

### Through

6. After the categories have been tentatively selected, students sort their cards.

7. After the sorting is completed, ask students to do a quick read of the cards in each group to confirm that they all address the same issue.

**Beyond**

8. Bring the students together as an entire class and ask each group to share their categories and the number of the cards that were put in each group. Record the categories and card number on the board, chart paper, or an overhead transparency.

9. Engage the students in a discussion concerning both the similarities and differences among the various categories identified and the placement of the cards.

## VARIATIONS

1. Once students are comfortable with the Reading Card Sort strategy lesson, they can be taught to use the strategy in their writing through the Writing Card Sort strategy.

2. Rather than the teacher generating the idea cards, students can assume this responsibility. As students engage in a thematic unit, they can record major or important ideas on separate cards. The cards can then be collected and numbered and serve as the basis for the Reading Card Sort strategy lesson.

**SAMPLE MATERIALS**

Growing Plants and Seeds Idea Cards

| | |
|---|---|
| 1. A fruit is the fleshy case around a seed. Apples, tomatoes, and peaches are fruits with seeds inside. We eat many fruits. Animals and insects do too. | 2. What tree is a couple? |
| 3. The wind carries pollen for some plants. They have small petals so that the wind can blow the pollen away. Some plants use insects to carry their pollen. | 4. Every day the little boy pulled up the weeds around the seed and sprinkled the group with water. |
| 5. Leaves have "sweat" pores. This helps them lose water. Cover a plant with a plastic bag. Fasten it around the stem with a string. Water the plant and put it in the sun. See what happens after a few hours. | 6. The old man said, "Grow, grow, little turnip. Grow sweet. Grow, grow little turnip. Grow strong." |
| 7. How do plants get water? The water they need rises from the ground through the roots into the stem, and then into the leaves and flowers. | 8. Many plants are in danger of dying out. If the last plant of a family is killed, we can never ever put it back on earth again. |
| 9. Peel the outer layer of dry skin from an onion. • Stick three toothpicks in the sides. • Rest the toothpicks in the rim of a jar with the roots of the onion facing down. • Fill the jar with water so it covers the bottom of the onion. Make sure the bottom is always covered. • Your onion plant will grow well in water and does not need to be planted in soil. • If you set the jar in light, the onion will grow a bright green stem. If the jar is set in a dark place, the stem will be yellow. | 10. Exploding flowers? Can it be? Yes. Scotch broom has flowers that explode. Each flower has five petals. Three of them stay closed up. They form a kind of envelope. Inside the envelope are the stamens and the pistil—waiting to explode. |
| 11. What tree will you find after a fire? | 12. You can arrange the plants you have grown in an attractive window garden display. Place a sweet potato plant in each end of the windowsill. Try to keep the potato itself out of direct sun. Tie a string along the sides of the window frame. Wrap the sweet potato vine around the string. As it grows, it will climb up the sides of the window on the string. |

| | |
|---|---|
| 13. Seeds are rather like packets of plant food with a tiny plant inside. The new plant begins to grow when conditions are just right. But some kinds of seeds only need water to get the message to start sprouting. | 14. If you are starting a plot where no garden has been before, the soil will need a lot of care before you can grow things. With a garden spade turn the soil over to break it up and let in light and air. A good soaking with water a while before you dig will help if the ground is hard. |
| 15. Squirrels carry away acorns, the seeds of the oak tree, and store them to eat later. They bury some in the ground and forget them. Oak trees are often planted in this way. | 16. The old beech tree is a family tree. Many different creatures make their home in this tree. |
| 17. Pull weeds out often—they use up food and space your plants needs. | 18. Make sure it is the right time of the year to plant. Some plants need a cool start, others do better when the ground is warm. |
| 19. With carbon dioxide, you can make apple seeds dive down and come up in a glass of water. Put a level teaspoonful of baking soda into a dry glass. Put three teaspoonfuls of vinegar into another glass half filled with water. Add several apple seeds to the soda glass. Now pour the vinegar and water mixture into the soda glass. Watch the fizz as the gas forms. What happens to the seeds? | 20. Once upon a time an old man planted a little turnip. |
| 21. Maybe you have no room for a garden plot or want a private growing place. You could make a whole garden in a window, if you have one, or in a collection of pots on a balcony or on a table inside near a window. | 22. One pitch black, very dark night, right after Mon turned off the light, I looked out my window only to see, a big brown owl up in my tree! And did it ever frighten me! |
| 23. Pumpkin seeds should be planted in spring or early summer. Buy the seeds in a packet or dry four or five fat ones from a pumpkin. | 24. At different times of the year you can grow different things. In some places it is warm all year round and plants will grow well at any time. In places where the ground freezes you will have to wait for warmer weather to garden outdoors. |
| 25. They are cattails. Cat's tails? No, not cat's tails, cattails. Cattails are plants. They are fun to play with. | 26. Animals and people eat some kinds of plant leaves. We eat cabbage, spinach, and lettuce. Tea is made of dried and fermented leaves. |
| 27. How can you change a pumpkin into another vegetable? | 28. A seed has three parts. Every seed has a seed coat, a baby plant, and food. The baby plant inside the seed will grow into a big plant. |

| | |
|---|---|
| 29. Heavy fruits like apples drop to the ground. Sometimes they stay right under the tree. Sometimes they bounce or roll away, and the seeds start to grow quite a way from the tree. | 30. What do seeds need for growing? They need ground that is warm and damp. |
| 31. People do not plant all seeds. Seeds may travel to places where they can grow. Seeds travel in many ways. | 32. "Rita is going to plant flowers in her window box," said Amanda. "Can I plant some in ours?" |
| 33. Make a desert home. Use a wide-mouthed jar. Cover the bottom with sand. Plant them in the sand. Cover the mouth of the jar with screen. Cactuses need plenty of light. They do not need much water. | 34. A little boy planted a carrot seed. |
| 35. When does a farmer plow his field with a steamroller? | 36. The ancient Egyptians had gardens in their towns. So did the Incas long ago in South America. |
| 37. Potatoes are good mashed, roasted, and fried. Did you know they make good hand puppets, too? | 38. When Tommy's mother came home, she got the surprise of her life. The whole house was full of plants and Tommy was still bringing in more. "What's going on here?" she gasped. "I told you," answered Tommy. "I'm a plant sitter. I take care of plants for people who are away on vacation." |
| 39. The cotton plant has many uses. The fibers are respun into thread or cleaned for cotton wool. Oil from the seeds is used in cooking, and cows eat the crushed seeds. | 40. Many plants can make new plants from parts of themselves. A piece of shoot, or a leaf, can often grow into a whole plant. |
| 41. The most important parts of a higher plant are the roots, the stem, and the leaves. | 42. Pitcher plants have leaves shaped like vases. Along the rim of each leaf is a sweet liquid. The liquid attracts insects. They crawl or fall inside. Once inside the insects cannot crawl out. The sides of the leaf are too slippery. The insect falls to the bottom. |
| 43. Trees that walk? How can that be? Trees can't walk! Trees have roots that keep them in one place. Yet people call mangroves "the trees that walk." | 44. And up came the turnip at last! |
| 45. Sweet potato vines are slow starters. Most potatoes take about six weeks before they begin to sprout green shoots. However, if your potato is going to grow, you should see tiny white roots within ten days. | 46. Tommy took care of the plants. He put those that needed sun on the sunny side. He watered them carefully—some a lot—and others just a little. |

# Semantic Mapping

## CONCEPT

Most texts contain "big ideas" that are interrelated to one another. The identification of these ideas and their interrelationships helps readers to better understand both the specific as well as the general meanings in what they are reading.

## MATERIALS

Several expository or informational texts that contain clearly developed ideas with connections
   among them
A road map of a particular geographical location
Mapping Grid (see Sample Materials)

## PROCEDURES

### Into

1. Show the road map to the students and discuss the purpose of such maps. Emphasize that road maps identify significant locations and the roads that connect them. List these purposes in the left-hand column.

2. After the various purposes have been identified and recorded, ask the students to discuss the techniques mapmakers use to express these purposes, for example, colors, shapes, lines, print, and so on. List these ways in the right-hand column.

3. Finally, ask the students what kinds of things get illustrated or included on a map and what things are left out. Discuss with the students that only the most important things—for example, roads, cities, towns, bodies of water, mountains, and the like—are included.

4. Discuss with the students that similar to mapmakers, authors also try and emphasize their major ideas and how they are connected. When reading a text, students should also look for major ideas and consider how these ideas are linked with one another.

**Through**

5. Read a short text to the students. Ask students to list the major ideas that are addressed as the text is being read.

6. Following the reading, discuss with the students the major ideas they have identified. List these on the board, chart paper, or an overhead transparency.

7. With help from the students, draw on the blackboard, chart paper, or an overhead transparency a "road map" of the major ideas that have been identified. Discuss what major ideas "go together" conceptually and what links exist among the ideas. Each major idea should have at least one link—line—that connects it to at least one other idea. As ideas are mapped and connections made, use the various mapmaker techniques previously discussed.

8. As the semantic map is constructed, emphasize that readers oftentimes differ as to the major ideas they identify and the links among them. Variation is a natural part of this process.

**Beyond**

9. Once students have a basic understanding of the Semantic Mapping strategy lesson, they can be asked to map texts in small groups or independently. Whenever possible, these group or individual maps should be shared with the class so as to highlight variation in the ideas and links that have been identified. Such variation supports students in developing a deeper understanding of what they have read as they encounter differing interpretations of a text.

## VARIATIONS

For students who need more support in the process of identifying and linking major ideas within a text, begin with the Web Concept Using Context strategy lesson before introducing Semantic Mapping.

**SAMPLE MATERIALS**

Mapping Grid:
Maps, Their Purposes, and Their Expressions

| Purposes That Maps Serve | Ways Mapmakers Express These Purposes |
|---|---|
| | |

# Text Sets

## CONCEPT

No text stands alone. Rather, each text is intertextually linked to a set of texts that are similar in some manner: topic, meaning, point of view, author, organizational structure, genre, text type, and so on. Readers make use of their encounters with previous texts and their knowledge of intertextuality when reading and comprehending texts.

## MATERIALS

Several texts that are similar in some manner: topic, meaning, organizational structure, genre, text type, and so on, such as:
*The Three Little Pigs*
*The Three Billy Goats Gruff*

de Paola, T. (1979). *Oliver Button is a sissy*. New York: Harcourt Brace Jovanovic.
Hoffman, M. (1991). *Amazing Grace*. New York: Dial.
Zolotow, C. (l972). *William's doll*. New York: Harper & Row.

Carlson, N. (1990). *Arnie and the new kid*. New York: Puffin.
Clements, A. (1988). *Big Al*. New York: Scholastic.
Komaiko, L. (1988). *Earl's too cool for me*. New York: Harper Trophy.

Or, several versions of the same story, such as the following, which all exist in several forms:
*The Three Little Pigs, The Three Billy Goats Gruff, The Ginger Bread Man, Henny Penny, The Teeny Tiny Woman,* and *The Little Red Hen*

Or, several books that present different perspectives on the same topic, such as:
Mayer, M. (1969). *Boy, was I mad!* Pleasantville, New York: Reader's Digest.
Simon, N. (1974). *I was so mad!* Niles, IL: Whitman.
Erickson, K., & Roffey, M. (1987). *I was so mad*. New York: Viking Penguin.

Mayer, M. (1983). *When I get bigger*. New York: Golden Press.
Goennel, H. (1987). *When I grow up*. Boston: Little Brown.

*The Three Little Pigs*
Scieszka, J. (1989). *The true story of the three little pigs*. New York: Penguin.

A Text Set Grid that identifies areas for comparison can be helpful when students are initially encountering this strategy. (See sample Text Set Grid for *The Three Little Pigs* and *The Great Big Enormous Turnip*.)

## PROCEDURES

### Into

1. Inform the students that they are going to be reading a number of texts that are similar in a number of ways. Students may read the texts individually or in groups; the teacher may read one text and have the students read the other; or the teacher may read all of the texts.

### Through

2. After the texts have been read, discuss with the students the similarities (and differences if appropriate) across the texts. List these similarities (and differences) on the board, chart paper, or an overhead transparency. Questions to lead off the discussion should be deliberately open ended:
   • What was the same about these stories/texts?
   • What information did you find presented in all of the stories/texts?
   • What are the similarities in the way these stories/texts were written?
   Or, if a text grid has been developed, introduce the grid to the students. Either as a class or in small groups, use the grid to identify the various ways in which the texts are similar.

3. After discussing as a class how the texts were similar, ask the students to identify which of the similarities are of major significance. Inquire as to whether the students have read or heard similar texts.

### Beyond

4. Conclude the lesson by having the students engage in the Structured Story strategy lesson in which they write their own texts to accompany the text set.

## SAMPLE MATERIALS

Text Set Grid for *The Three Little Pigs* and *The Three Billy Goats Gruff*

| Text Characteristic | The Three Little Pigs | The Three Billy Goats Gruff |
|---|---|---|
| Setting | | |
| Characters | | |
| Problem | | |
| Villain | | |
| Response to Problem | | |
| Final Solution | | |
| What was the author trying to teach you? Why did the author write this story? | | |

# Structured Stories

## CONCEPT

No text stands alone. Rather, each text is intertextually linked to a set of texts that are similar in some manner: topic, meaning, organizational structure, genre, text type, and so on. Writers make use of their encounters with previous texts and their knowledge of intertextuality when writing new texts.

## MATERIALS

A text set—a group of texts that are similar in some manner—topic, meaning, organizational structure, genre, text type, and so on—that has been previously read (see Text Sets strategy lesson)
Blank books

## PROCEDURES

### Into

1. Engage students in the Text Sets strategy lesson and identify similarities among the texts. These similarities should be listed on the board, chart paper, or an overhead transparency.

### Through

2. Inform the students that they are going to write their own stories using the similarities in the texts read. Essentially, they are going to be adding a new text to the text set. This may be done individually, in small groups, or as an entire class.
3. Have students brainstorm all of the topics that might be written about. List these on the board, chart paper, or an overhead transparency.
4. Each student or group then selects the topic of interest and writes and illustrates a text, using the similarities discussed during the Text Sets strategy lesson.

**Beyond**

5. After the texts have been revised and edited, they are copied into the blank books and the pages are illustrated.
6. Give students/groups the opportunity to share their texts and to discuss how their text is similar to those in the text set.

## VARIATIONS

Some students may need additional support and find the writing of an entire text too difficult. In such cases, students may simply write an additional episode or event to be added to an existing story within a text set.

# Time Lines

## CONCEPT

Reading requires synthesizing and organizing information. As readers attempt to comprehend text, they identify key ideas and attempt to logically organize them in order to make meaningful connections.

## MATERIALS

A text that presents a series of chronological events (e.g., historical materials, biographies, etc.)
Slips of paper

## PROCEDURES

### Into

1. Have the students read the text.

### Through

2. Give the students several slips of paper and have them identify an important event on each of the slips of paper.

### Beyond

3. Have the students use the cards to organize their events in chronological order.

## VARIATIONS

The teacher can demonstrate how to utilize scale on a time line to visually demonstrate a variety of time units.

# Venn Diagrams

## CONCEPT

The purpose for reading significantly impacts the types of relationships readers develop with texts. Readers search for ways in which some ideas in a text are both similar as well as different from other ideas in the same text or across texts being read.

## MATERIALS

Any text(s) that readers will find easy to understand. Major ideas and their interrelationship to one another should be clearly identifiable.
Venn diagram

## PROCEDURES

### Into

1. The teacher or the students read the text(s).
2. Provide students the opportunity to respond in a general way to the meanings generated from the reading.
3. Identify particular ideas, issues, characters, events, and so on in the text(s) to compare and contrast.

### Through

4. Have the students identify ways in which particular ideas, issues, characters, and the like are similar. On the overhead, blackboard, or chart paper, write these shared attributes in the overlapping section of the Venn diagram.
5. Students then identify ways in which particular ideas, issues, characters, and so on are different. Record those attributes that are different or not shared on the areas of the Venn diagram where the circles do not overlap.

### Beyond

6. With the students, identify other contexts in which they might use the strategy.

**VARIATIONS**

Venn diagrams can be easily created using software such as Inspiration or KidsInspiration. These software applications have ready-made templates that are easily manipulated and result in a visually attractive product.

# Writing Card Sort

## CONCEPT

Writing involves a process of building conceptual links among major ideas within the text.

## MATERIALS

A variety of reading materials on a particular topic that the class is studying
Index cards or slips of paper

## PROCEDURES

### Into

1. Before engaging the students in the Writing Card Sort strategy lesson, it is helpful if students have had experiences with the Reading Card Sort strategy lesson as well as the Card strategy lesson.

2. Inform the students that they are going to be investigating an issue related to a particular topic or thematic unit. Depending on the needs of the teacher and the students, the entire class may explore the same issue or students may be put into small groups to research different topics or individual students may select their own individual topics.

3. Review the students' experiences with the Reading Card Sort strategy lesson. Give particular attention to the fact that different ideas were written on different cards, yet the cards could be related in some general manner.

4. As students read the various materials on their topic(s), they should look for major ideas that the authors are presenting. Each idea should be briefly summarized on a separate card. If is also helpful if students include the material being cited for later reference.

5. Before beginning to record the major ideas on cards, it is helpful if students first peruse and skim a variety of materials. This general reading will give them a "feel" for the ideas being presented on the topic and help them to better understand the difference between major and minor ideas.

**Through**

6. Once the students have had the necessary time to identify and record major ideas related to the topic, bring them together as a class.

7. Tell the students that, similar to what was done with in the Reading Card Sort strategy lesson, they are to read all of the cards that have been generated. Then, based on similarities in content, the cards should be sorted into piles.

8. Before the actual sorting begins, it can be helpful if students first generate a list of possible sorting categories after all of the cards have been read. If students need additional support, these potential categories can be shared with the entire class or in small groups.

9. After the categories have been tentatively selected, students sort their cards.

10. After the sorting is completed, ask students to do a quick read of the cards in each group to confirm that they all address the same general issue.

11. Similar to what the students did in the Card strategy lesson, the students decide which group of cards will be written about first, which group will be written about second, and so on. Then, the ideas within each group are arranged based on the order in which they will be written about.

12. Using the cards as a guide, students draft their inquiry paper. As with the Card strategy lesson, students will need to more fully develop and extend the major ideas on the cards.

13. If necessary, students may return to the original source of any idea card if they need more information or need to refresh their memories. However, when possible, students should try to rely primarily on the cards. This will support them in putting the ideas into their own words as they expand and elaborate on the ideas represented on the cards. Returning too often to the source of the card oftentimes leads students to copy from the text rather than to find their own language for the ideas presented.

**Beyond**

14. After drafts have been completed, students should be given the opportunity to share what they have written. This sharing can be done with a partner, in small groups, or with the entire class.

15. If the drafts are to be published, engage the students in a variety of strategy lessons in the Writing Revision section and Using Conventions of Written Language section.

# Reader Response Strategies

# Add, Zoom, Flashback, Squeeze, X-Tend

(Adapted from Waikowhai Intermediate School, New Zealand, 1995)

## CONCEPT

Readers come to more fully understand what they have read through the process of recalling what has been read with other readers.

## MATERIALS

A story or an article that the students will find easy to comprehend
Retelling cards (see Sample Materials)

## PROCEDURES

### Into

1. Introduce the text to be read to the students. Inform the students that after the text has been read, they are going to be asked to recall what has been read in a variety of ways. Briefly discuss the five types of recall in which the students are to be engaged:

   Add:       carry on the retelling of the story
   Zoom:      add more detail to what the last person said
   Flashback: go back to something already retold and carry on the story from there
   Squeeze:   summarize what has been retold so far
   X-tend:    add personal comments, reflections, and/or evaluations concerning what has been read

2. The text can either be read aloud by the teacher, in small groups, or individually.

### Through

3. Once the text has been read, either as an entire class or in small groups, depending on the needs of the students, a student begins to retell what has been read. After a portion has been shared, a second student selects one of the retelling cards and adds to the retelling based on the directions on the card.

4. The teacher or group leader will need to monitor each student's retelling so as to keep the strategy lesson "moving." Occasionally, some students may want to add, zoom, flashback, squeeze, or x-tend in too much detail or not enough. Depending on the

length of the text and time constraints, students need to be encouraged to "wrap it up" or extend what they have shared.

### Beyond

5. The various types of retelling can be used whenever students have read the same text and then are asked to share with other students in the class. Chapters, articles, videotapes, and the like from social sciences and science should be considered as well as literature.

## VARIATIONS

Rather than students taking turns selecting retelling cards, the teacher may assign different cards to different students, depending on the needs and abilities of the students.

SAMPLE MATERIALS

| | |
|---|---|
| **ADD**<br><br>CARRY ON RETELLING THE STORY/TEXT. | **ZOOM**<br><br>ADD MORE DETAIL TO WHAT THE LAST PERSON SAID. |
| **SQUEEZE**<br><br>SUMMARIZE WHAT HAS BEEN RETOLD SO FAR. | **X-TEND**<br><br>ADD PERSONAL COMMENTS, REFLECTIONS, AND/OR EVALUATIONS ABOUT THE STORY/TEXT. |
| **FLASHBACK**<br><br>GO BACK TO SOMETHING ALREADY RETOLD AND CARRY ON THE STORY/TEXT FROM THERE. | |

# Author's Chair

(Adapted from Graves & Hansen, 1983)

## CONCEPT

Writers rely on their readers to help them celebrate what they have written.

## MATERIALS

Final drafts

## PROCEDURES

### Into

1. Discuss with students that one of the purposes of the Author's Chair is to celebrate the work of the writer and to tell the writer what is liked about the piece. Emphasize the role of the audience in responding.

### Through

2. The author reads the text aloud to the class or a small group of students. Authors may want to practice reading their texts before coming before the class or group.
3. After the author has read the piece, students take turns identifying what they liked and why. It is important to discuss why something is liked so that the author understands what made it effective.
4. Students repeat the process until all pieces have been read and each student has received response.

### Beyond

5. Using chart paper, the teacher lists all of the characteristics that students liked in the pieces that were shared. Students can refer to this What We Like Wall Chart when drafting future texts.

# Circle Check Out

(Adapted from Heffernan, 2004)

## CONCEPT

Writers rely on their readers to help them celebrate what they have written. In turn, readers learn about the writing process by considering what writers do in their texts.

## MATERIALS

Final drafts

## PROCEDURES

### Into

1. Discuss with students that the purpose of the Circle Check Out is to provide writers the opportunity to share a particular part of something they have written.
2. Ask students to read through something they have written and to identify a section to share. The students can select something they particularly like, or the teacher can specify that students should identify something the class has been working on, such as:
   - strong openings or endings
   - well-crafted paragraphs
   - character development
   - use of strong, vivid descriptive language
   - action scenes
   - use of dialogue
   - humorous or frightening events
   - plot development
   - something new that the writer is attempting to do

   The point here is that students will only identify and share a portion of what they have written, not the entire text as is commonly the case with the Author's Chair strategy lesson.
3. Before coming to the Circle Check Out, it is helpful if students first read through several times the piece they wish to share with the class.

**Through**

4. The author reads the text portion aloud to the class or a small group of students and discusses why it was shared. Other students may also want to comment about the strength of what was read.

**Beyond**

5. The teacher may want to put up a bulletin board that contains student writing as it relates to particular writing issues, such as those listed in step 2.

# Character Development in Reading

## CONCEPT

Understanding the major characters in a story is a key factor in understanding the overall story. Proficient readers consider the dimensions of major characters to better help them understand the plot of the story.

## MATERIALS

A short story with well-defined and developed characters

## PROCEDURES

### Into

1. Discuss with the students the idea that understanding the personalities, motives, likes and dislikes, and so on of the major characters in a story helps in understanding the overall story.
2. Select a story with which the students are well familiar. This can be a story the students have read in class or be a movie or television show.
3. With the students, identify the main characters in the story and list these on the board, chart paper, or an overhead transparency.
4. Select one character and have students brainstorm everything that they know about the character's personality. The teacher should contribute to the discussion of the character as well. List the personality traits on the board, chart paper, or an overhead transparency.
5. With student assistance, draw a web of the character using the most important ideas from the character list that was brainstormed. Discuss with the students the various links and relationships that have been represented in the web.

### Through

6. Give students a short story to read. As students read the story, they are to focus on a particular character. This character may be selected by the teacher or by individual students.

7. After the story has been read, ask students to brainstorm and list the major traits of the character they have selected. Provide students the opportunity to share what they have brainstormed.

8. Using their lists, students web the character selected.

### Beyond

9. Either as a class or in small groups—it works best if students in each group have all focused on the same character—students share their webs. As webs are shared, both the differences and similarities in the webs should be discussed.

10. Discuss with the students the similarities and differences in the webs and how different readers may understand the same character in both similar and unique ways.

## VARIATIONS

1. To help students see the way in which characters can evolve and change within a story, students can be asked to engage in several webbings for a character. This variation works best with longer stories or chapter books. Using the Character Web Grid, at designated points in the story, ask students to stop reading and to web a main character. Allow students to share their webs and to discuss how their webs are both similar and different to previous webs they have generated for the character.

2. Once readers become comfortable webbing characters from what they read, they can be introduced to the Sketching Character strategy lesson and learn to web characters for their writing.

**SAMPLE MATERIALS**

Character Web Grid

Name of Story: _____

Name of Character: _____

| 1. Web what you know about the character at this point. | 2. Web what you know about the character at this point. |
|---|---|
| 3. Web what you know about the character at this point. | 4. Web what you know about the character at this point. |

# Literature Response Groups

## CONCEPT

Just as writers "talk" to readers through what they have written, readers "talk" to authors through their responses to what they have read.

## MATERIALS

Literature selections will vary depending on the way in which literature is integrated into the classroom curriculum:
- Book Sets: Multiple copies of the same piece of literature—usually enough so that each of the students participating in the Literature Response Group has a copy of the text.
- Text Sets: These sets consist of groupings of two or more texts that are conceptually linked around common concepts or generalizations. For example, the following books could be part of a text set highlighting the struggle that individuals face when attempting to "be true to themselves." (See the Text Sets strategy lesson)
  de Paola, T. (1979). *Oliver Button is a sissy*. New York: Harcourt Brace Jovanovich.
  Hoffman, M. (1991). *Amazing Grace*. New York: Dial.
  Zolotow, C. (l972). *William's doll*. New York: Harper & Row.
  Or, the following text set can be used to focus on "not judging a book by is cover."
  Carlson, N. (1990). *Arnie and the new kid*. New York: Puffin.
  Clements, A. (1988). *Big Al*. New York: Scholastic.
  Komaiko, L. (1988). *Earl's too cool for me*. New York: Harper Trophy.
- Author Studies: A collection of books written by the same author.

## PROCEDURES

### Into

1. Present the literature piece to the students through a short book talk.
2. Students select the Literature Response Group they want to participate in, depending on the literature selection that interests them. Or, the teacher may assign students to a particular group.

3. The teacher develops both the conceptual and linguistic background the students will need to understand the new piece of material. Into activities may help tap into the students' understanding of the topic or issue related to the text. For example, students may discuss experiences they might have had that are similar to that of the main character in the story. Or, the teacher may provide experiences to develop the students' background, that is, showing a video related to the book, or having students predict what the book will be about from looking at the pictures.

## Through

4. The literature selection is read. Depending on the reading proficiency of the students and the length of the text, reading can take various forms:
   • The teacher reads the book aloud to the students.
   • Students read with a partner.
   • Individual students read the book prior to beginning the Literature Response Group.
   • For longer books, the teacher might want to divide the book into smaller chunks and bring students together for discussions after they have read each section.

## Beyond

5. In Reader Response Groups, the students respond to the reading. To get students started, the teacher might suggest that the group consider some of the following questions:
   • What was my purpose for reading this text?
   • What did I learn from reading this text?
   • Why did the author write this text? What was the author trying to tell me?
   • What parts did I like best? What parts were my favorites? Why did I like these particular parts?
   • What parts did I like least? Why did I dislike these parts?
   • Did this text remind me of other texts I have read? How was this text both similar or dissimilar to other texts?
   • What would I change in this text if I had written it? What might the author have done to have made this text better, more understandable, more interesting?
   • Are there things/parts that I did not understand? What can I do to better understand these parts?

# Interpretations

(Original idea from Mitzi Lewison, personal communication;
adapted from Kucer, Silva, & Delgado-Larocco, 1995)

## CONCEPT

Comprehension involves a transaction between the reader and the text. Background knowledge can affect the way a reader comprehends text. Social interaction gives readers the opportunity to negotiate meaning and develop deeper understandings of the text.

## MATERIALS

Any text that the teacher anticipates students will find difficult to comprehend
Interpretation Grids (see Sample Materials)

## PROCEDURES

### Into

1. Before reading the text, tap into the students' background knowledge by brainstorming information they know about the concept or topic highlighted in the reading.
2. Have the students illustrate their ideas about the reading topic using the Interpretation Grid.
3. Have students write their ideas about the reading topic using the Written Interpretation Grid.
4. Once students have their own illustrations and written interpretations, give them the opportunity to share with others their interpretations. Discuss their similarities and differences.

### Through

5. Read the text with the students. Ask the students to think about the author's interpretation of the concept or topic. Have the students add what they think is the author's interpretation to the Illustrative and Written Interpretation Grids.
6. Give students the opportunity to share their understandings of the author and discuss similarities and differences.

7. Read the difficult text a second time. Have the students underline their favorite phrases and share these with others.

8. Have the students circle the phrases that they find confusing or difficult to understand.

9. Using the Multiple Interpretations Grid, have the students record one phrase that they identified as confusing or difficult to understand.

10. Ask the students to write down their best guess as to what they think the particular phrase might mean.

11. Have students share their difficult phrase with others. Ask other students to write down what they think the difficult phrase might mean.

**Beyond**

12. Reread the interpretations and select the one that makes most sense.

13. Reread the text and determine how well the interpretation works.

## SAMPLE MATERIALS

Interpretation Grid:

Illustrative Interpretation of Concept or Topic

Material: _____

| Illustrate what YOU think. | Illustrate what the AUTHOR thinks. |
| --- | --- |
| | |

Interpretation Grid:

Written Interpretation of Concept or Topic

Material: _____

| Write what YOU think. | Write what the AUTHOR thinks. |
|---|---|
|  |  |

Interpretation Grid:

Multiple Interpretations

A phrase that I am unclear about is:

My interpretation is:

Another possible interpretation is:

Another possible interpretation is:

Another possible interpretation is:

# Save the Last Word for Me

(Adapted from Short, Harste, & Burke, 1996)

## CONCEPT

Comprehension involves a transaction not only between the reader and the text, but also between reader and reader. Other readers as well as the author influence how a text is understood.

## MATERIALS

Reading material
Index cards or slips of paper

## PROCEDURES

### Into

1. Introduce the reading material to the students. Let the students know that as they read, they are to select parts from the text that they would like to bring to discuss in the reader response groups.
2. Students should be encouraged to identify parts of the text that they find interesting, points with which they particularly agree or disagree, significant new learnings, points of confusion, and so on.
3. On one side of the index card or scrap paper, students write the part of the text that has been selected for response and the page where the part is located. Students only need to write enough words, phrases, or sentences that would allow others to locate the quote in the text. It can be helpful if the page number on which the issues to be responded to is located. This makes it easier to return to the text when the response is discussed.
4. On the other side of the card or paper, students respond to the quote they have selected. Again, students need only write enough so that they will remember what they want to share about the quote.

**Through**

5. Give students time to read the text and to complete their response cards.

6. Have the students go through their cards and put them in the order they would like to discuss them, going from most to least important.

7. Explain to the students that they will be taking turns reading their quotes and having others react to them *before* they discuss the response to their own quotes—thus saving the last word for themselves

8. Have the first student begin by sharing his or her own quote. After other members of the group respond to the quote, the first student responds to his or her own quote.

**Beyond**

9. Students continue taking turns reading and responding to the quotes. If someone else shares a student's top quote before his or her turn, the student chooses his or her next quote.

# Say Something

(Adapted from Short, Harste, & Burke, 1996)

## CONCEPT

Readers develop deeper understandings as they interact both with the text as well as with others. Readers "talk" to the author and with other readers to come to a fuller understanding of what they are reading.

## MATERIALS

This strategy can be used with any reading material. When introducing the Say Something strategy lesson to students for the first time, it is particularly helpful to select a piece of material that the teacher knows will be likely to spur discussion among the group. For this first reading, it is also helpful to have identified stopping places in the reading with a pencil or a sticky note.

## PROCEDURES

### Into

1. Inform students that they will be reading and discussing a reading selection with a partner.
2. Let students know that they will be stopping at various points in the text to "say something" to one another about what they have read. Students can respond by making connections to personal life experiences evoked by the reading, relating the reading to previously read texts, making predictions about what is to come, asking questions to clarify the meaning of the text, and so on. In order to provide an example of how Say Something is used in everyday life, discuss with the students how most people talk about a movie or a television show they may have recently seen.
3. Pair students in the class.

### Through

4. The text is read to the previously selected stopping point. The teacher can read the text, students can take turns reading aloud, or students can read the text silently.

5. When reaching the stopping point has been reached, ask the students to turn to their partner and "say something" about the text.

**Beyond**

6. Continue reading and stopping to say something at the stopping points that have been selected throughout the text.

## VARIATIONS

1. As students become more comfortable with the strategy, have the students decide where they will stop to say something.
2. Rather than asking students to say something, students can be asked to "write something."

# Making Text Connections

(Adapted from Keene & Zimmermann, 1997)

## CONCEPT

Comprehension is more than simply being able to literally recall the ideas put forth by the author. Comprehension also involves the reader making connections between the text and himself or herself, between the text and the world, and between the text and other texts previously read or written.

## MATERIALS

Several well-structured texts that reflect ideas and language that are easily accessible to the students. The texts should also provide numerous opportunities for students to make text-to-self, text-to-world, and text-to-text connections.
A Making Text Connections Grid for the recording of text connections (see Sample Materials)

## PROCEDURES

### Into

1. Read to the class a short text that is of interest to the students. Periodically throughout the reading, stop and discuss your own text-to-self, text-to-world, and text-to-text connections. Record these connections on the blackboard underneath the appropriate column heading: text-to-self connections, text-to-world connections, and text-to-text connections.
2. Once students understand the kinds of connections that are possible, encourage their participation at the stopping points in the reading. Record student connections using the grid.

### Through

3. Give students a second text to independently read and a copy of the Making Text Connections Grid.
4. Students are to read the text and record connections that they are able to make between the text and themselves, the world, and other texts they have read or written.

**Beyond**

5. When the reading is completed, give students the opportunities to share each type of connection. Record these on the board so that all students can see the various types of connections their classmates have made.

## VARIATIONS

If students experience difficulty in making text-to-text connections, engage them in the Text Set strategy lesson or the Structured Stories strategy lesson.

**SAMPLE MATERIALS**

Making Text Connections Grid

Text: _____

| Text-to-Self Connections | Text-to-World Connections | Text-to-Text Connections |
|---|---|---|
|  |  |  |

# Reading and Writing Block Strategies

# Extra Words

(Adapted from Goodman & Burke, 1980)

## CONCEPT

Reading is a process of identifying the core meanings or ideas in the text being read. Proficient readers are able to identify those words that are central to the author's message and those words that are less important.

## MATERIALS

Several texts that are well structured and readable and contain sentences students will find rather complex. Texts with descriptive language are particularly useful.

## PROCEDURES

### Into

1. Ask the students how they handle a text that contains numerous long or complex sentences. The purpose here is to discover how students handle such complex language structures.
2. Discuss with the students that sometimes authors use "extra" words in what they write. The purpose of these "extra" words is to give the reader a fuller understanding of the ideas being written about. At times, however, these extra words can make it difficult to understand the main idea that the author is attempting to make.
3. One way to handle a text that is difficult to understand is to skip the extra words and to focus on those words that are central to the author's message.
4. On an overhead projector, show the students a short text with complex sentence structures. As a group, read each sentence and ask the students which words are "extra." Cross out these words and discuss with the students why these words are "extra."

### Through

5. Give the students a copy of a new text and ask them to independently cross out the "extra" words. This may be done independently or in small groups, depending on the degree of support the students need.

6. After the independent reading, show the text on an overhead projector. For each sentence, ask a student to share what words were crossed out and why. Cross out these words on the transparency.

**Beyond**

7. As students read various texts throughout the year, occasionally ask them to identify and share words that they feel are "extra."

# Reader-Selected Miscues

(Adapted from Watson, 1980)

## CONCEPT

Proficient readers monitor their reading for meaning. When meaning is disrupted, they utilize a variety of strategies to work through the disruption.

## MATERIALS

Any text that is of interest to the students and that contains some language and/or concepts that students may initially find challenging. The students may read the same or a variety of texts, depending on the experience and needs of the students and the needs of the teacher.
Problem and Solution Grid (see Sample Materials)

## PROCEDURES

### Into

1. Identify the reading with which the students are going to be engaged. Tell the students that when they encounter a difficulty in their reading, they should "mark" the difficulty in some manner. This may involve putting a bookmark at the page or a sticky notes under the problem, underlining the difficulty, or recording the difficulty on a slip of paper or in a reading log, and so on.

### Through

2. After the reading, provide students the opportunity to review the troublesome spots they have identified. Ask each student to select several to share. The exact number to be selected will vary depending on the particular group of students who are experiencing this strategy lesson.
3. Ask a student to share one difficulty with the class or the group doing the reading. The student should discuss the nature of the difficulty and read the paragraph or surrounding sentences in which the difficulty was encountered. List the problem on the following Problem and Solution Grid.
4. For each problem listed, discuss several strategies that the reader might use to solve the problem—for example, read on and return, read previous sentence or paragraph, substitute something that makes sense. List these strategies on the grid.

**Beyond**

5. After various difficulties and solutions have been listed, ask students to return to the text they have read. Using the various strategies identified, students attempt to solve the problems they have identified. The number of problems to be solved will vary depending on the student and the text being read.

6. Give students the opportunity to share their solutions to the problems.

7. As solutions are shared, begin a Reading Strategy Wall Chart.

## VARIATIONS

1. When first introducing this strategy lesson to the students, it is helpful if all students have the same text. This makes it easier to identify difficult parts to solve.

2. Before introducing the Reader-Selected Miscues strategy lesson, it is helpful if the students have first experienced the Selected Deletion/Multiple Known Concepts strategy lesson. The teacher can then make links between the various strategies learned in the Selected Deletion and the Reader-Selected Miscues strategy lessons.

**SAMPLE MATERIALS**

Problem and Solution Grid

| Difficulty | Possible Solutions |
|---|---|
|  |  |

# Reading Wall Chart

(Adapted from Kucer, 1995; Kucer et al., 1995)

## CONCEPT

Encountering "unknowns" is a natural part of the reading process, even for proficient readers. When readers are confronted with something they do not recognize or understand, they utilize a variety of strategies to work through the problem.

## MATERIALS

Any materials with which the students will encounter something they do not recognize or understand

## PROCEDURES

### Into

1. The Reading Wall Chart strategy lesson works best in conjunction with the Reader-Selected Miscues strategy lesson.
2. As students read the text, ask them to record things that they do not initially recognize or understand. If they are ultimately able to figure out the unknowns, students should record how they were able to do so as well.

### Through

3. Periodically, ask students to share their reading problems and solutions. On a large sheet of chart paper, record the various strategies they have discovered to work their way through a text. Add to the Wall Chart whenever the opportunity arises.
4. Review the strategies on the Wall Chart throughout the school year and encourage students to use the strategies when reading.

### Beyond

5. Once a substantial number of reading strategies have been recorded, the teacher will want to type them on $8\frac{1}{2} \times 11"$ paper and distribute them to the students. Students can then refer to the chart whenever they encounter difficulties during their reading.

**VARIATIONS**

When reading aloud to the students, the teacher can "think aloud" strategies that are used to work through difficult parts of the text. (See Think Aloud strategy lesson.) The teacher points out and discusses how these strategies are similar to those that students have identified on the Wall Chart.

## SAMPLE MATERIALS

Reading Strategy Wall Chart

1. Stop reading → think about it → make a guess → read on to see if the guess makes sense.

2. Stop reading → reread the previous sentence(s) or paragraph(s) → make a guess → continue reading to see if the guess makes sense.

3. Skip it → read on to get more information → return and make a guess → continue reading to see if the guess makes sense.

4. Skip it → read on to see if what you do not understand is important to know → return and make a guess if it is important; do not return if it is not important.

5. Put something in that makes sense → read on to see if it fits with the rest of the text.

6. Stop reading → look at the pictures, charts, graphs, and so on → make a guess → read on to see if the guess makes sense.

7. Sound it out (focus on initial and final letters, consonants, known words within the word, meaningful word parts) → read on to see if the guess makes sense.

8. Stop reading → talk with a friend about what you do not understand → return and continue reading.

9. Stop reading → look in a glossary, dictionary, encyclopedia, or related books on the topic → return and continue reading.

10. Read the text with a friend.

11. Stop reading.

# Selected Deletion/Multiple Known Concepts

(Adapted from Goodman & Burke, 1980)

## CONCEPT

Reading is a process of predicting upcoming text structures, meanings, and words based on what has been previously read. Proficient readers use previous context and the print itself to predict individual words.

## MATERIALS

A text that is well structured, readable, but unfamiliar to the reader. At least initially, the text should be one that the reader can handle with some ease. Throughout the text, delete words, phrases, clauses, and/or sentences and replace them with a line of a standard length. It is also helpful to number each blank for easy reference. Deletions should be carefully selected such that the reader will be able to make use of context—before and after—to predict what might be put in the blanks. A text with pictures can provide additional support for the reader. (see Sample Materials)

## PROCEDURES

### Into

1. Inform the students that they are going to read a story in which words, phrases, clauses, and/or sentences have been deleted and replaced by a line. Be sure that students are aware that a standard line length has been used for all blanks. That is, the line length does not indicate how many words have been deleted.
2. Give the students the opportunity to peruse the entire story before starting to read.

### Through

3. The students read the piece aloud together (see Choral Reading strategy lesson). When they encounter a blank, the students are to say something that makes sense and continue reading.
4. The teacher plays a supportive role in this strategy, reading aloud with the students and keeping the pace flowing. When a blank is encountered, the teacher pauses, lets the readers predict, and then begins reading aloud again with the students.

**Beyond**

5. After the entire text has been read, discuss the range of predictions for each blank and list them on the board. Ask the students to support their predictions using the text and their background knowledge. All predictions are evaluated in terms of whether "they sound like language" and "make sense."

6. Allow students the opportunity to read aloud the text a second time, putting in their favorite predictions.

7. Discuss with the students the usefulness of this strategy. Highlight the fact that this strategy can be used when reading a text containing unknown or unrecognized words. Remind the students that an unknown or unrecognized word is similar to the blanks in the text that they recently read.

## VARIATIONS

1. Once students become familiar with the strategy, they can work in small groups, pairs, or individually without direct teacher mediation.

2. A follow-up strategy lesson that provides less support for the student is Predicting Word Meanings and Reader-Selected Miscues strategy lessons.

## SAMPLE MATERIALS

*The Great Big Enormous Turnip*
(Tolstoy, 1976)

Once upon a time an old man planted a little turnip. The old man said, "Grow, grow, little turnip. Grow sweet. Grow, grow, little turnip. Grow strong." And the turnip grew up sweet and strong and big and enormous. Then one day the old man went to pull it **1** _____. He pulled—and pulled again. But he could not **2** _____ it up. He called the old woman. The old woman pulled the **3** _____ man. The old man pulled the turnip. And they pulled—and pulled again. But **4** _____ could not pull it up. So the old woman called her **5** _____. The granddaughter pulled the old woman. The old woman pulled the old man. The old man pulled the **6** _____. And they pulled— and pulled again. But they could **7** _____ pull it up. The granddaughter called the black dog. The black dog pulled the **8** _____. The granddaughter pulled the old woman. The old woman pulled the old man. The old man pulled the turnip. And they pulled—and pulled again. But they could not pull it up. The black dog called the **9** _____. The cat pulled the dog. The black dog pulled the **10** _____. The granddaughter pulled the old woman. The old woman pulled the old man. The old man pulled the turnip. And they pulled—and pulled again. But they **11** _____ pull it up. The cat called the mouse. The **12** _____ pulled the cat. The cat pulled the dog. The black dog pulled the granddaughter. The granddaughter pulled the **13** _____. The old woman pulled the old man. The old man pulled the turnip. They pulled—and pulled again. And up came the **14** _____ at last!

# Synonym Substitution

(Adapted from Goodman & Burke, 1980)

## CONCEPT

Reading is a constructive and meaning-making process. Readers translate the author's surface structure (language) into their own surface structure (language) and at the same time maintain the author's meaning.

## MATERIALS

A text that is well structured, readable, and—initially—familiar to the reader. Throughout the text there should be predictable words, phrases, clauses, and/or sentences that have been underlined. It is also helpful to number each blank for easy reference. Selection of these points should be done carefully such that the reader can make use of the previous context to predict what is underlined and then to generate a substitution. Use of a text with pictures included provides additional support for less-proficient readers. (see Sample Materials)

## PROCEDURES

### Into

1. Inform students that they will be reading aloud a story with which they are familiar. In the story, certain words, phrases, clauses, and/or sentences have been underlined.
2. Discuss with the students what the story is about. Then, let them peruse the entire story.
3. Before reading is initiated, tell them that they are not to read what is underlined, but instead must supply something that means the same thing at these points in the text.

### Through

4. The teacher and the students orally read the text. The teacher's role is to maintain the pace, to read chorally with the students, but not to provide substitutions. When an underlined word is encountered, the teacher pauses so students can provide substitutions, and then continues reading with the students.

**Beyond**

5. After the entire text has been read, discuss the range of substitutions for each underlined item and list them on the board.
6. Allow the students the opportunity to read aloud the text a second time, putting in
   their favorite substitutions.

## VARIATIONS

For English-language learners, the Synonym Substitution strategy lesson can be difficult if
they are not familiar with the vocabulary and concepts that appear in the text.

## SAMPLE MATERIALS

*The Three Little Pigs*
(Scott Foresman, 1976)

Once upon a time there were three little pigs. One day the three little pigs left home. Each little pig wanted to build a house. The first little pig made a house of straw. The second **1** <u>little</u> pig made a house of sticks. The third little pig made a house of **2** <u>bricks</u>. A big bad wolf saw the little pigs. "A little pig will make a good **3** <u>lunch</u> for me," he said. The **4** <u>big</u> bad wolf went to the house of the first little pig. The **5** <u>wolf</u> called, "Little pig, little pig, let me come in." "Not by the hair of my chinny chin chin!" **6** <u>said</u> the first little pig. "Then I'll huff and I'll puff and I'll blow your house in!" 7 <u>called</u> the wolf. So he huffed and he puffed and he blew the **8** <u>house</u> in. But the first little pig got away. He ran into the **9** <u>woods</u> to hide. The big bad wolf went to the house of the second little pig. The wolf called, "Little pig, little pig, let me come in." "Not by the hair of my chinny chin chin!" **10** <u>said</u> the second little pig. "Then I'll huff and I'll puff and I'll blow your house in!" called the wolf. So he huffed and he puffed and he blew the **11** <u>house in</u>. But the second little pig got away. He ran into the woods to hide. The **12** <u>big bad</u> wolf went to the house of the third little pig. The wolf called, "Little pig, little pig, let me come in." "Not by the hair of my chinny chin chin!" said the third little pig. "Then I'll huff and I'll puff and I'll blow your house in!" called the **13** <u>wolf</u>. So he huffed and he puffed and he huffed and he puffed. But the wolf **14** <u>couldn't</u> blow the house in. The wolf **15** <u>got</u> on top of the house. He called, "Little pig, little pig! I'll come down the chimney and eat you up!" The third little pig took the **16** <u>cover</u> off the pot of water. The water was **17** <u>very</u> hot. The little pig called, "Come on down!" The wolf slid down the chimney. He landed in the water with a big splash. And that was the end of the **18** <u>big bad wolf</u>.

# Think Aloud

## CONCEPT

Proficient readers utilize a number of reading strategies to process text. Emergent and struggling readers often are not aware of many of the strategies used by proficient readers to monitor and comprehend text.

## MATERIALS

A reading passage that contains points of difficulty for the reader and that would provide the teacher with several opportunities to model one or two strategies for monitoring comprehension. Preview the passage and identify points to stop and "think aloud" or discuss how the student uses these strategies to comprehend text.

Index cards with the definition of the strategies to be demonstrated during the think-aloud. (See Table 2.22, Reading Strategies and Processes.) For example, to demonstrate how to make inferences based on visual and linguistic cues, the teacher might write the following on an index card:

> Look at the picture and the first
> letter of the word. Guess!

## PROCEDURES

### Into

1. Introduce the students to the reading passage you have prepared to model the selected strategies.

### Through

2. Read the passage, stopping at previously identified points to think aloud ways in which you use a particular strategy. For example, the teacher might say: "When I am not sure of a word, I look at the pictures and then look at the word. I see if the word starts with the first sound of the object in the picture. I then try the word to see if it makes sense."

3. After completing the reading of the passage, read each strategy description on the index card and discuss the strategies with the students.

4. Have the students work in partners to reread the text and practice the newly discussed strategies.

**Beyond**

5. Next time the students are reading a text, remind them to use the strategies.

## VARIATIONS

Students can add record strategies they use on the Reading Wall Chart. (See Reading Wall Chart strategy lesson.)

# Writing Wall Chart

(Adapted from Kucer, 1995; Kucer et al., 1995)

## CONCEPT

Encountering "writer's block" is a natural part of the composing process, even for proficient writers. All writers occasionally encounter points in their written drafts where they do not know what to write next or have difficulty expressing an idea. When proficient writers are confronted with these difficulties, they utilize a variety of strategies to work through the problem.

## MATERIALS

A piece of writing to be assigned

## PROCEDURES

### Into

1. Introduce the students to the writing assignment previously decided on. This assignment can be related to a particular topic being studied within a thematic unit or within a content area, such as science or social sciences. Or, the topics may be one decided on by individual students.
2. Tell the students that as they write, they should try and be aware of what they do when they are having difficulty knowing what to write about next or in putting their ideas into language.

### Through

3. After drafts have been completed, ask the students to share how they handled the problem with finding ideas or language when writing.
4. On a large sheet of chart paper, record the various strategies the students have discovered to work their way through a text.
5. Throughout the year when students are writing, encourage them to try out these strategies when they encounter problems. Additionally, ask them for new strategies to add to the wall chart.
6. Review the strategies on the wall chart throughout the school year and encourage students to use the strategies when writing.

**Beyond**

7. Once a substantial number of writing strategies have been recorded, the teacher will want to type them on $8\frac{1}{2} \times 11"$ paper and distribute them to the students. Students can then refer to the chart whenever they encounter difficulties during their writing.

## VARIATIONS

When engaging the students in teacher, shared, or guided writing, the teacher can think aloud strategies that are used to work through difficult parts of the text. The teacher points out and discusses how these strategies are similar to those that students have identified on the Wall Chart.

**SAMPLE MATERIALS**

Writing Strategy Wall Chart

1. Brainstorm possible ideas and jot them down on paper. Select one of the ideas and try it out.

2. Reread what you have written so far and see if an idea comes to mind.

3. Skip ahead to a part that you know what you will write about. Come back to the problem later.

4. Write it as best you can and return later to make it better.

5. Write it several different ways and choose the one that you like the best.

6. Write whatever comes into your mind.

7. Talk about it/conference with a friend.

8. Read other texts to some new ideas.

9. Stop writing for a while and come back to it later.

# Using Context Strategies

# Concept Webs

## CONCEPT

Readers not only bring their background knowledge to the reading act, they also develop knowledge through the very act of reading. Much of this knowledge is developed in the form of concepts. Concepts can be conceived as webs of meaning focused on a central idea.

## MATERIALS

A variety of texts on the same topic, issue, or concept

## PROCEDURES

### Into

1. When introducing Concept Webs, it can be helpful if students have experienced the Semantic Mapping or Cloning an Author strategy lessons.
2. Inform the students that they are going to be reading a variety of materials on a particular topic, issue, or concept. Introduce students to the concept, such as "conflict" or "photosynthesis," on which they are to focus.
3. Before reading begins, ask students to individually brainstorm and list all that they currently know about the concept. Give students the opportunity to share these ideas with one another, either with a partner, in small groups, or with the entire class.
4. After the brainstorming, students are to web their ideas. Webbing involves the students in drawing a diagram that links all of their brainstormed ideas based on their relationships. Once again, allow students time to share their webs.

### Through

5. Students are given time to read various materials on the concept under consideration. This reading of materials may take place over several days. As students discover new and relevant information, they list the information on a piece of paper.
6. Using relevant information from their previous list of ideas and web, as well as the new information generated, students draw a second web.

**Beyond**

7. Students share their initial and final webs and discuss how their understanding of the concept has change.

## VARIATIONS

1. For students who may need additional support, the development of the initial and final concept web can be done as an entire class. In this case, all brainstormed ideas before and after the reading are listed by the teacher on the board, an overhead transparency, or chart paper. With assistance from the student, the teacher draws the diagram using the ideas listed.

2. Once students have developed in-depth knowledge of the concept, they can be asked to share their knowledge through nonlinguistic forms. The students can illustrate the concept or be asked to perform the concept. The movement to nonlanguage forms frequently leads to new insights on the part of the students.

# Predictable Books

## CONCEPT

Reading is a process of predicting language and meaning based on the language and meaning previously read. Written language becomes more predictable or more easily anticipated as the reader becomes more and more familiar with the language and content of the author.

## MATERIALS

A text that makes use of repetitive and/or cumulative episodes, events or ideas and makes use of repetitive and/or cumulative syntactic and semantic patterns. Pictures should also be redundant—tell the same story—as the print. When selecting predictable texts for the students, the following factors should be considered:

- The match between the language of the reader and the language of the author.
- The match between the background of the reader and the background of the author.
- The use of repetitive and/or cumulative episodes, events, or ideas.
- The use of repetitive and/or cumulative syntactic and semantic patterns.
- The relationship between the text and the illustrations.

## PROCEDURES

### Into

1. Give the students copies of the predictable book and ask them to "read" all of the pictures to discover what the story is going to be about. This is oftentimes referred to as a "picture walk."
2. Ask the students to predict and discuss the storyline based on the pictures. List student predictions on the board or overhead.

### Through

3. Tell the students that you are going to read the book aloud to them and they should read aloud with you. As students become increasingly familiar with the text, stop

reading the highly predictable parts and allow students to chorally read without teacher support.

### Beyond

4. After the students have read the book with you, allow time for them to respond to the book. Some possible responses might be:
   - What did you like best about the book? What was your favorite part?
   - What did you like the least about the book? What would you change in the story if you could?
   - Does this story remind you of any other stories? Is this story like other stories that you know about? How are these other stories like the story that we just read?
   - Why do you think the author wrote this story? What was the author trying to teach you?
   - Were there things in the story that you had difficulty understanding or reading? Let's see if we can figure out ways to find what these things mean or say.
5. Give the students the opportunity to reread the book aloud with a friend or in small groups.

## VARIATIONS

1. If students are in need of additional support, after the picture walk, discuss each page with the students. During this discussion, informally use some of the language of the text that is found on each page.
2. If students are more proficient, they can chorally read the text, read in pairs, or read independently.

# Predicting Word Meanings

(Adapted from Atwell & Rhodes, 1984)

## CONCEPT

Reading is a process in which individual words are defined by the context in which they are found. Proficient readers use their background knowledge and the surrounding context to determine and expand the meanings of words.

## MATERIALS

A well-structured text containing words whose meanings the reader may not know or whose meanings are different from those known to the reader. The context in which the words are found should support the reader in predicting what the words might mean. (see Sample Materials)

A Word Analysis Grid with four columns. The first column contains a list of words from the text whose meanings the reader may not know or whose meanings are different from those known to the reader. The second column is for prereading predictions and the third for postreading predictions. The final column is for recording evidence supporting postreading predictions. (see Sample Materials)

## PROCEDURES

### Into

1. Inform the students that they are going to be reading a text in which they may encounter words whose meanings they do not know or that are being used in ways that may be new to them.
2. Distribute the Word Analysis Grid to the students. Individually or in groups of two or three, students write predictions for what the words might mean. Or, the words may be listed on the board or shown on an overhead. The teacher reads each word, asks the class for predictions, and records the predictions.
3. If students work individually or in groups, allow them to share their predictions. These predictions should be recorded on the board or an overhead. Discuss with the students the rationale behind their predictions.

**Through**

4. Give students the text from which the words were taken. Individually or in groups of two or three, students read the text. They return to the word list and using the text as a guide, students record the meanings of the words in the postreading prediction column based on the context in which they are found. In the fourth column, students support their predictions using information from the text and their background.

5. Provide students the opportunity to share their postreading predictions and evidence. Compare and contrast these with their prereading predictions.

**Beyond**

6. Discuss with students how they used context to generate their postreading predictions. Explicitly refer to meanings in the text that supported their postreading predictions.

7. Discuss with students that when they encounter words that they do not know, they can use context to help them predict what the words might mean.

## VARIATIONS

1. If students are reading a text that has been photocopied, they can underline in the text the evidence used for their postreading predictions.

2. Once students are comfortable with this strategy, introduce them to the Reader-Selected Miscues strategy lesson.

**SAMPLE MATERIALS**

Word Analysis Grid

| Word | Prereading Prediction | Postreading Prediction | Evidence |
|------|----------------------|------------------------|----------|
| pickle | | | |
| raise | | | |
| stretch | | | |
| pitch | | | |
| chase | | | |
| scale | | | |
| planish | | | |

## "Making a Bowl"

When a silversmith wants to make a bowl, he must decide on the technique he will use. He can choose to raise the bowl, or to stretch it. In either case, he will start out with a flat, circular piece of metal and, by hammering a certain way, he will shape the disc into a bowl.

If he has decided to raise the bowl, he will begin at the center and work his way out toward what will be the rim, hammering on what will be the outside of the bowl.

If he has decided to stretch the bowl, he will hammer outward from the center; this time on what will become the inside of the bowl.

Metal becomes harder after it has been hammered for a while. To keep the metal pliable, the silversmith will heat the disc with a torch. Often, the torch fire will leave black scale over the metal. To remove this, the smith will drop the piece into an acid solution or pickle. The pickle will clean off the scale and the smith can continue hammering.

When the bowl shape is complete, the smith starts to planish the piece to remove any hammer marks and to make the finished bowl smooth and shiny. Using a special planishing hammer, the smith taps lightly all around the piece several times. Each of these little hammer blows evens out the surface of the bowl. At this point, the bowl will be done.

Occasionally, the smith may want to add a decorative finish or design. To do this, he will fill the bowl with hot pitch. After the pitch has cooled and hardened, the smith will use a chisel-like tool to chase the design he wants. The pitch will hold the shape of the bowl while pressure is applied to the chasing. When the design is complete, the pitch is heated and poured out. The bowl is cleaned and it is done.

# Selected Deletion/Single Known Concept

(Adapted from Goodman & Burke, 1980)

## CONCEPT

Reading is a process of integrating meanings across the text to form a coherent whole. This integration involves the evaluation of past meanings in the light of current and predicted meanings.

## MATERIALS

A text that is well structured, readable, but unfamiliar to the reader. The text should focus on a single concept, event, or issue with which the reader is familiar both conceptually and linguistically. As the text progresses, the reader should be provided with more and more information about the topic. If the concept, event, or issue is explicitly stated, a standard length blank in the text should replace it.

Divide the text into sections. Each section should provide the reader with additional information about the deleted concept. (see Sample Materials)

A Prediction Grid for students to record their predictions and the information used to form/support their predictions. (see Sample Materials)

## PROCEDURES

### Into

1. Inform the students that they are going to read a text on a concept, event, or issue with which they are familiar. The concept, event, or issue, however, has been replaced by a blank. Make sure that students understand that the same word is to fit in all of the blanks in the text.

### Through

2. Reveal the first part of the text. Initially, it is helpful if the text is shown to the students on an overhead transparency or on the chalkboard. Ask the students to read the first section and write a prediction for what might go in the blank in the left-hand column of the Prediction Grid. Students are to support their prediction—provide evidence—using the text and their background knowledge. This support is recorded in the right-hand column of the grid.

3. Give students the opportunity to share their predictions. List the predictions and support on the board or overhead transparency. All predictions are evaluated in terms of whether "they sound like language" and "make sense."

4. Reveal the second section of the text. Students read this section and record a prediction. This prediction may be the same as their previous prediction or it may be different based on the new information.

5. Before sharing new predictions, review with the students their previous predictions. Ask the student who made each prediction whether or not it still makes sense and why or why not. If the student has rejected the previous prediction, cross it out.

6. Students share and support any new predictions. These are discussed and recorded on the Prediction Grid.

7. Continue throughout the text in this manner—reading, evaluating previous predictions, generating and supporting new predictions, and so on.

**Beyond**

8. When the entire text has been read, allow various students to reread the text using their final predictions. Ask the students if the predictions make sense in the entire text.

## VARIATIONS

Rather than sharing each prediction as it is made, students read the entire text individually or in a group. After the text has been read, students share and support their final predictions.

## SAMPLE MATERIALS

"The ____"

I was really mad. I mean REALLY MAD! When I got home from school I discovered that all of my ____ was missing! Someone had come into the kitchen and taken all of my ____ .

In the morning before I went to school, it had been on the table. Now, not one piece of my ____ was on the table. Not one piece! Who could have taken it?

I had baked the ____ myself and it took a long time to make. I had not even burned it. The ____ was a beautiful, golden brown.

I had wanted to have a slice of ____ after school with butter and jelly. But, someone had taken it. Maybe the person had even eaten all of it. Now, I would have to be hungry until dinnertime. I was really made all right.

"Pat"
(Adapted from Anderson, Reynolds, Schallert, and Goetz, 1977)

Pat slowly got up from the mat, planning the escape. Pat hesitated a moment and thought. Things were not going well.

What was most bothersome was being held, especially since the charge had been weak. Pat considered what to do in the present situation.

Pat was aware that it was because of the early roughness that the penalty had been so severe–much too severe from Pat's point of view. The situation was becoming frustrating; the pressure had been grinding for too long. Pat was being ridden unmercifully.

Pat was getting angry now and felt it was time to make the move. Success or failure would depend on what Pat did in the next few seconds.

Prediction Grid

| Prediction | Support |
|---|---|
| 1. | |
| 2. | |
| 3. | |
| 4. | |

# Selected Deletion/Multiple Unknown Concept

(Adapted from Goodman & Burke, 1980)

**CONCEPT**

Reading is a process through which readers are introduced to new ideas and concepts. Therefore, learning is the result of many reading experiences.

**MATERIALS**

A text that is well structured, readable, but unfamiliar to the reader. The text should focus on a single concept, event, or issue with which the reader is unfamiliar both conceptually and linguistically. As the text progresses, the reader should be provided with more and more information about the topic. Underline the concept in the text every time it occurs. Then, divide the text into sections. Each section should provide the reader with additional information about the deleted concept. (see Sample Materials)

A Prediction Grid for students to record their predictions and the information used to form/support their predictions. (see Sample Materials)

**PROCEDURES**

### Into

1. Inform the students that they are going to read a text about a concept, event, or issue with which they are unfamiliar. The concept has been underlined for them. As they read the text, the students will be "taught" about the topic.

### Through

2. Reveal the title of the text. At least initially, the text should be shown to the students on an overhead transparency or on the chalkboard. Ask the students to read the title—or read it to them if they will be unable to pronounce the word—and write what they understand the word means in the left-hand column of the Prediction Grid. Students are to support their prediction—provide evidence—using the text and their background knowledge. This support is recorded in the right-hand column of the grid.

3. Give the students the opportunity to share their predictions. List the predictions and support on the board or overhead transparency. All predictions are evaluated in terms of whether "they sound like language" and "make sense."

4. Reveal the second section of the text. Students read the next section of and record a prediction. This prediction may be the same as their previous one or it may be different based on the new information.

5. Review their list of previous predictions. Ask the student who made each prediction whether or not it still makes sense and why or why not. If the student has rejected the previous prediction, cross it out.

6. Students share and support any new predictions. These are discussed and recorded on the Prediction Grid.

7. Continue throughout the text in this manner—reading, evaluating previous predictions, generating and supporting new predictions, and so on.

**Beyond**

8. When the entire text has been read, allow various students to reread the text using their final predictions. Ask the students if the predictions make sense in the entire text.

## VARIATIONS

Rather than sharing each prediction as it is made, students read the entire text individually or as a group. After the text has been read, students share and support their final predictions.

**SAMPLE MATERIALS**

"Terracing"
(Adapted from Burke, 1976)

Early mountain farmers in many parts of the world studied and learned from their environment. As they looked around, they saw raised, level places, or natural terraces on mountainsides. A terrace, jutting out from the mountain, caught soil and water that would otherwise run down the slope. Here plants grow better than on steep land.

Early farmers living in mountainous areas were always looking for flat places or terraces to farm. Trying to grow plants on the sides of the mountains was too difficult. Many times, however, there were not enough flat places on the sides of the mountains. Or, the natural terraces were so small in size that not much could be grown on them. As the number of farmers living on the mountains became larger, the farmers needed to find a way to grow more food.

The farmers learned to dig flat places into the sides of the mountains. Then, they were able to plant food on these flat places. Even though the farmers had made these flat places, they also called them terraces. Just like the natural terraces, these terraces dug by the farmers also caught soil and water and became good places to grow crops.

Prediction Grid

| Prediction | Support |
|---|---|
| 1. | |
| 2. | |
| 3. | |
| 4. | |

# Writing Revision Strategies

# Revision Circle

## CONCEPT

Writers rely on readers to clarify their meanings and to help them determine whether the purposes and needs of the audience are being met.

## MATERIALS

Drafts of student writing that are to be published
Writing Conference Form (see Sample Materials)
Aliki. (1986). *How a book is made*. New York: Harper & Row.

## PROCEDURES

### Into

1. Discuss with the students that they are going to be selecting something they have written to revise, edit, and publish. Read *How a Book Is Made* to give the students an understanding of the publishing process.

2. After students have selected a piece of writing to bring to publication, discuss with them that one of the purposes of the Revision Circle is to ask for general feedback in terms of how well their writing makes sense to others. Emphasize the role of the audience in responding and asking questions.

3. Introduce the Writing Conference Form. The nature of this form will vary depending on the needs of the students and the teacher. Demonstrate the role of the writer and the audience by reading a piece to the class and having the students respond. Use the Writing Conference Form to record the students' responses.

### Through

4. When three or four students are ready for a writing conference, have students meet at a small table.

5. One student reads his or her piece aloud to the rest of the group.

6. When the author is finished, the group members share what they liked about the piece. This positive response is often overlooked in writing conferences. However, writers need to know what is good about their texts so that they can continue doing it in future writings.

7. To give the author more freedom to reflect on the audience's comments, responses can be noted on the Writing Conference Form by the teacher or an assigned scribe.

8. The audience then responds in terms of ways to improve the piece. Students may ask questions about parts of the piece that were unclear, identify ideas that might be further developed, discuss the order in which ideas were presented, and so on. It is important that when suggested revisions are shared that there is also a discussion of *how* the changes might be accomplished. Students need to know both what to change as well as how to change it.

9. Students repeat the process until all pieces have been read and each student has received response.

### Beyond

10. Students leave the circle and decide on what to revise based on the audience's responses.

11. After all revisions for meaning have been finished, engage the students in one or more of the following editing strategy lessons in the Using Conventions of Written Language section.

12. Once texts have been revised and edited, the students can be engaged in the Author's Chair strategy lesson to celebrate what they have written.

## VARIATIONS

Students may choose to come to a Revision Circle to ask for help with a particular problem. The audience can support the writer by brainstorming possible solutions to the problem posed by the writer.

**SAMPLE MATERIALS**

Writing Conference Form

| Author: | Date: |
|---|---|
| Title: | |
| Things we liked: | Things we think would improve the piece: |

# Having a Conference With Yourself

(Adapted from Atwell, 1998)

**CONCEPT**

Writers reflect and improve the meaning of a piece by reflecting on what is being written.

**MATERIALS**

Rough drafts
Chart paper

**PROCEDURES**

### Into

1. The teacher discusses with the students that writers constantly reread their drafts and make decisions as to the strengths and weaknesses of their own texts.
2. Inform the students that they will be starting a chart, Revision Questions, that lists strategies they can use when rereading their own work.

### Through

3. The teacher demonstrates self-conferencing by reading one of his or her drafts with the students. For a demonstration conference, it might be helpful to only focus on one writing concern, that is, deciding if an idea has been fully developed. It is important to think aloud for the students the types of questions a writer might be asking of himself or herself during the process of reading. These might include:
   - Do I need to add more information?
   - Do I need to take out information that is not needed or does not add to the piece?
   - Should I reorder the information that I have written?

### Beyond

4. Have the students brainstorm other questions that may be useful when revising their own writing. List these questions on the Revision Questions Wall Chart. Students should be helped to recall useful questions that others have asked during Revision

Circle Conferences. Depending on the writing assignment and what the teacher is trying to highlight, the questions asked will vary.

5. Have the students engage in a self-conferencing prior to bringing a piece to the Revision Circle.

6. Periodically, revise the Revision Questions Wall Chart that has generated by the students. The teacher helps students understand that self-conferences can address a number of concerns: purpose, beginnings, endings, information, leads, language, and the like.

# Writing Expansion

## CONCEPT

Writing involves a process of expanding those ideas that are more important in a text.

## MATERIALS

A rough draft
Index cards or slips of paper

## PROCEDURES

### Into

1. Share with the students a rough draft that is in need of further development.
2. With the students, identify those ideas that need to be expanded. Select one to revise.
3. Ask students to brainstorm all of the new information that might be added to the underdeveloped part of the text. List these ideas on the board, chart paper, or an overhead transparency.
4. Decide with the students which of the brainstormed ideas should be included in the text and in what order. Number each idea based on the order in which it is to be included.
5. On the board or an overhead transparency, rewrite the section of the text with the new ideas included.

### Through

6. Students read a rough draft they have written and identify something that needs to be further developed.
7. On index cards or slips of paper, students record new ideas to be included in the text.
8. Once new ideas have been identified, students arrange the cards in the order in which the ideas are to be added.

9. Students revise their drafts, including the new information on the cards.

**Beyond**

10. Give students the opportunity to share the portion of their rough drafts that were revised and the revised draft where the new information was added.

# Minicognitive Writing Strategies

(Adapted from Atwell, 2002; Dorn & Soffos, 2001)

## CONCEPT

Writers employ a number of strategies to construct and revise meaning. These strategies can occur at any point in time during the drafting and revising process.

## MATERIALS

Sample of student writing or published writing that demonstrates the use of the strategy to be demonstrated.

## PROCEDURES

### Into

1. The teacher decides on a particular meaning-based aspect of writing with which the students need additional support. Ministrategy lessons to support strategy development can focus on a variety of topics and problem-solving strategies:
   • How to generate and organize writing ideas
   • How to expand, extend, and elaborate writing ideas
   • How to organize and integrate meaning to form a cohesive text
   • How to use relevant background knowledge to generate meaning
   • How to plan predicting and plan future meaning based on what has been written
   • How to monitor and evaluate meaning as text is being generated
   • How to revise when meaning is lost or purposes are not realized
   • How to use a variety of strategies to revise text
   • How to use a variety of strategies to encountering blocks
   • How to use writing to explore ideas and discover new meanings
   • How to reflect and respond to what is being written
   • How to vary the manner in which text is written based on different purposes, intentions and audiences
   (See the Minilinguistic Writing strategy lessons for a focus on conventions.)

2. Introduce the ministrategy by discussing the strategy's purpose or focus. The introduction is aimed at helping the students understand how writers engage in a particular strategy to solve certain writing problems.

**Through**

3. Demonstrate the strategy to the students. Strategies can be demonstrated in various ways:
   • Conduct a think-aloud to help students see how the teacher uses this particular strategy as a writer
   • Use a piece produced by a student to show how a student peer has successfully the used the strategy
   • Read a text to illustrate how a published author has used the strategy.
   When conducting a think-aloud or using student examples, it is best to use an overhead transparency or chart paper so that all students can see the materials used in the demonstration.

**Beyond**

4. The teacher then coaches the students into applying the strategy used during the demonstration. Students can:
   • Apply the strategy to their own writing
   • Look for additional examples of the strategy in other published or student writing

**VARIATIONS**

When working with more-proficient writers, the students can use spiral notebooks to take notes of the points presented in the minilesson.

# 6

# Teaching the Sociocultural Dimension of Literacy

The sociocultural dimension of literacy is concerned with the reader and writer as text user and text critic. Sociocultural strategy instruction, therefore, helps children to understand how (1) texts are used in various contexts for various purposes and functions, and how (2) texts reflect or highlight particular viewpoints and ignore others. Although the linguistic, cognitive, and developmental dimensions are always present in all strategy instruction, sociocultural strategy lessons highlight the communal and ideological dimension of literacy.

The sociocultural strategy lessons are organized around the following themes:

- Text Contexts, Functions, and Characteristics: strategy lessons that help students to see the relationship among the circumstances, purposes, and features found in written language.
- Let's Get Critical: strategy lessons that help students to examine texts with an analytical eye and to see beyond the surface.
- Language and Power: strategy lessons that help students to see the link between the way language is expressed and who is in authority.

**Text Contexts, Functions, and Characteristics
Strategies**

# Reading Across the Disciplines

## CONCEPT

Writers vary their texts linguistically and conceptually depending on their identities and purposes.

## MATERIALS

Various texts from varying disciplines, such as literature, sciences, social studies, and mathematics

Discipline Analysis Grid (see Sample Materials)

## PROCEDURES

### Into

1. Introduce the students to two of the disciplinary texts. Because students are usually very familiar with literary texts, it is best to include a literary text when first introducing this strategy lesson.
2. Distribute to the students copies of the Discipline Analysis Grid and show the grid on the board or an overhead transparency. Discuss with the students the idea that "reading is not reading" and that how we read depends on the text being read and our purpose for reading.
3. Select a question from the grid and with the students compare and contrast the two disciplinary texts selected. List the characteristics for each text on the grid.

### Through

4. Review with the students the remaining questions on the grid. Then, in small groups, ask students to either (a) complete the entire grid, (b) assign one question per group to complete, or (c) assign the same question to all groups.
5. Once the grid or question has been completed, each group shares their findings and the teacher records these on the grid on the board or an overhead transparency.

**Beyond**

6. Discuss with the students why the two texts are so different. Why did the authors produce such very different texts? Help students to understand that the discipline itself has a significant impact on the way in which a text gets written.

7. This pairing of disciplines can be repeated with any subject area the teacher feels students need support in reading.

## VARIATIONS

1. The teacher is encouraged to add other questions to the grid as appropriate.

2. A number of linguistic as well as cognitive strategy lessons can be used to support the Reading across the Disciplines strategy lesson:

   Linguistic Strategy Lessons: Aiding the Text, Previewing, Reading Text Signals, Writing Text Signals

   Cognitive Strategy Lessons: Flowcharts, Semantic Mapping, Venn Diagrams, Concept Webs

**SAMPLE MATERIALS**

Discipline Analysis Grid

| Questions | Discipline: | Discipline: |
|---|---|---|
| What is the purpose of the text? What is the text trying to teach you? | | |
| What kinds of ideas are found in the text? | | |
| What background knowledge should be used to understand the text? | | |
| What kinds of language or words are used in the text? | | |
| What kinds of text aids—headings, subheadings, illustrations, pictures, charts—are used? Why are these text aids used or not used? | | |
| How are the ideas in the text arranged or structured? | | |

# Functions of Literacy

(Adapted from Halliday, 1973)

## CONCEPT

Proficient readers and writers are able to use written language for a variety of purposes to meet a variety of needs in their lives.

## MATERIALS

Materials will vary depending on the function of literacy activity. See Sample Materials for the various functions of literacy and corresponding classroom activities.

## PROCEDURES

### Into

1. As demonstrated by the variety of activities in the Functions of Literacy Activity grid, into procedures will differ depending on the particular activity selected. As with all literacy lessons, the focus of into procedures is on helping students enter into the activity.

### Through

2. As with the into procedures, through procedures will vary depending on the function of literacy activity. The focus of any through procedure is on helping students move from the beginning to the end of the activity.

### Beyond

3. After the function of literacy activity has been completed, it can be helpful to debrief with the students. During the debriefing, students can discuss how they went about completing the activity, problems they may have encountered, and how they worked their way through the problem to a solution.

## SAMPLE MATERIALS

Functions of Literacy Activities

| Language Function | Classroom Literacy Activities |
|---|---|
| *Instrumental*: "I want" Literacy used as a means of getting things; satisfying material needs | Sign-up charts for activities or interest centers; picture collages with captions: things I want for my birthday, Christmas, and so on; play stores, gas stations, and the like; posters and advertisements; use of paper money; ordering supplies; things I want lists; listing of things needed for a project; shopping lists; birthday and holiday lists; library book lists; want ads; yellow pages; recipe ingredients list |
| *Regulatory*: "Do as I tell you/How it must be" Literacy used to control the behaviors, feelings, or attitudes of others | Directional and traffic signs; rules for care of pets, plants, and so on; written directions; schedules, notes to and from others; laws and rules; letter writing to governmental officials; newspaper editorials and letters to the editor; suggestion box; instructions and recipes; arts and crafts "how-to" books; road maps |
| *Interactional*: "Me and you/Me against you" Literacy used to interact with others; forming and maintaining personal relationships; establishing separateness | Letters, e-mails, and faxes to and from friends and relatives; friendship books; message boards; notes between and among teachers and students; class post office; pen pals; shared reading experiences; notes on home bulletin board or refrigerator; Dear Abby column |
| *Personal*: "Here I come" Literacy used to express individuality and uniqueness; awareness of self; pride and shame | Books about self and family; pictures of self and family with captions; personal experience stories; family or class albums with captions; writing and illustrating "about me" books; what I want to be when I grow up stories; journals and diaries; student of the week bulletin board; autobiographies; family histories; Dear Abby column |
| *Heuristic*: "Tell me why" Literacy used to explore the environment; to ask questions, to seek and test knowledge | Question box; concept books; science experiments; research/inquiry projects; surveys and interviews; predicting the weather; model building; question and answer books |
| *Imaginative*: "Let's pretend" Literacy used to create new worlds; to leave the here and now | Creative dramatics; Readers' Theatre; storytelling and writing; puppetry; science fiction books; jokes, riddles, and puns; comic books; word games; crossword puzzles |
| *Informative*: "I've got something to tell you" Literacy used as a means of communicating information to someone who does not possess the information | Bulletin boards; notes to others; reference materials; encyclopedias and dictionaries; newspapers and magazines, expert groups; book, record, movie reviews; television and movie guides; concept books; Web sites |

# Literacy Use Audit

## CONCEPT

Proficient readers and writers use written language for a variety of purposes to meet a variety of needs in their lives.

## MATERIALS

Literacy Activities Log (see Sample Materials)

## PROCEDURES

### Into

1. Because reading and writing are so frequently used, students oftentimes are unaware of how literacy permeates their everyday lives. Discuss with the students that they—including their teacher—are going to be detectives for the next several days. They are going to be documenting their use of reading and writing outside of school. The number of activities and days students document will vary depending on the needs of the teacher and students.

2. Distribute the Literacy Activities Logs to the students, the number of pages depending on the number of activities and days to be documented.

3. Explain each of the four columns to the students. In the Reading and/or Writing Activity column, students list a single reading or writing activity in which they were engaged. Of course, some literacy events may actually involve both reading and writing. In the second column, Other People Involved, the students record the names of other individuals if they were part of the reading or writing. For example, a student and a sibling might look in a television guide to decide which program to watch. Under Location, where the literacy activity took place is recorded. Finally, the purpose or Reason for Reading and/or Writing is listed in the final column, such as deciding what television program to watch.

4. At this point, the teacher will probably want to specify that school-related literacy activities should not be recorded. The purpose of the literacy strategy lesson is to see how reading and writing are used outside of the school context.

5. It can be helpful if the teacher specifies how many literacy activities should be recorded each day or specifies that only the most important literacy activities are to be listed. For example, the teacher might direct the students to list the three most important activities each day.

**Through**

6. After the first day of documenting literacy use, the teacher and students should share what they have recorded. This sharing will serve several purposes. First, it will allow the teacher to see if students are understanding the use of the Literacy Activities Log and what is to be recorded in each column. The sharing also allows the students to gain insight into the various kinds of literacy activities that can be recorded.

**Beyond**

7. After the documenting of literacy activities has been completed, allow students time to look over their logs. Ask them to share with the class any patterns that they have discovered. For example, students may discover that much of their literacy use is related to entertainment or that other people are frequently involved when they read outside of school.
8. The teacher and students might want to generate student and/or class profiles of their literacy use. The number or percentage of times in which other people were involved, the various locations, and the reasons for reading or writing can be calculated. Individual student profiles can be compared and contrasted with other students as well as with the class profile.

**VARIATIONS**

Students might also want to document the use of literacy in their own communities through the Neighborhood Literacy Walks strategy lesson.

## SAMPLE MATERIALS

### Literacy Activities Log

Name: _____    Date: _____

| Reading and/or Writing Activity | Other People Involved | Location | Reason for Reading and/or Writing |
|---|---|---|---|
|  |  |  |  |
|  |  |  |  |
|  |  |  |  |
|  |  |  |  |

# Neighborhood Literacy Walks

(Power & Hubbard, 2003)

## CONCEPT

Proficient readers and writers use written language for a variety of purposes to meet a variety of needs in their lives. Because reading and writing are so prevalent, literacy use is oftentimes not "seen."

## MATERIALS

Neighborhood Literacy Log (see Sample Materials)

## PROCEDURES

### Into

1. Because reading and writing are so frequently used, students oftentimes are unaware of how literacy permeates their everyday lives. Discuss with the students that they—including their teacher—are going to be detectives for the next several days. They are going to be documenting the use of reading and writing in their neighborhoods. Of course, some literacy events may actually involve both reading and writing. The number of activities and days students document will vary depending on the needs of the teacher and students.

2. Distribute the Neighborhood Literacy Logs to the students, the number of pages depending on the number of activities and days to be documented.

3. Explain each of the four columns to the students. In the Reading and/or Writing Activity column, students list a single reading or writing activity they observed. In the second column, Other People Involved, the students record the names of other individuals if they were part of the reading or writing. For example, two individuals might be reading the schedule at a bus or subway stop. Under Location, where the literacy activity took place is recorded. Finally, the purpose of Reason for Reading and/or Writing is listed in the final column, such as finding out when the next bus or subway is scheduled to stop at a particular location.

4. It can be helpful if the teacher specifies how many literacy activities should be recorded each day or specifies that only the most important literacy activities are to be listed.

For example, the teacher might direct the students to list the three different types of activities observed each day.

## Through

5. After the first day of documenting neighborhood literacy use, the teacher and students should share what they have recorded. This sharing will serve several purposes. First, it will allow the teacher to see if students are understanding the use of the Neighborhood Literacy Log and what is to be recorded in each column. The sharing also allows the students to gain insight into the various kinds of literacy activities that can be recorded.

## Beyond

6. After the documenting of neighborhood literacy activities has been completed, allow students time to look over the logs. Ask them to share with the class any patterns that they have discovered. For example, students may discover that much of the literacy use observed is related to entertainment or advertisements, or that other people are frequently involved when they read outside of school.

7. The teacher and students might want to generate neighborhood profiles of literacy use. The number or percentage of times in which other people were involved, the various locations, and the reasons for reading or writing can be calculated.

## VARIATIONS

1. Rather than recording neighborhood literacy activities, students might use cameras to capture literacy use. These pictures can then be shared in class and a bulletin board constructed that shows how literacy is used for different purposes in the students' community.

2. Students might also want to document their own literacy use outside of school through the Literacy Use Audit strategy lesson.

**SAMPLE MATERIALS**

Neighborhood Literacy Log

Name: _____     Date: _____

| Reading and/or Writing Activity | Other People Involved | Location | Reason for Reading and/or Writing |
|---|---|---|---|
|  |  |  |  |
|  |  |  |  |
|  |  |  |  |
|  |  |  |  |

# Signs and Their Contexts

## CONCEPT

Environmental print—such as street and traffic signs, advertisements, billboards, business names, and the like—is located in specific environments for specific reasons. Proficient readers use the environmental context to predict what environmental print might say.

## MATERIALS

Various types of environmental print that have been cut from magazines, newspapers, and so on. These signs can be laminated to preserve them for repeated use.

Various "settings" or background scenes, such as photographs of city, suburban, and rural views, that have been taken from magazines, newspapers, and the like. These settings can also be laminated to preserve them for repeated use.

## PROCEDURES

### Into

1. Ask students to reflect on and discuss the kinds of environmental print or signs that they encounter in their neighborhoods and surroundings. This reflection and discussion can be enhanced if students have experienced the Neighborhood Literacy Walks strategy lesson.
2. During this discussion, ask students to consider what kinds of print are located in what kinds of settings and why. List these reasons on the board or an overhead transparency.

### Through

3. Students are put into small groups and the various signs and settings are distributed.
4. Ask students to place the various signs in the settings in which they would most likely be located.
5. As students put the signs in their settings, a recorder should list the reasons for the matching of signs and settings.

**Beyond**

6. Allow the groups of students to share their signs and settings placements and the reasons for the matches.

## VARIATIONS

Ask students to consider what kinds of new signs might be needed. Ask students to create these signs as well as the settings in which they would be found.

# Let's Get Critical Strategies

# Boys Will Be Boys; Girls Will Be Girls

## CONCEPT

Authors frequently write in ways that challenge stereotypical norms in our society.

## MATERIALS

A text set of books and/or articles in which male and female characters resist being positioned in stereotypical ways, such as:

de Paola, T. (1979). *Oliver Button is a sissy*. New York: Harcourt Brace Jovanovich.
Hoffman, M. ( 1991). *Amazing Grace*. New York: Dial.
Munsch, R. (1980). *The paper bag princess*. Toronto, Canada: Annick.
Waber, B. (1972). *Ira sleeps over*. New York: Scholastic.
Zolotow, C. (l972). *William's doll*. New York: Harper & Row.
Character Analysis Grid (see Sample Materials)

## PROCEDURES

### Into

1. Begin the strategy lesson by having the students discuss the behaviors that are typically associated with boys and with girls. List these on the board or overhead transparency under the headings "boys" and "girls."
2. Ask the students to consider who is advantaged and disadvantaged by these stereotypical behaviors.
3. Read aloud to the students one of the books or articles from the text set. Ask the students to consider the main character's behavior and what gender norms were challenged.
4. Ask students to identify the character who was violating gender norms. List the character on the Character Analysis Grid.
5. Students identify the behavior(s) that violated gender norms and the norms being violated. The teacher also lists these on the Grid.

**Through**

6. In small groups, distribute copies of the Character Analysis Grid and books and/or articles from the text set. Ask students to read each book and/or article and to complete the grid.

7. Allow students to share their findings. Record these on the Character Analysis Grid that was used previously.

**Beyond**

8. Over the next several days or weeks, have students keep track of students in the class who violate gender norms and the reactions to such violations. Periodically, provide students with the opportunity to share their observations.

## VARIATIONS

The Boys Will Be Boys; Girls Will Be Girls strategy lesson can be used with any group of texts in which groups of individuals violate stereotypical norms, such as norms that are related to race, ethnicity, socioeconomics, nationality, sexual orientation, and so on.

## SAMPLE MATERIALS

### Character Analysis Grid

| Character | Behavior | Norms That Were Challenged |
|-----------|----------|-----------------------------|
|           |          |                             |
|           |          |                             |
|           |          |                             |
|           |          |                             |

# Class Conflict Stories

(Adapted from Levin, 2003)

## CONCEPT

Writers use the writing process to explore their world and to discover solutions to problems they may experience.

## MATERIALS

No special materials are required for teaching this strategy lesson.

## PROCEDURES

### Into

1. The teacher and/or students identify various conflicts that have arisen in the class. These conflicts are recorded on the board or an overhead transparency.
2. A conflict is selected for examination. With guidance from the teacher, the students discuss their various understandings of the conflict and possible causes. As the facilitator of this discussion, the teacher attempts to keep his or her biases in check so as to encourages various voices and perspectives from the students.

### Through

3. Once the issue has been thoroughly examined and discussed, the students brainstorm possible solutions. The teacher lists these solutions on the board or overhead transparency. The strengths and weaknesses of each solution are then discussed.
4. In small groups, in pairs, or individually, students select a solution. The students then write about the conflict and the solution that has been selected. If appropriate, the conflict and solution can be illustrated as well.

### Beyond

5. Students are provided the opportunity to share their Class Conflict Stories with the class.
6. The teacher may want to assemble the stories into a Class Conflict Story Book. This book can then be placed in the class library for students to read during their free time.

## VARIATIONS

1. Once students have experience with the Class Conflict strategy lesson, a Class Conflict Wall Chart can be created. The teacher places a piece of chart paper labeled Class Conflicts on the wall or bulletin board. As conflicts arise that need to be addressed, students record the conflict on the chart. These conflicts can then be used as topics for writing.

2. The teacher and students can also identify stories in which similar conflicts have been examined. The conflicts and resolutions in the stories can be compared and contrasted with the resolutions written by the students.

# Critical Response

## CONCEPT

Effective and proficient readers are sensitive to how various characters are "positioned" within a text based on such factors as power, gender, ethnicity, socioeconomics, sexual orientation, appearance, and so on.

## MATERIALS

Various text that position characters based on such factors as power, gender, ethnicity, socioeconomics, sexual orientation, appearance, and so on. The following books, for example, lend themselves to an examination of gender positioning:

Hazel, N., & Harste, J. (1982). *My icky picky sister*. Pinellas Park, FL: Willowisp.
Munsch, R. (1988). *Love you forever*. Scarborough, Ontario: Firefly Books.
Silverstein, S. (1964). *The giving tree*. New York: Harper & Row.
Waber, B. (1972). *Ira sleeps over*. New York: Scholastic.

## PROCEDURES

### Into

1. As in a typical Literature Response strategy lesson, the text is introduced to the students. Students read and respond to the book. If a Text Set is used, students can read and respond to each individual book.

### Through

2. After the initial responses, the teacher asks the students to return to the text(s) and consider a variety of questions related to the text(s) read. For the previously cited books, questions related to gender might be:
   - How did the female character—for example, sister, mother, tree—behave toward the male character—for example, brother, son?
   - How did the male character—for example, brother, son—behave toward the female character—for example, sister, mother?

- Why do you think the author had the female character behave as she did? Why was the female positioned as she was?
- Why do you think the author had the male character(s) behave as he did? Why was the male positioned as he was?
- Who is advantaged and who is disadvantaged by such stereotypes?
- What alternate behaviors might the female and male character exhibit?

**Beyond**

3. Ask the students to reflect on classroom incidents that reflect behaviors that are gender based, such as who is allowed or encouraged to participate in certain activities and who is discouraged.

4. Discuss the reasons behind inclusion and exclusion. Who is advantaged and disadvantaged by such behaviors.

5. Students read other texts and look for both stereotypical and stereotypical-defying behaviors.

6. Students monitor classroom activities, behaviors, and incidents that relate to the issue that has been examined in the books read.

# Exploring Critical Issues

(Adapted from Kucer, Silva, & Delgado-Larocco, 1995; Leland, Harste, Ociepka, Lewison, & Vasquez, 1999)

## CONCEPT

All texts reflect a particular perspective, stance, or position. Readers more fully comprehend a text when they are able to understand "where the author is coming from."

## MATERIALS

A text set of materials—books, magazines, newspapers, records/CDs, videos/DVDs—related to a particular critical issue, such as the struggle to be true to yourself and the consequences of doing so:

> de Paola, T. (1979). *Oliver Button is a sissy*. New York: Harcourt Brace Jovanovich.
> Hoffman, M. (1991). *Amazing Grace*. New York: Dial.
> Zolotow, C. (1972). *William's doll*. New York: Harper & Row.

Or, the danger in judging someone by their appearance:

> Carlson, N. (1990). *Arnie and the new kid*. New York: Puffin.
> Clements, A. (1988). *Big Al*. New York: Scholastic.
> Komaiko, L. (1988). *Earl's too cool for me*. New York: Harper Trophy.

Critical Issues Reading Grid (see Sample Materials)

## PROCEDURES

### Into

1. Introduce the text set to the students. Discuss with them the fact that all of the texts are related in some manner. Distribute the Critical Issues Reading Grid to the class and explain the various categories.

2. If the students are not familiar with such grids and their use, the teacher might want to complete part of the grid with the class.

3. If students are in need of the additional support, the teacher reads one of the texts to the class.

4. After the text is read, the teacher and students collaboratively complete the grid for the text. It can be helpful if the grid is on the blackboard, chart paper, or an overhead transparency.

**Through**

5.  In groups or individually, the students read the texts and complete the grid. Inform the students that they should not complete the box at the bottom of the grid.

**Beyond**

6.  As a class, the teacher and students discuss what was recorded in each section of the grid for each text. The teacher records these responses on the grid.

7.  Once the class grid has been completed, ask the students to consider the question in the box at the bottom of the grid. If students are unfamiliar with analyzing texts in this manner, the teacher may need to supply additional support by contributing ideas to the discussion.

8.  Record the various ways in which the texts are alike.

9.  Ask the students if they have ever had similar experiences in their lives or know someone who has had similar experiences.

## SAMPLE MATERIALS

Critical Issues Reading Grid
"Go Where You Wanna Go, Be What You Wanna Be"

| Issue: | Grace | Oliver | William |
|---|---|---|---|
| Desire/Goal: | | | |
| Problem/Obstacle: | | | |
| Advocate/Support: | | | |
| Outcome: | | | |

What do the three stories, *Amazing Grace*, *Oliver Button Is a Sissy*, and *William's Doll* all have in common?

Critical Issues Grid
A Book and Its Cover

| Issue: | Big Al | Earl | Philip |
|---|---|---|---|
| Appeared To Be: | | | |
| Reaction of Other Characters: | | | |
| Changing Event: | | | |
| New Perspective: | | | |

What do the three stories, *Big Al*, *Earl's Too Cool for Me*, and *Arnie and the New Kid* all have in common?

# Gendered Fairy Tales

## CONCEPT

It is not uncommon for writers to have their characters behave and think in stereotypical ways. Proficient readers are sensitive to the ways in which various groups of individuals are positioned within the stories that they read.

## MATERIALS

Munsch, R. (1980). *The paper bag princess*. Toronto, Canada: Annick.
Various fairy tales in which there are both female and male characters, such as:
    *Cinderella*
    *Snow White and the Seven Dwarfs*
    *Hanzel and Gretel*
Character Analysis Grid (see Sample Materials)

## PROCEDURES

### Into

1. Introduce one of the fairy tales to the students. Ask them if they are familiar with the story.
2. Distribute the Character Analysis Grid to the students and have them write down the name of the fairy tale being introduced. Tell them that as you read the fairy tale to them, they are to identify the various characters and their significant or important behaviors.
3. Read aloud the fairy tale to the students. When finished, provide the students with time to complete the grid.
4. On the blackboard, chart paper, or an overhead transparency, record on the Character Analysis Grid the various characters that the students have identified.
5. After all major characters have been listed, ask the students to discuss the significant or important behaviors of each character. List these behaviors on the grid as well.

**Through**

6. Form the students into small groups and provide them with several fairy tales to read.

7. As the students read the fairy tales, they are to once again identify the various characters and their significant or important behaviors. These characters and behaviors should be added to the Character Analysis Grid.

8. After all fairy tales have been read and the grid completed, ask the students to look for any patterns of behavior that might exist among any of the characters.

**Beyond**

9. A spokesperson for each group shares one of the fairy tales read and the characters and behaviors identified. The teacher records these findings on the Character Analysis Grid that was used previously for the story read aloud to the students.

10. After the various groups have reported their findings, the class looks for and discusses any patterns of behavior that might exist among any of the characters.

11. Read to the students the story *The Paper Bag Princess*. Ask the students to consider how the princess's behaviors are different from the behaviors of the female characters in the previously read stories.

12. As a class, list the various characters and behaviors in *The Paper Bag Princess*. Provide students with the opportunity to discuss how the princess was different than the female characters in the other fairy tales.

13. Discuss with the students who "wins" and who "loses" when various groups of individuals are positioned in these ways.

## VARIATIONS

The Gendered Fairy Tales strategy lesson can be used with any group of texts in which groups of individuals are positioned in stereotypical ways based on such characteristics as race, ethnicity, socioeconomics, nationality, sexual orientation, and so on.

**SAMPLE MATERIALS**

Character Analysis Grid

| Text | Character | Behaviors |
|------|-----------|-----------|
|      |           |           |
|      |           |           |
|      |           |           |
|      |           |           |

# Uncovering Hidden Meanings

## CONCEPT

All texts reflect "hidden" meanings or ideologies. Readers more fully or deeply comprehend a text when they are able to understand the author's unstated or implicit beliefs.

## MATERIALS

Two texts that explicitly reflect two points of view on a particular issue or topic, such as:

Scieszka, J. (1989). *The true story of the three little pigs*. New York: Penguin.

Scott Foresman. (1976). *The three little pigs*. Glenview, IL: Scott Foresman.

Two texts whose points of view on a particular issue or topic are hidden or not made explicit, such as:

Kraus, R. (1945). *The carrot seed*. New York: Scholastic.

Tolstoy, A. (1976). *The great big enormous turnip*. Glenview, IL: Scott Foresman.

Hidden Meanings Grid (see Sample Materials)

## PROCEDURES

### Into

1. To introduce the Uncovering Hidden Meanings strategy lesson, begin with two texts that explicitly address the same issue or topic in very different ways. Two texts that reflect this characteristic are *The Three Little Pigs* and *The True Story of the Three Little Pigs*.

2. The teacher can read the two stories to the class or have students read the texts in small groups or individually.

3. After the texts have been read, have the students contrast the very different perspective of the two texts. In the left-hand column of the grid, the teacher will want to list the various issues that are being contrasted. This listing can be predetermined by the teacher if necessary or grow out of the discussion with the students. List these differences on a Hidden Meanings Grid. The teacher will want to help students become sensitive to not just the different content, but also the language that the author uses to frame the content.

4. Once the grid has been completed, discuss with the students the differences between the two texts. An adult version of a completed grid is included with the other sample materials.

## Through

5. Discuss with the students that not all texts are as explicit in their perspectives as *The Three Little Pigs* and *The True Story of the Three Little Pigs*. Oftentimes, perspectives are hidden and have to be uncovered.

6. Introduce to the students two texts that have less obvious contrasting perspectives, such as *The Great Big Enormous Turnip* and *The Carrot Seed*. Again, the teacher can read the two stories to the class or have students read the texts in small groups or individually.

7. As a class, small groups, or independently, students complete the Hidden Meanings Grid with the two texts. The teacher may predetermine the issues to be addressed or allow the students to do this on their own.

8. After the grid has been completed, students are given the opportunity to share the meanings that they have uncovered.

9. Using the completed grid as a guide, discuss with the students the differences between the two texts. An adult version of a completed grid for *The Great Big Enormous Turnip* and *The Carrot Seed* is also included with the other sample materials.

## Beyond

10. Throughout the school year, after a text has been read, ask the students to consider the position or point of view that the author has taken on the topic under consideration. Help students to consider both the content and the language itself. Discuss with the students the viewpoints that are "hidden" or not explicitly addressed by the author.

**SAMPLE MATERIALS**

Hidden Meanings Grid

| Issue | Text: | Text: |
|---|---|---|
|  |  |  |
|  |  |  |
|  |  |  |
|  |  |  |

An Analysis of Pigs and Wolves

| Issue | The Three Little Pigs | The True Story |
|---|---|---|
| Storyteller: | unidentified and uninvolved, but one that is all knowing | wolf who was a participant in the story and has a point of view |
| Storyteller's Agenda: | to retell the "facts" of an event | to persuade an audience to accept a different set of "facts" |
| Use of Language: | "facts" are presented in a "objective" manner; use of "distant" and uninvolved language | "facts" are presented in a persuasive manner; use of involved language inviting understanding and sympathy |
| Intended Audience: | an audience that is fearful of wolves but not of pigs<br><br>an audience that can be easily persuaded by the "facts" told in an objective manner | an audience that has heard the pig's but not the wolf's perspective<br><br>an audience sympathetic with the pig's perspective<br><br>an audience skeptical or hostile to the wolf's perspective<br><br>an audience that is more fearful of wolves than pigs |
| Historical Context: | an audience that historically is fearful of wolves | an audience that historically is fearful of wolves |

An Analysis of Turnips and Carrot Seeds

| Issue | Turnip | Carrot Seed |
|---|---|---|
| Power: | individual efforts may not lead to success; power is realized through collaboration | individual persistence and hard work leads to success; power is realized through individual initiative |
| Interpersonal Relationships: | individuals are part of a community; all members of a community have a valuable role to play; the community can accomplish tasks that an individual cannot; individuals of diverse backgrounds can collaborate in order to accomplish a goal; community involves helping an individual accomplish his or her goal | the community attempts to thwart individual efforts; do not expect support from community members |
| Initiative: | initiative is demonstrated by seeking assistance and support when necessary; lack of success calls for seeking additional support and trying again | initiative is demonstrated by the individual persevering in the face of opposition; success takes time |
| Use of Language: | the repetition of episodes with a new character being added each time reflects the collaborative nature of the community | the repetition of episodes with a new family member voicing discouragement |
| Intended Audience: | a community whose existence depends on collaboration among its members | a community whose existence depends on each member seeking his or her own success |

# Inquiry Charts

(Adapted from Hoffman, 1992)

**CONCEPT**

Understanding frequently involves taking on one perspective or stance rather than another perspective or stance. Readers' knowledge is more fully developed when they understand the various perspectives on a topic or issue.

**MATERIALS**

Various reference materials—books, magazines, newspapers, records/CDs, videos/DVDs—on a particular topic that reflect different points of view.
Inquiry Chart (see Sample Materials)

**PROCEDURES**

**Into**

1. The Inquiry Chart strategy lesson works best when students are involved in the study or investigation of a particular topic or issue.
2. Either before the inquiry begins, or after the students have begun their investigation, ask students what questions they would like to explore or have "answered." Oftentimes, students ask more penetrating questions after they have had the opportunity to study the topic for a while. List students questions on the board, chart paper, or an overhead transparency.
3. Review the questions with the students, consolidating those questions that are essentially variations of one another.
4. Ask the students which questions they would like to investigate. Students may need to be helped to understand that some questions are more significant or critical than others. Once questions have been identified, list these on the top row of the Inquiry Chart.

**Through**

5. Introduce students to the various research materials that are available for their inquiry. If students have access to the school or community library and/or web sites, the availability of these resources should be discussed as well.

6. Depending on the instructional context, the teacher may have each student answer some or all of the questions or form research teams that answer some or all of the questions.

7. Give students the time necessary to investigate their questions and write their "answers" on the Inquiry Chart.

**Beyond**

8. Bring the students together to share their answers to the questions. It is helpful if the teacher records the various answers on a large inquiry chart that has been drawn on the board, chart paper, or overhead transparency.

9. As various questions are answered, help the students to see that different research materials have provided them with different answers. Discuss with the students why such variation might exist.

## VARIATIONS

Individually or in research teams, students may select their own topics and inquiry questions to explore.

## SAMPLE MATERIALS

Inquiry Chart
Inquiry Questions

| Research Materials | Question One | Question Two | Question Three | Question Four |
|---|---|---|---|---|
|  |  |  |  |  |
|  |  |  |  |  |
|  |  |  |  |  |
|  |  |  |  |  |
|  |  |  |  |  |

# Points of View

## CONCEPT

All characters in a text reflect particular points of view or perspectives. These views oftentimes are related to the various social groups to which the character belongs, such as gender,
socioeconomic status, culture, and the like. Readers more fully comprehend a text when they
are able to understand these various perspectives.

## MATERIALS

Two texts that explicitly reflect two points of view on a particular issue or topic, such as:
   Scieszka, J. (1989). *The true story of the three little pigs*. New York: Penguin.
   Scott Foresman. (1976). *The three little pigs*. Glenview, IL: Scott Foresman.
   Or a single text in which the various characters explicitly express differing points of view,
      such as:
   Browne, A. (1998). *Voices in the park*. New York: DK Publishing.
   Point of View Grid (see Sample Materials)

## PROCEDURES

### Into

1. To introduce the Points of View strategy lesson, begin with two texts that explicitly
   address the same issue or topic in very different ways. Two texts that reflect this
   characteristic are *The Three Little Pigs* and *The True Story of the Three Little Pigs*.
2. The teacher can read the two stories to the class or have students read the texts in
   small groups or individually.
3. In the left-hand column of the grid, the teacher lists the various issues or events and
   characters that are being contrasted. This listing can be predetermined by the teacher
   if necessary or grow from the discussion with the students. Across the top of the grid,
   the various characters whose views are to be contrasted are listed. It can be helpful
   if the grid is on the blackboard, chart paper, or an overhead transparency so that all
   students can easily see what is written.
4. After the texts have been read, have the students discuss the very different perspective
   of the characters in the two texts. The students will also want to consider why each

character holds the view that he or she does. List these differences and reasons on the Points of View Grid. The teacher should help students become sensitive to not just the different content, but also the language that the author uses to frame the content.

## Through

5. Discuss with the students that sometimes characters within the same story may have differing points of view, such as the characters in the book *Voices in the Park*.

6. Introduce the text to the students. Again, the teacher can read the story to the class or have students read the text in small groups or individually.

7. As a class, in small groups, or independently, students complete the Point of View Grid for the text. The teacher may predetermine the issues or events and characters to be addressed or allow the students to do this on their own.

8. After the grid has been completed, students are given the opportunity to share their ideas. List these ideas on a grid. Again, it can be helpful if the grid is on the blackboard, chart paper, or an overhead transparency so that all students can easily see what is written.

## Beyond

9. Throughout the school year, after a text has been read, ask the students to consider the points of view of various characters.

## VARIATIONS

The Multiple Voices strategy lesson extends the Points of View strategy lesson by engaging students in the writing of stories that reflect alternate perspectives.

**SAMPLE MATERIALS**

Point of View Grid
Characters

| Issue/Event | | | | |
|---|---|---|---|---|
| | | | | |
| | | | | |
| | | | | |
| | | | | |
| | | | | |

# Multiple Voices

## CONCEPT

All characters in a text reflect particular points of view or perspectives. These views often-times are related to the various social groups to which the character belongs, such as gender, socioeconomic status, culture, and so on. Readers more fully comprehend a text when they are able to understand these various perspectives.

## MATERIALS

Two texts that explicitly reflect varying points of view on a particular issue or topic, such as:
    Scieszka, J. (1989). *The true story of the three little pigs*. New York: Penguin.
    Scott Foresman. (1976). *The three little pigs*. Glenview, IL: Scott Foresman.
  Or a single text in which the various characters explicitly express differing points of view, such as:
    Browne, A. (1998). *Voices in the park*. New York: DK Publishing.

## PROCEDURES

### Into

1. Before teaching this strategy lesson, it is helpful if students have experienced the Points of View strategy lesson.
2. Read aloud to the students several stories that reflect varying points of view or a single text in which multiple viewpoints are expressed.
3. Discuss with the students the various views expressed and list these on the board, chart paper, or an overhead transparency.
4. Discuss why such different view points might exist about the same event.

### Through

5. Identify a story that the students have previously read. Review the story with the student, listing the major characters and their behaviors on the board or an overhead transparency.
6. Discuss whose point of view is represented in the story.

7. Students can then write a second story that expresses the viewpoint of another character, such as is the case with *The True Story of the Three Little Pigs*. Or, they can rewrite the story and include differing perspectives as in *Voices in the Park*.

8. Give students the opportunity to share their stories and discuss the various points of views expressed.

**Beyond**

9. Throughout the school year, after a text has been read, ask the students to consider the points of view represented by the various characters.

# Outrageous Viewpoints

(Adapted from Wollman-Bonilla, 1998)

## CONCEPT

Many times individuals or groups seek to censor or "hide" texts that address controversial, social, and/or economic problems within our society.

## MATERIALS

A variety of reading materials that some individuals have assumed are too "outrageous" for students to read because they address controversial, social, and/or economic problems in our society, such as:

Bunting, E. (1991). *Fly away home*. New York: Clarion.
Bunting, E. (1994). *Smoky night*. New York: Harcourt Brace.
dePaola, T. (1979). *Oliver Button is a sissy*. New York: Harcourt Brace Jovanovich.
Greenfield, E. (1978). *Honey, I love and other love poems*. New York: Crowell.
Hoffman, M. (1991). *Amazing Grace*. New York: Dial.
Munsch, R. (1980). *The paper bag princess*. Toronto, Canada: Annick.
Paterson, K. (1977). *Bridge to Terabithia*. New York: Crowell.
Ringgold, E. (1991). *Tar beach*. New York: Crown.
Taylor, M. (1976). *Roll of thunder, hear my cry*. New York: Dial.
Turner, A. (1987). *Nettie's trip south*. New York: Macmillan.
Zolotow, C. (1972). *William's doll*. New York: Harper & Row.
Outrageous Viewpoints Grid (see Sample Materials)

## PROCEDURES

### Into

1. Select one of the "outrageous" texts to read to the class. Discuss with the students that some adults have considered this book to be too outrageous or inappropriate for students to read.

2. As the text is read, ask the students to consider what might make the book outrageous to some adults. Why might adults think these issues are outrageous?

3. Give students the opportunity to share their reasons for thinking some adults might think the text is outrageous. Record their responses on the Outrageous Viewpoints Grid.

## Through

4. Form the students into small groups. Give each group several outrageous viewpoints texts and each student an Outrageous Viewpoints Grid.

5. Each group reads the various books, discusses what is outrageous about the book and why, and then completes the Outrageous Viewpoints Grid.

## Beyond

6. A spokesperson for each group shares the group's Outrageous Viewpoints Grid with the class.

7. Engage the students in a discussion concerning when and why it might be appropriate to keep certain texts from certain individuals. Who gets to determine what texts others can and cannot read?

**SAMPLE MATERIALS**

Outrageous Viewpoints Grid

| Name of Text | "Outrageous Viewpoint" | What Makes the Viewpoint "Outrageous" |
|---|---|---|
|  |  |  |
|  |  |  |
|  |  |  |
|  |  |  |
|  |  |  |
|  |  |  |
|  |  |  |
|  |  |  |
|  |  |  |
|  |  |  |

# I Seem To Be, But Really I Am

(Adapted from Koch, 1970)

**CONCEPT**

Writers use the writing process to explore and at times to reveal their various identities, both public and private.

**MATERIALS**

A short story about how an individual appeared to be one way when in fact he or she was quite different, such as in:

Carlson, N. (1990). *Arnie and the new kid*. New York: Puffin.
Clements, A. (1988). *Big Al*. New York: Scholastic.
Komaiko, L. (1988). *Earl's too cool for me*. New York: Harper Trophy.

**PROCEDURES**

**Into**

1. Engage the students in a discussion about how appearances can oftentimes be deceiving. Objects, events, and people may seem to be one way when in fact they are quite different. Discuss various objects, events, and/or people that are different than they appear.

2. Discuss with the students why people might "hide" their inner selves. What might cause people to reveal their inner selves?

3. Read aloud to the students a short story about an individual who appeared to be one thing, but in fact was quite different.

4. Discuss with the students the differences between appearances and reality in the book.

**Through**

5. Introduce the students to the following repetitive two-line form:
   I seem to be _____
   But really I am _____

6. Ask several students to share how they appear to be and how they really are. Write these on the board, chart paper, or an overhead transparency.

7. Students are to write their own individual poems about how they appear and how they really are. They may use the two-line form or structure their poem in any way they choose. The important point is that they address both how they appear and how they really are.

8. Students may also be provided the opportunity to illustrate their poems, showing both their appearances and their realities.

**Beyond**

9. Provide students the opportunity to share their poems and illustrations. An interesting alternative is to have one student read the poem of another unidentified student. The class then guesses the author of the poem.

**VARIATIONS**

The same procedure can be used with such topics as "I used to be, but now I am" or "When I was little I, but now that I'm big I."

# Writing About Critical Issues

(Adapted from Heffernan, 2001)

## CONCEPT

All texts reflect a particular perspective, stance, or position. One way in which individuals explore alternate perspectives, stances, or positions is through the writing process.

## MATERIALS

Critical Issues Writing Grid (see Sample Materials)

## PROCEDURES

### Into

1. Students need to have experienced the Exploring Critical Issues strategy lesson before beginning this strategy lesson.
2. Review with the students the critical issue text set, the Critical Issues Reading Grid, and the theme that was addressed in the texts from the Exploring Critical Issues strategy lesson.
3. Discuss with the students that they are going to be writing their own stories to be added to the critical issue text set. On the board or an overhead transparency, show students the Critical Issues Writing Grid. Keeping in mind the books in the Critical Issues Reading Grid, ask students to brainstorm various desires or goals characters in a story might have. Encourage students to consider desires or goals that reflect those found in the Reading Grid. List these on the Writing Grid.
4. For each of the desires or goals listed, students brainstorm possible problems/obstacles that might be encountered. These are listed on the Writing Grid as well.
5. Ask the students to consider who might be an advocate/supporter for the character and list these.
6. Finally, students brainstorm possible outcomes for the various desires and goals. Help students to understand that all stories do not necessarily end "happily ever after." Record these possible outcomes.

**Through**

7. Using the Critical Issues Writing Grid as a guide, students write a story to be added to the text set. It is important that the grid be used as a support system, not as a rigid framework that must be followed. Students should be encouraged to move beyond the grid in their thinking and writing when possible.

**Beyond**

8. Allow the students to share their critical issue stories. Discuss with the students how each story fits with the critical issue text set previously read.

## SAMPLE MATERIALS

Critical Issues Writing Grid

| Desire/Goal | Problem/Obstacle | Advocate/Supporter | Outcome |
|-------------|------------------|--------------------|---------|
|             |                  |                    |         |

# Problem Posing

(Adapted from McLaughlin & DeVoogd, 2004)

## CONCEPT

All texts reflect a particular perspective, stance, or position. Readers more fully comprehend a text when they are able not only to understand the author's perspective but also to consider alternatives as well.

## MATERIALS

Challenging the Text Grid (see Sample Materials)

## PROCEDURES

### Into

1. Introduce the students to the text to be read. Narrative as well as expository texts can be used for the Problem Posing strategy lesson.
2. Individually, in small groups, or as a teacher read-aloud, the introduced text is read.
3. Engage the students in a Literature Response Group Strategy lesson with the text. Some possible questions to explore might be:
   • What was my purpose for reading this text?
   • What did I learn from reading this text?
   • Why did the author write this text? What was the author trying to tell me?
   • What parts did I like best? What parts were my favorite? Why did I like these particular parts?
   • What parts did I like least? Why did I dislike these parts?
   • Did this text remind me of other texts I have read? How was this text both similar or dissimilar to other texts?
   • What would I change in this text if I had written it? What might the author have done to make this text better, more understandable, more interesting?
   • Are there things/parts that I did not understand? What can I do to better understand these parts?

**Through**

4. Discuss with the students that they are going to take a second look at the text. This time, not only will they consider the author's views, but they will also consider other possible views as well.

5. Give students a copy of the Challenging the Text Grid. It is helpful if the grid is also shown on the board, chart paper, or an overhead transparency.

6. Read the questions to the students, clarifying what each question means as necessary.

7. Either as a class, in small groups, or individually, ask students to revisit the text and to record the author's views for the four questions. Give students the opportunity to share their responses.

8. Ask students to consider and to record their responses to the four questions listed in the Alternate Views column of the Grid. Give students the opportunity to share their responses.

**Beyond**

9. As a class, students compare and contrast the Author's Views with possible Alternate Views.

10. Discuss with the students the idea that texts represent some points of views and ignore or hide others. Throughout the year, as various texts are read, ask students to reflect on the views presented and possible alternates.

**SAMPLE MATERIALS**

Challenging the Text Grid

Name: _____          Text: _____

| Author's Views | Alternate Views |
|---|---|
| Who or what is the focus of the text? | What other focuses might be possible? |
| What point of view or perspective is presented? | What other points of view or perspectives are missing or discounted? |
| What does the author want the reader to believe or think? | What other beliefs or thoughts are possible? |
| What actions might be taken based on the author's views? | What actions might be taken based on alternate views? |

# Language and Power Strategies

# Exploring Written Dialects

(Adapted from Delpit, 1990; Y. Goodman, 2003)

## CONCEPT

Writers know how to vary their use of language based on their audience.

## MATERIALS

Various published as well as student-written materials that contain "nonstandard" forms of
English. The following books contain examples of nonstandard English-language forms:
Joseph L. (2000). *The color of my words*. New York: HarperCollins.
McKissack, P. (1986). *Flossie and the fox*. New York: Scholastic.
McKissack, P. (1989). *Mirandy and brother wind*. New York: Random House.
Stanley, D. (1996). *Saving Sweetness*. New York: Putnam.
Stanley, D. (1999). *Raising Sweetness*. New York: Putnam.
Informal and Formal English Grid (see Sample Materials)

## PROCEDURES

### Into

1. Read to the class a published story that contains examples of nonstandard forms of
English.
2. Using the Informal and Formal English Grid on the board, chart paper, or an overhead
transparency, list examples of the nonstandard forms of English. Discuss with the
students that there oftentimes are various ways of expressing the same idea in English
(or any language). The manner in which ideas are expressed may vary depending
on the context and the audience. For example, the way in which students express
themselves on the playground or in e-mails to friends might differ from the way in
which they would express the same ideas to their parents or other adults at home or
to their teachers at school.
3. For each of the examples listed, which might be referred to as "informal English,"
ask the students for the more "formal English" way of expressing the same idea. How
might these ideas, for example, be expressed to a teacher? List the formal English
counterpart next to the informal English form. There may be numerous ways in which
the ideas can be expressed more formally and these should be listed.

**Through**

4. On the board, chart paper, or an overhead transparency, share a sample of a student-written text that contains informal uses of English. Begin by discussing with the students the strengths of the paper and what they like about it.

5. Ask students to identify any examples of informal English and underline them as they are identified. The teacher can also underline examples that the students may not recognize as being informal.

6. As was done with the published text, ask students for more formal ways in which the ideas can be expressed. List these on the Informal and Formal English Grid.

7. Throughout this process, it is important students understand that the informal forms of English or not "wrong," "bad," or "incorrect." Rather, they are simply alternate ways of expressing the same idea. However, in some formal contexts, students will want or need to use more formal expressions of English.

**Beyond**

8. Either in groups or individually, ask students to read through texts they have written and to underline forms that they believe are informal. Give students the opportunity to share these forms with other students in the class.

9. Students generate more formal alternatives for their informal written language expressions.

## VARIATIONS

1. Rather than begin with examples of informal English, begin with formal English examples. Read a published story to the students that contains standard forms. Ask the students how they might express some of the ideas using informal English. List the formal and the informal forms on the Informal and Formal English Grid.

2. In order to help students understand the role of power and authority in language use, engage them in the Power and Language Forms strategy lesson.

## SAMPLE MATERIALS

Informal and Formal English Grid

| Examples of Formal English | Examples of Informal English |
|---|---|
|  |  |

# Dialect Dictionaries
# (Adapted from Delpit, 1998)

## CONCEPT

Writers know how to vary their use of language based on their audience.

## MATERIALS

Various published as well as student-written materials that contain "nonstandard" forms of
   English. The following books contain examples of nonstandard English-language forms:
   Joseph L. (2000). *The color of my words*. New York: HarperCollins.
   McKissack, P. (1986). *Flossie and the fox*. New York: Scholastic.
   McKissack, P. (1989). *Mirandy and brother wind*. New York: Random House.
   Stanley, D. (1996). *Saving Sweetness*. New York: Putnam.
   Stanley, D. (1999). *Raising Sweetness*. New York: Putnam.
   Booklets with blank pages for each student in the class

## PROCEDURES

### Into

1. Before engaging students in the Dialect Dictionaries strategy lesson, it is helpful if
   students have first experienced the Exploring Written Dialects strategy lesson.

2. Discuss with the students the various purposes that dictionaries can serve, for example,
   spelling, definitions, grammar, and so on. Inform the students that they are going to
   be making Dialect Dictionaries. In Dialect Dictionaries, students record informal and
   formal ways of expressing the same idea.

3. Read to the class a published story that contains examples of nonstandard forms
   of English. List these nonstandard forms on the board, chart paper, or an overhead
   transparency.

4. Discuss with the students the standard or more formal way in which these ideas can
   be expressed. List these standard forms next to or underneath the informal forms.

**Through**

5.  Distribute the blank booklets and inform the students that throughout the school year they will be keeping a list of various informal and formal ways of expressing the same idea. Ask students if they know of any examples of such informal and formal forms of language use. The teacher should share examples from the students' own use of language if the students are unaware of any examples.

6.  Students should list any examples that are shared in their Dialect Dictionaries.

**Beyond**

7.  Throughout the year when nonstandard or standard forms with nonstandard counterparts of language are encountered, the teacher and students should discuss these forms and add them to their Dialect Dictionaries.

8.  In those instructional settings when formal language is required, such as during the publishing of student texts, the teacher should encourage the use of the Dialect Dictionaries to standardized student writings.

# Power and Language Forms

(Adapted from Delpit, 1990; Y. Goodman, 2003)

## CONCEPT

The language that individuals or groups are "allowed" to use is affected by other individuals or groups that are in positions of power or authority.

## MATERIALS

A videotape of a television program in which nonstandard forms of English are used. Certain situational comedies frequently contain nonstandard forms of English.
A videotape of a television newscast.

## PROCEDURES

### Into

1. Before beginning the Power and Language Forms strategy lesson, it can be helpful if students have first experienced the Exploring Written Dialects strategy lesson.
2. Introduce students to the television program that is about to be shown. Ask students if they have seen the program and what they think about the series.
3. As the students view the program, they are to write down all forms of English that are "nonstandard" or what might be called "informal" in nature. If necessary, show a portion of the program and then identify and discuss any nonstandard forms of English that were used.
4. After viewing the program, students share the informal forms of English that were identified. List these forms on the board or an overhead transparency.
5. Ask the students if they know individuals, including themselves, or groups of individuals that use the forms listed.

### Through

6. Before viewing the television newscast, inform the students that they are to contrast the forms of English used in the newscast with the forms used in the television program.

7. After the viewing, discuss with the students the differences in language forms that were observed in the television program and the newscast. Ask students why they did not observe uses of nonstandard forms of English in the newscast.

8. Discuss with the students why the language used in the television program differs from that used in the newscast. Ask students who makes the decision as to what forms of language are acceptable in different situations. Help students to understand that "acceptable" language forms are often a reflection of the situation and those individuals in positions of power rather than a reflection of the language itself.

**Beyond**

9. Throughout the following weeks, ask students to observe and record when certain individuals "correct" the language forms of other individuals. Students should record who is correcting whom, the nature of the correction, and the situation in which the correction occurs.

10. Give students the opportunity to share their observations. Discuss who has the right/power to correct the language of others and why.

## VARIATIONS

If the students are bilingual and/or biliterate, the strategy lesson can be done with two different languages rather than with different dialects.

# Sell It!

(Adapted from Comber, 2001; O'Brien, 1994)

## CONCEPT

Writers use language in particular ways to convince readers to accept as "true" particular ideas.

## MATERIALS

Various advertisements that have been taken from magazines and newspapers, a videotape of several television commercials, or an audiotape of radio commercials.

## PROCEDURES

### Into

1. Begin by sharing several print advertisements with the students. Ask students what they know about advertisements or commercials in general and where they are typically located or found.
2. Allow students to more closely examine, listen to, or watch a particular advertisement. During this process, ask the students to consider the following questions:
   - How do you know what is being advertised?
   - How do you know whom the product is for? Which words and pictures tell you that?
   - What do the advertisers want you to think about the product? Which words and pictures tell you that?
   - Who produces these advertisements?
   - How do the advertisers try and convince you that you need the product? Which words and pictures tell you that?

### Through

3. As students share their various answers to these questions, list the advertising techniques and language forms on the board, chart paper, or overhead transparency.
4. Using the various techniques and language forms discovered, have students produce their own advertisements or commercials. These may be advertisements for newspapers and magazines, the radio, or television.

**Beyond**

5. As the advertisements or commercials are shared, ask the class to look for the techniques and language forms used to sell the product. Discuss these after the sharing.

## VARIATIONS

Another way in which students can be helped to "deconstruct" advertisements is by pairing advertisements with texts written for children that present another perspective (Vasquez, 2003). For example, advertisements that show only girls playing with dolls might be paired with *William's Doll* (Zolotow, 1972) and the perspectives compared and contrasted.

# Signs, Functions, and Power

## CONCEPT

Hiding behind all instances of print are issues of authority. Proficient readers understand that signs represent many "meanings" beyond their literal meanings.

## MATERIALS

Multiple copies of photographs of various street signs, advertisements, business signs, and so on. Various signs can be found in newspapers and magazines. Or, students can take pictures of signs found in their communities.

## PROCEDURES

### Into

1. Introduce several types of signs to the students. Ask them what each sign "means."
2. Discuss with the students why these signs are "put up" and what purposes they are intended to serve—for example, control traffic, encourage consumption, provide information, and so on.
3. Ask the students who has the authority to put up such signs. Highlight the idea that typically only certain people have the "right" to display certain signs, such as store owners, government officials, businesses, etc.

### Through

4. Organize the students into small groups and give each group a variety of signs. A spokesperson for each group should be identified as well as a recorder.
5. Ask students to group the signs in terms of their shared purposes or functions that have been previously discussed. The recorder should list the purposes identified for each group.
6. Allow a spokesperson for each group to share their findings with the class.

7. Students return to their groups and group the signs in terms of who has the authority or power to put up the sign. The recorder should list the authorities identified for each group.

8. Allow a spokesperson for each group to share his or her findings with the class.

**Beyond**

9. Give the students the opportunity to do a literacy walk around the classroom and school. Students record the various kinds of print that they observe displayed on the walls, bulletin boards, doors, and other places.

10. As a class or in small groups, students share the various kinds of print they located and discuss the purposes of the print.

11. Discuss with students who has the authority to display the print they encountered.

# III

# Putting It All Together

# 7

# A Dimensional Literacy Curriculum

In the previous chapters, we presented various strategy lessons to promote the development of the linguistic, cognitive, and sociocultural dimensions of literacy. The individual strategy lessons were addressed in a general manner so that they could be easily adapted to meet the needs of a diverse student population. In this chapter, we provide a general curricular framework into which the strategy lessons might be embedded. In those instructional contexts in which teachers have some say over the curriculum, we encourage teachers to adapt and modify the framework as necessary. For teachers working within more prescribed settings, the strategy lessons may need to be used within an established curriculum. In either case, it is ultimately the teacher that rouses the curriculum to life by providing students with experiences that engage their hearts and their minds.

On a curricular level, many educators have advocated that students encounter four types of literacy experiences on a regular basis: thematic or inquiry units; teacher reading and student response; independent reading and student response; and independent writing, conferencing, and publishing (see Table 7.1). A range of instructional time that has been found to be appropriate is suggested for each curricular component. It is within these components that various linguistic, cognitive, and sociocultural strategy lessons will be encountered by the students.

## THEMATIC OR INQUIRY UNITS

In many respects and in contrast to other disciplines, reading and writing have no inherent content in and of themselves. A wide range of materials and experiences can be used for the teaching and learning of literacy. Going back to at least the time of Dewey (1938), many educators have proposed the use of themes as the basis for instruction. Given a variety of names (e.g., integrated units, project approach, inquiry studies) and reflecting various theoretical orientations, the general focus being advocated here is on the exploration of topics or issues to promote the development of both literacy (linguistic, cognitive, sociocultural) and conceptual knowledge (Banks, 1991; Freeman, & Freeman, 2002; Kucer et al., 1995; Manning, Manning, & Long, 1994; Short, Harste, & Burke, 1996).

When selecting topics of study, it is important to consider the quality of experiences that the topic can provide. Dewey (1938) suggested that quality experiences are those that take up something from those experiences that have gone before and modify in some way the quality of those experiences that come after. Quality experiences promote desirable future experiences in the students.

**TABLE 7.1**

Literacy Curricular Components

| Component | Characteristics | Time |
|---|---|---|
| Thematic or Inquiry Units | Students explore and critique topics and issues of interest using various disciplines (literature, social science, science) and multiple communication systems (language, art, music, mathematics, movement). Materials include diverse types of texts (narratives, expositions, dramas, poems) and various resources (magazines, newspapers, records, audiotapes, songs, computer programs, books, filmstrips, videotapes, movies, simulation games). The focus is on literacy development (learning about literacy, learning literacy, and learning through literacy) and critical content development (generalizations, concepts, and facts). | 1–2 1/2 hours |
| Teacher Reading and Student Response | Teacher oral reading of theme-related books, stories, articles, and so on. Students are given opportunities to respond and to critique the reading. | 15–45 minutes |
| Independent Reading and Student Response | Student silent reading of self-selected books, stories, magazines, student published texts, and the like. Students are given opportunities to share and to critique what is read with the class. | 15 minutes–1 hour |
| Independent Writing, Conferencing, and Publishing | Student writing, conferencing, revision and editing, and publishing on self-selected topics. | 30 minutes–1 1/2 hours |

Recently, critical theorists have pushed topic-centered literacy curricula from simply a "study of" to a "critique of" (e.g., Buckingham & Sefton-Green, 1994; Comber & Simpson, 2001). This shift was demonstrated by the various sociocultural strategy lessons presented in chapter 6. In their review of critical literacy research and professional literature, Lewison, Flint, and Sluys (2002) proposed that inquiry units reflect four overlapping and interrelated qualities. First, the units help students to understand "the everyday through new lenses" (pp. 382–383). Current knowledge and beliefs are examined and even challenged. The units also help students to understand the topic from multiple viewpoints or through various lenses. Perspectives not commonly considered or heard are given consideration. Third, inquiry units help students to move beyond their own personal experiences to those that are more group or socially based. Topics are examined in terms of power, dominance, and privilege. Finally, inquiry units involve "taking a stand and promoting social justice" (p. 387). Students are engaged in activities that have an impact on their worlds (Edelsky, 1999).

Another traditional limitation of many themes has been their focus on facts and figures rather than more global forms of knowledge. Although facts and figures can begin to form the basis for understanding, they fall short in offering the depth of understanding necessary for a fuller and more textured knowing to occur. Themes must also support students in the development of higher types of knowledge in the form of concepts and generalizations.

Figure 7.1 illustrates these various "levels" of content knowledge and their interrelationship (Banks, 1991, 1993; Kucer, 2005; Kucer, Silva, & Delgado-Larocco, 1995; Silva &

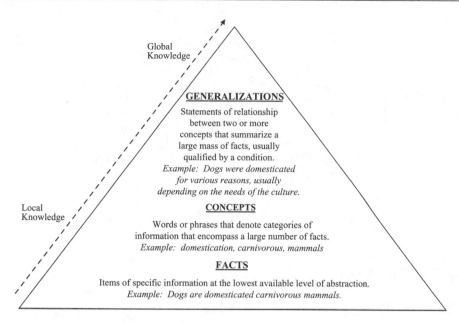

FIG. 7.1.   Forms of content knowledge.

Delgado-Larocco, 1993; Silva & Kucer, 1997). Facts are the lowest or narrowest level of content knowledge and represent specific pieces of information. Dogs are domesticated carnivorous mammals, for example, is a fact. Concepts as we have seen embody a large number of facts. Domestication, carnivorous, and mammals are all concepts. Although it is possible to "give" students a fact, a concept or web of meaning is usually developed through multiple experiences with the concept in various contexts. Generalizations are the most global forms of knowledge that indicate a relationship among two or more concepts and that summarize a large number of facts. Dogs were domesticated for various reasons, usually depending on the needs of the culture, is a generalization. Similar to concepts, generalizations develop over space and time through multiple experiences with various interrelated concepts.

As illustrated in Fig. 7.2 (Kucer et al., 1995), the development of a critical understanding of higher forms of knowledge is at the center of the thematic curriculum. The communication systems—art, music, language, mathematics, and movement—as well as the thinking processes commonly used in the disciplines— literature, social sciences, and sciences—are the vehicles through which such critical understandings are developed. The content or "stuff" of the curriculum is drawn from those disciplines that are relevant to the topic.

Conceptual and generalizable knowledge are developed and refined throughout the theme as students recycle and revisit key ideas and meanings in different contexts using different lenses and materials in different activities. No one experience, no one text can result in a well-formed concept or generalization; the experiences and texts interacted with must be numerous and ongoing. Additionally, concepts and generalizations are dynamic, not static in nature. For all of us, children as well as adults, knowledge evolves over time; the notion of mastering a concept or generalization makes little sense. Rather, knowledge continues to grow and change as students experience various exploratory activities using various communication systems and thinking processes. Figure 7.3 (Kucer et al., 1995) illustrates this transactive process.

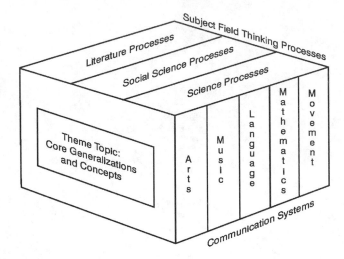

FIG. 7.2.   An integrated view of the curriculum.

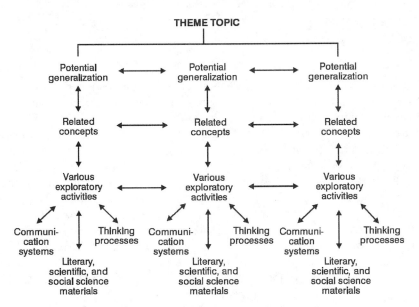

FIG. 7.3.   The interrelationship among theme topic, generalizations, concepts, activities, materials, thinking processes, and communication systems.

In one third-grade bilingual and bicultural class in Southern California, for example, the students explored the topic of immigration (Kucer et al., 1995; Kucer & Silva, 1997). Given the controversial nature of the issue in California and the wealth of material available, it would have been relatively easy for the teacher to focus on individual instances in which immigration was an issue. However, the teacher built on and extended these firsthand experiences of the students and helped them to develop broader understandings. In addition to learning facts and figures about immigration, students also developed knowledge about a number of concepts (e.g., immigrants, contributions, conflict, change) and generalizations (e.g., immigrants have made significant contributions to society; immigration can lead to conflict and change among

**TABLE 7.2**

Immigration Theme Strategies

| Linguistic | Cognitive | Sociocultural |
|---|---|---|
| • Previewing<br>• Aiding the Text | • Reading Strategy Wall Chart<br>• Selected Deletion/Multiple Known Concept<br>• Literature Response Groups<br>• Life Story Time Line | • Inquiry Charts<br>• Exploring Critical Issues |

various groups within a society; there are many reasons why people immigrate to one country from another).

As the students investigated the reasons for and the impact of immigration, they were engaged in a number of linguistic, cognitive, and sociocultural strategy lessons. (See Table 7.2.) Socioculturally, students critically examined the various reasons that immigrants came to the United States and the various routes they traveled through the use of Inquiry Charts. They read various text sets on immigration as part of Exploring Critical Issues strategy lessons. Cognitively, students expanded their ability to manage difficult parts of a text through the use of the Reading Wall Chart as well as Selected Deletion/Multiple Known Concept activities. Students also responded to the immigration texts sets while engaged in Literature Response Groups. Students published their own immigration stories using Life Story Time Lines. Finally, the linguistic strategy lessons of Previewing and Aiding the Text helped students increase their proficiency with expository texts. They learned the various functions of such text aids as headings, subheadings, graphs, and charts and how to use them when reading and writing.

As strategy lessons were implemented, the teacher also varied the degree of support provided based on the developmental needs of the students. With certain activities or particular students, the teacher initially supplied a great deal of mediation and collaboration. In other circumstances, students were more independent and assumed a larger share of the responsibility for the activity. In these cases, the teacher served as a guide when necessary. To support students in gradually internalizing literacy processes, the teacher and students engaged in cognitive strategies such as Shared Reading, Guided Reading as well as Shared Writing and Guided Writing. Linguistic strategies included the use of Language Experience and Phonics Generalizations strategies.

As is evident in this classroom, learning about the dimensions of literacy was seamlessly integrated throughout the units of study. The strategy lessons supported students' linguistic, cognitive, and sociocultural literacy growth. At the same time, the activities helped students construct conceptual and generalizable knowledge about the topic under study.

Some teachers and students may be constrained in their choice of thematic topics. Mandated curricula within their school districts may determine what topics are addressed. In such cases, the stories in the basal reader or chapters in the social science or science textbooks can serve as the foundation for the selection of topics. Basal readers and literature anthologies frequently group stories around central topics, issues, or themes. By their very nature, social science and science chapters are topic centered.

In schools where content standards define the curricula, these standards can serve as the foundation for topic selection and for the identification of thematic concepts and generalizations. For example, to teach an immigration unit similar to the one we previously described, a teacher in Texas might identify social studies learning standards (Texas Education Agency, n.d., TEKS Grade 3) such as the ones presented in Table 7.3. A teacher knowledgeable of the mandated social studies standards can further support the development of higher types of

**TABLE 7.3**

Sample Immigration Unit Third Grade Standards (TEKS)

*Social Studies*

*Knowledge and Skills*

(3.1) History. The student understands how individuals, events, and ideas have influenced the history of various communities.

(3.2) History. The student understands common characteristics of communities, past and present.

(3.3) History. The student understands the concepts of time and chronology.

(3.5) Geography. The student understands the concepts of location, distance, and direction on maps and globes.

(3.7) Economics. The students understands the concepts of an economic system.

(3.11) Citizenship. The student understands the impact of individual and group decisions on communities in a democratic society.

(3.12) Culture. The student understands ethnic and/or cultural celebrations of the United States and other nations.

(3.14) Culture. The student understands the importance of writers and artists to the cultural heritage of communities.

(3.16) Social studies skills. The student applies critical-thinking skills to organize and use information acquired from a variety of sources including electronic technology.

(3.18) Social studies skills. The student uses problem-solving and decision-making skills, working independently and with others, in a variety of settings.

*English as a Second Language (ESL)*

The following expectations apply to the second language learner at his or her level of proficiency in English.

(3.7) Reading/variety of texts. The student reads widely for different purposes in varied sources.

(3.9) Reading/comprehension. The student uses a variety of strategies to comprehend selections read aloud and selections read independently.

knowledge as these standards are reframed in terms of concepts and generalizations related to immigration. Similarly, the teacher would refer to the English language arts standards in order to identify appropriate literacy standards. The sample reading standards identified in Table 7.3 can naturally be taught within the context of strategies such as the Literature Response Groups and Exploring Critical Issues identified earlier in the immigration unit. As part of the thematic planning, the teacher would also need to consider ways of assessing the students to demonstrate achievement of these standards.

## TEACHER READING AND STUDENT RESPONSE

Teachers, regardless of the age of their students, should read to them. Students need to hear the sounds of language and the expression of ideas in forms they may not yet be able to read on their own. This oral reading may be related to the theme under study or something the students have requested; it may be chapter books, short stories, magazines, newspaper articles, or poems.

Teacher reading also allows for the demonstration of various strategies, processes, and stances involved in reading and comprehending. In the third-grade bilingual classroom, when the teacher read a sentence that did not make sense, she used various strategies from the Reading Strategy Wall Chart to determine what the sentence meant. If she changed a word without altering the author's meaning, she linked her behavior to the Synonym Substitution strategy lesson. When particular ideas evoked internal responses, the teacher engaged in various Reader Response strategy lesson.

As well as reading and demonstrating, teachers should also provide opportunities for students to engage in critical response to what they have heard. Like the stance of critique taken in the thematic units, teachers support students in systematically analyzing what is being read, regardless of who is doing the reading.

## INDEPENDENT READING AND STUDENT RESPONSE

On a regular basis, students need occasions to explore their own interests and read for the pure pleasure of reading. The block of time devoted to independent reading and the chance to share their critical responses demonstrates the value placed on self-selected reading. In our society, we often hear various groups—teachers, parents, politicians—lament the lack of reading abilities of the population in general. Certainly, it is the case that many individuals find reading to be problematic in their lives. Just as important and problematic is the desire to read or the lack thereof. It probably would not be an overstatement to say that there exist just as many individuals who can read but do not—reluctant or resistant readers—as there are individuals who cannot read but want to—struggling readers. Providing students with regular and ongoing opportunities to read for pleasure and to share this pleasure with others is one avenue to address motivational issues (Gambrell, 1996). Interest can motivate even struggling or reluctant readers to pursue texts that may be beyond their reading abilities (Allen, 2000). Finally, because we tend to become good at what we enjoy doing, research has consistently demonstrated that increased amounts of reading is related to increased student reading achievement (Allington, 2001).

For self-selected reading to be successful, there needs to be a wide range of reading materials on various topics, in different text types and genres, and from various resources (e.g., books, magazines, newspapers). If students are developing biliteracy, written materials in various languages should also be available. It is important to keep in mind that the purpose of this reading experience is to help students to discover and explore their interests. Therefore, care should be taken not to require students to demonstrate and display their knowledge of what has been read. Book reports, written summaries, and the like are best avoided. Teacher time is better spent helping students locate materials that are appropriate to their abilities and interests (Fielding & Roller, 1992).

This does not mean, however, that students should not have the opportunity to share and respond to what they read. Time should be set aside for students to share their thoughts about the readings. On a regular basis, the third-grade bilingual teacher formed her student into Reader Response Groups where students discussed what they had read during Independent Reading.

## INDEPENDENT WRITING, CONFERENCING, AND PUBLISHING

Blocks of time when students can engage in self-selected writing topics, conferencing, and publishing must also be part of the daily classroom routine. If our goal is to develop independent writers, students must be provided multiple writing experiences on topics about which they care deeply. Additionally, children, as we have learned from writing teachers such as Atwell (1990, 1998, 2002), Calkins (1994), and Graves (1983, 1994), need regular and frequent time in which to engage in the process. Students need to know that they will have both opportunities and periods of time to compose and to reflect on their writing. Although independent writing and much of the writing that occurs as part of a thematic differ as to topic, they do not differ in terms of process. Self-selected writing and thematic writing both involve a cycle in which students compose, share their work through conferencing with others, revise, edit, publish, and celebrate (Short et al., 1996). This cycle can be supported by such strategy lessons as Brainstorming Writing Ideas, Character Development in Writing, Editors' Table, and Publishing and Celebrating.

For students who lack the experience in writing about topics they choose, the teacher may need to provide additional support to make this curricular component effective. Developing a list of possible writing topics with students can be a helpful first step. Even more important, the teacher should help students discover where writers locate or discover their topics, as in the Brainstorming Writing Ideas strategy lesson. Almost any experience, topic, and interest holds the possibility for writing, if students develop and live a "writerly life" (Calkins, 1994). Dyson (2003) argued that such open-ended writing and reading activities are critical in that they serve as points in the school day where "unofficial" literacy topics can enter the classroom. However, as Moje (2000) noted, students often will not automatically bring into the classroom setting such unsanctioned forms of literacy. Teachers may need to explicitly encourage their use.

## CONCLUSION AND SUMMARY

In this concluding chapter, we have attempted to demonstrate how linguistic, cognitive, and sociocultural strategy lessons might be embedded within a curricular framework that meets the developmental needs of various students. As with the strategy lessons, we are confident that teachers will adapt the curricular components to the context within which they instruct and their students learn. We are also confident that teachers will develop and add their own strategy lessons to those that have been addressed in this book. Despite current attempts to standardize both teachers and learners, as well as teaching and learning, the dimensions of literacy call for much more dynamic and contextualized educational settings.

# References

Adler, S. (1993). Aprons and attitudes: A consideration of feminism in children's books. In H. Claire, J. Maybin, & J. Swann (Eds.), *Equality matters* (pp. 111–123). Bristol, England: Multilingual Matters.

Allen, J. (2000). *Yellow brick roads: Shared and guided paths to independent reading 4–12.* Portland, ME: Stenhouse.

Allen, V. (1991). Teaching bilingual and ESL children. In J. Flood, J. Jensen, D. Lapp, & J. Squire (Eds.), *Handbook of research on teaching the English language arts* (pp. 356–364). New York: Macmillan.

Allington, R. (2001). *What reading matters for struggling readers: Designing research-based programs.* New York: Longman.

Anderson, A., & Stokes, S. (1984). Social and institutional influences on the development and practice of literacy. In H. Goelman, A. Oberg, & F. Smith (Eds.), *Awakening to literacy* (pp. 24–37). London: Heinemann.

Anderson, R., & Nagy, W. (1996). Word meanings. In R. Barr, M. Kamil, P. Mosenthal, & P. D. Pearson (Eds.), *Handbook of reading research: Volume II* (pp. 690–724). Mahwah, NJ: Lawrence Erlbaum Associates.

Anderson, R., Reynolds, R., Schallert, D., & Goetz. (1977). Frameworks for comprehending discourse. *American Educational Research Journal, 14,* 367–382.

Anderson, R., & Shifrin, Z. (1980). The meaning of words in context. In R. Spiro, B. Bruce, & W. Brewer (Eds.), *Theoretical issues in reading comprehension* (pp. 331–348). Hillsdale, NJ: Lawrence Erlbaum Associates.

Anderson, R., Spiro, R., & Anderson, M. (1978). Schemata as scaffolding for the representation of information in connected discourse. *American Educational Research Journal, 14,* 367–382.

Atwell, M. (1980). *The evolution of text: The interrelationship of reading and writing in the composing process.* Unpublished doctoral dissertation, Indiana University, Bloomington.

Atwell, M., & Rhodes, L. (1984, May). Strategy lessons as alternatives to skills lessons in reading. *Journal of Reading,* pp. 700–705.

Atwell, N. (1998). *In the middle: New understandings about writing, reading, and learning.* Portsmouth, NH: Heinemann.

Bailey, M. H. (1967). The utility of phonic generalizations in grades one through six. *The Reading Teacher, 20,* 413–418.

Banks, J. (1991). *Teaching strategies for ethnic studies.* Boston: Allyn & Bacon.

Banks, J. (1993, June–July). The canon debate, knowledge construction, and multicultural education. *Educational Researcher, 22,* 4–14.

Bank Street College of Education. (Ed.). (1965). Bill Evers and the Tigers. In *My city* (pp. 237–243). New York: Macmillan.

Barrs, M., & Pidgeon, S. (Eds.). (1994). *Reading the difference: Gender and reading in elementary classrooms.* York, ME: Stenhouse.

Bell, K. (2003). *From the heart*. Toronto, Ontario: Pippin Publishing.

Bender-Peterson, S., & Lach, M. (1990). Gender stereotypes in children's books: Their prevalence and influence on cognitive and affective development. *Gender and Education, 2*, 111–123.

Berdiansky, B., Cronnel, B., & Koehler, J. (1969). *Spelling-sound relations and primary form-class descriptions for speech-comprehension vocabularies of 6–9 year-olds* (Technical Report No. 15). Inglewood, CA: Southwest Regional Laboratory for Educational Research and Development.

Bernhardt, E. (2000). Second-language reading as a case study of reading scholarship in the 20th century. In M. Kamil, P. Mosenthal, P. D. Pearson, & R. Barr (Eds.), *Handbook of reading research: Volume 3* (pp. 791–811). Mahwah, NJ: Lawrence Erlbaum Associates.

Bigelow, W. (1989). Discovering Columbus: Rereading the past. *Language Arts, 66*, 635–643.

Bigelow, W., Miner, B., & Peterson, R. (1991). Rethinking Columbus. In W. Bigelow, B. Miner, & R. Peterson (Eds.), *Rethinking schools*. Milwaukee, WI: Rethinking Schools.

Bigelow, W., & Peterson, B. (Eds.). (1998). *Rethinking Columbus: The next 500 years*. Milwaukee, WI: Rethinking Schools.

Brandt, D. (1990). *Literacy as involvement: The acts of writers, readers, and text*. Carbondale: Southern Illinois University Press.

Brandt, D. (1998). Sponsors of literacy. *College Composition and Communication, 49*, 165–185.

Bransford, J., & Johnson, M. (1973). Considerations of some problems of comprehension. In W. Chase (Ed.), *Visual information processing* (pp. 383–438). New York: Academic.

Brinkley, E. (1998). What's religion got to do with attacks on whole language? In K. Goodman (Ed.), *In defense of good teaching* (pp. 57–71). York, ME: Stenhouse.

Brisk, M. E., & Harrington, M. M. (2000). *Literacy and bilingualism: A handbook for all teachers*. Mahwah, NJ: Lawrence Erlbaum Associates.

Bruner, J. (1986). *Actual minds, possible worlds*. Cambridge, MA: Harvard University Press.

Bruner, J. (1974). The ontogenesis of speech acts. *Journal of Child Language, 2*, 1–19.

Buck, C. (1977). Miscues of non-native speakers of English. In K. Goodman (Ed.), *Miscue analysis: Applications to reading instruction* (pp. 91–96). Urbana, IL: National Council of Teachers of English.

Buckingham, D., & Sefton-Green, J. (1994). *Cultural studies goes to school: Reading and teaching popular media*. Bristol, PA: Taylor & Francis.

Calkins, L. (1994). *The art of teaching writing* (2nd ed.). Portsmouth, NH: Heinemann.

Carrasquillo, A., Kucer, S. B., & Abrams, R. (2004). *Beyond the beginnings: Literacy interventions for upper elementary English language learners*. Clevedon, England: Multilingual Matters LTD.

Cazden, C. (1988). *Classroom discourse: The language of teaching and learning*. Portsmouth, NH: Heinemann.

Cazden, C. (1992). *Whole language plus*. New York: Teachers College.

Chamot, A. U., & El-Dinary, P. B. (1999). Children's learning strategies in language immersion classrooms. *The Modern Language Journal, 83*(3), 319–338.

Chomsky, C. (1970). Reading, writing, and phonology. *Harvard Educational Review, 40*, 287–309.

Clay, M. (1975). *What did I write?* London: Heinemann.

Clymer, T. (1996). The utility of phonic generalizations in the primary grades. *The Reading Teacher, 50*, 182–187.

Coles, G. (2000). *Misreading reading*. Portsmouth, NH: Heinemann.

Comber, B. (2001). Negotiating critical literacies. *School Talk, 6*, 1–2.

Comber, B., & Simpson, A. (Eds.). (2001). *Negotiating critical literacies in classrooms*. Mahwah, NJ: Lawrence Erlbaum Associates.

Cummins, J. (1988). Language proficiency, bilingualism and academic achievement. In P. Richard-Amato (Ed.), *Making it happen: Interaction in the second language classroom* (pp. 382–395). New York: Longman.

Cummins, J. (1991). Interdependence of first- and second-language proficiency in bilingual children. In E. Bialystok (Ed.), *Language processing in bilingual children* (pp. 70–89). Cambridge, UK: Cambridge University Press.

Cunningham, J. (2001). Essay book review: The National Reading Panel Report. *Reading Research Quarterly, 36*, 326–335.

Cunningham, J., & Fitzgerald, J. (1996). Epistemology and reading. *Reading Research Quarterly, 31*, 36–60.

Cunningham, P. M. (2005). *Phonics they use* (4th ed.). New York: Longman.

de Beaugrande, R. (1980). *Text, discourse, and process*. Norwood, NJ: Ablex.

de Beaugrande, R. (1984). *Text production*. Norwood, NJ: Ablex.

DeFord, D. (1981). Literacy: Reading, writing, and other essentials. *Language Arts, 58*, 652–658.

Delpit, L. (1990). Language diversity and learning. In S. Hynds & D. Rubin (Eds.), *Perspectives on talk and learning* (pp. 247–266). Urbana, IL: National Council of Teachers of English.

Delpit, L. (1998). What should teacher do? Ebonics and culturally responsive instruction. In T. Perry & L. Delpit (Eds.), *The real ebonics debate: Power, language, and the education of African-American children* (pp. 17–26). Boston: Beacon Press.

Devine, J. (1994). Literacy and social power. In B. Ferdman, R. M. Weber, & A. Ramirez (Eds.), *Literacy across languages and cultures* (pp. 221–237). Albany: State University of New York Press.

Dewey, J. (1938). *Experience and education*. New York: Collier.

Dorn, L. J., & Soffos, C. (2001). *Scaffolding young writers*. Portland, ME: Stenhouse

Dyson, A. H. (2003). *The brothers and sisters learn to write: Popular literacies in childhood and school cultures*. New York: Teachers College Press.

Edelsky, C. (Ed.). (1999). *Making justice our project*. Urbana, IL: NCTE.

Ehri, L., & Nunes, S. (2002). The role of phonemic awareness in learning to read. In A. E. Farstrup & S. J. Samuels (Eds.), *What research has to say about reading instruction* (3rd ed., pp. 110–139). Newark, DE: International Reading Association.

Ehri, L., Nunes, S., Willows, B., Yaghoub-Zadeh, A., & Shanahan, T. (2001). Phonemic awareness instruction helps children learn to read: Evidence from the National Reading Panel's meta-analysis. *Reading Research Quarterly, 36*, 250–287.

Emans, R. (1967). The usefulness of phonic generalizations above the primary grades. *The Reading Teacher, 20*, 419–425.

Enciso, P. (1994). Cultural identity and response to literature: Running lessons from Maniac Magee. *Language Arts, 71*, 524–533.

Fashola, O., Drum, P., Mayer, R., & Kang, S. (1996). A cognitive theory of orthographic transitioning: Predictable errors in how Spanish-speaking children spell English words. *American Educational Research Journal, 33*, 825–843.

Ferdman, B. (1990). Literacy and cultural identity. *Harvard Educational Review, 60*, 181–204.

Fielding, L., & Roller, C. (1992). Making difficult books accessible and easy books acceptable. *The Reading Teacher, 45*, 678–685.

Fitzgerald, J. (1995). English-as-a-second-language learners' cognitive reading processes: A review of research in the United States. *Review of Educational Research, 65*, 145–190.

Fletcher, R., & Portalupi, J. (1998). *Craft lessons*. Portland, ME: Stenhouse.

Fountas, I., & Pinnell, S. (1996). *Guided reading*. Portsmouth, NH: Heinemann.

Freedbody, P., & Luke, A. (1990). Literacies' programs: Debates and demands in cultural context. *Prospect: The Australian Journal of TESOL, 5*, 7–16.

Freeman, D., & Freeman, Y. (1994). Between worlds: Access to second language acquisition. Portsmouth, NH: Heinemann.

Freeman, D. E., & Freeman, Y. (2002). *Closing the achievement gap*. Portsmouth, NH: Heinemann.

Freeman, D. E., & Freeman, Y. S. (2004). *Essential linguistics*. Portsmouth, NH: Heinemann.

Gambrell, L. (1996). Creating classroom cultures that foster reading motivation. *The Reading Teacher, 50*, 14–25.

Gee, J. (1996). *Social linguistics and literacies: Ideology in discourses* (2nd ed.). New York: Falmer.

Gilbert, P. (1989). *Writing, schooling, and deconstruction: From voice to text in the classroom*. London: Routledge.

Goldenberg, C. (1992/1993). Instructional conversations: Promoting comprehension through discussion. *The Reading Teacher, 46*, 316–326.

Goodman, K. (1996). *On reading*. Portsmouth, NH: Heinemann.

Goodman, K. (Ed.). (1998). *In defense of good teaching*. York, ME: Stenhouse.

Goodman, K., & Goodman, Y. (1978). Reading of American children whose language is a stable rural dialect of English or a language other than English (NIE-C-00-3-0087). Washington, DC: U.S. Department of Health, Education and Welfare.

Goodman, Y. (2003). *Valuing language study: Inquiry into language for elementary and middle school students*. Urbana, IL: National Council of Teachers of English.

Goodman, Y., & Burke, C. (1980). *Reading strategies: Focus on comprehension*. New York: Owens.

Graves, D. (1983). *Writing: Teachers and children at work*. Portsmouth, NH: Heinemann.

Graves, D., & Hansen, J. (1983). The author's chair. *Language Arts, 60*, 176–183.

Graves, D. H. (1989). *Experiment with fiction*. Portsmouth, NH: Heinemann.

Graves, D. H. (1994). *A fresh look at writing*. Portsmouth, NH: Heinemann.

Halliday, M. A. K. (1973). *Explorations in the functions of language*. London: Arnold.

Hancock, L., & Biddle, N. (1994, November). Red, white—and blue. *Newsweek, 130*, p. 54.

Harste, J., Woodward, V., & Burke, C. (1984). *Language stories and literacy lessons*. Portsmouth, NH: Heinemann.

Heath, S. (1982). What no bedtime story means: Narrative skills at home and school. *Language in Society, 11*, 49–76.

Heath, S. (1983). *Ways with words: Language, life, and work in communities and classrooms*. Cambridge, UK: Cambridge University Press.

Heffernan, L. (2001). Writing as a tool for change. *School Talk, 6*, p. 5.

Heffernan, L. (2004). *Critical literacy and writer's workshop: Bringing purpose and passion to student writing*. Newark, DE: International Reading Association.

Henkin, R. (1995). Insiders and outsiders in first-grade writing workshops: Gender and equity issues. *Language Arts, 72*, 429–434.

Hoffman, D. (1996). Culture and self in multicultural education: Reflections on discourse, text, and practice. *American Educational Research Journal, 33*, 545–569.

Hoffman, J. (1992). Critical reading/thinking across the curriculum: Using I-charts to support learning. *Language Arts, 69*, 121–127.

Holdaway, D. (1979). *The foundations of literacy*. Sydney, Australia: Ashton Scholastic.

Jimenez, R., Garcia, G., & Pearson, P. D. (1995). Three children, two languages, and strategic reading: Case studies in bilingual/monolingual reading. *American Educational Research Journal, 32*, 31–61.

Jimenez, R., Garcia, G., & Pearson, P. D. (1996). The reading strategies of bilingual Latino/a students who are successful English readers: Opportunities and obstacles. *Reading Research Quarterly, 31*, 90–112.

Just, M. A., & Carpenter, P. (1987). *The psychology of reading and language comprehension*. Newton, MA: Allyn & Bacon.

Kagan, S. (1994). *Cooperative Learning*. San Juan Capistrano, CA: Resources for Teachers, Inc.

Kamler, B. (1993). Constructing gender in the process writing classroom. *Language Arts, 70*, 95–103.

Keenan Ochs, E. (1977). Making it last: Repetition in children's discourse. In S. Ervin-Tripp & C. Mitchell-Kernan (Eds.), *Child discourse* (pp. 125–138). New York: Academic.

Keene, E. O., & Zimmermann, S. (1997). *Mosaic of thought: Teaching comprehension in a reader's workshop*. Portsmouth, NH: Heinemann.

Kintsch, W. (1998). *Comprehension: A paradigm for cognition*. Cambridge, UK: Cambridge University Press.

Koch, K. (1970). *Wishes, lies, and dreams: Teaching children to write poetry*. New York: Random House.

Krashen, S. (1985). *The input hypothesis*. Beverly Hill, CA: Laredo Publishing Company.

Kraus, R. (1945). *The carrot seed*. New York: Scholastic.

Kucer, S. B. (1983a). Text coherence from a transactional perspective. In J. Niles & L. A. Harris (Eds.), *Searchers for meaning in reading/language processing and instruction* (pp. 104–110) (Thirty-second Yearbook of the National Reading Conference). Rochester, NY: NRC.

Kucer, S. B. (1983b). *Using text comprehension as a metaphor for understanding text production: Building bridges between reading and writing*. Unpublished doctoral dissertation, Indiana University, Bloomington.

Kucer, S. B. (1986). Helping writers get the "big picture." *Journal of Reading, 30,* 18–24.

Kucer, S. B. (1995). Guiding bilingual students "through" the literacy processes. *Language Arts, 72,* 20–29.

Kucer, S. B. (2001). *Dimensions of literacy: A conceptual base for teaching reading and writing in school settings.* Mahwah, NJ: Lawrence Erlbaum Associates.

Kucer, S. B. (2005). *Dimensions of literacy: A conceptual base for teaching reading and writing in school settings* (2nd ed.). Mahwah, NJ: Lawrence Erlbaum Associates.

Kucer, S. B., Silva, C., & Delgado-Larocco, E. (1995). *Curricular conversations: Themes in multilingual and monolingual classrooms.* York, ME: Stenhouse.

Labov, W. (1973). The boundaries of words and their meanings. In C. J. Bailey & R. Shuy (Eds.), *New ways of analyzing variation in English* (pp. 340–373). Washington, DC: Georgetown University.

Leland, C., Harste, J., Ociepka, A., Lewison, M., & Vasquez, V. (1999). Exploring critical literacy: You can hear a pin drop. *Language Arts, 77,* 70–77.

Levin, D. E. (2003). *Teaching young children in violent times: Building a peaceable classroom* (2nd ed.). Educators for Social Responsibility/National Association for the Education of Young Children. Gabriola Island, BC, Canada: New Society Publishers.

Lewison, M., Flint, A., & Sluys, K. (2002). Taking on critical literacy: The journey of newcomers and novices. *Language Arts, 79,* 382–392.

Luke, A. (1995). When basic skills and information processing just aren't enough: Rethinking reading in new times. *Teachers College Record, 97,* 95–115.

Luke, A. (1998). Getting over method: Literacy teaching as work in "new times." *Language Arts, 75,* 305–313.

Mandler, J., & Johnson, N. (1977). Remembrance of things pansed: Story structure and recall. *Cognitive Psychology, 9,* 111–151.

Manning, M., Manning, G., & Long, R. (1994). *Theme immersion: Inquiry-based curriculum in elementary and middle schools.* Portsmouth, NH: Heinemann.

Mayer, M. (1976). *Ah-choo.* New York: Dial.

McDermott, R. (1995). Culture as disability. *Anthropology and Education Quarterly, 26,* 324–348.

McLaughlin, M., & DeVoogd, G. (2004). *Critical literacy: Enhancing students' comprehension of text.* New York: Scholastic.

Moline, S. (1995). *I see what you mean.* York, ME: Stenhouse.

Moje, E. (2000). "To be part of the story": The literacy practices of gangsta adolescents. *Teachers College Record, 102,* 651–690.

Moss, B. (1994). Creating a community: Literacy events in African-American churches. In B. Moss (Ed.), *Literacy across communities* (pp. 147–178). Cresskill, NJ: Hampton.

New London Group. (1996). A pedagogy of multiliteracies: Designing social futures. *Harvard Educational Review, 66,* 60–92.

O'Brien, J. (1994). Show Mum you love her: Taking a new look at junk mail. *Reading, 28,* 43–46.

Ogle, D. S. (1986). K-W-L: A teaching model that develops active reading of expository text. *Reading Teacher, 39,* 564–570.

Orellana, M. F. (1995). Literacy as a gendered social practice: Tasks, text, talk, and take-up. *Reading Research Quarterly, 30,* 674–708.

Pennycook, A. (2001). *Critical applied linguistics: A critical introduction.* Mahwah, NJ: Lawrence Erlbaum Associates.

Peregoy, S., & Boyle, O. (2005). *Reading, writing, and learning in ESL.* Boston: Pearson Education.

Piazza, C. L. (2003). *Journeys.* Upper Saddle River, NJ: Merrill Prentice Hall.

Power, B., & Hubbard, R. (2003). Documenting neighborhoods. *Language Arts, 80,* 222.

Pressley, M. (1998). *Reading instruction that works: The case for balanced teaching.* New York: Guilford.

Pressley, M., Goodchild, F., Fleet, J., Zajchowski, R., & Evans, E. (1989). The challenges of classroom strategy instruction. *The Elementary School Journal, 89,* 301–342.

Purcell-Gates, V. (1996). Stories, coupons, and the TV Guide: Relationships between home literacy experiences and emergent literacy knowledge. *Reading Research Quarterly, 31,* 406–428.

Purcell-Gates, V., L'Allier, S., & Smith, D. (1995). Literacy at the Harts' and the Larsons': Diversity among poor, inner city families. *The Reading Teacher, 48*, 572–578.

Read, C. (1971). Pre-school children's knowledge of English phonology. *Harvard Educational Review, 41*, 1–34.

Read, C. (1975). *Children's categorization of speech sounds in English*. Urbana, IL: NCTE.

Reder, S. (1994). Practice-engagement theory: A sociocultural approach to literacy across languages & cultures. In B. Ferdman, R. M. Weber, & A. Ramirez (Eds.), *Literacy Across Languages & Cultures* (pp. 33–74). Albany: State University of New York Press.

Rumelhart, D. (1975). Notes on a schema for stories. In D. Brown & A. Collins (Eds.), *Representation and understanding: Studies in cognitive science* (pp. 211–236). New York: Academic.

Rumelhart, D. (1980). Schemata: The building blocks of cognition. In R. Spiro, B. Bruce, & W. Brewer (Eds.), *Theoretical issues in reading comprehension* (pp. 33–58). Hillsdale, NJ: Lawrence Erlbaum Associates.

Rumelhart, D. (1984). Understanding understanding. In J. Flood (Ed.), *Understanding reading comprehension* (pp. 1–20). Newark, DE: IRA.

Saunders, W., & Goldenberg, C. (1999). The Effects of Instructional Conversations and Literature Logs on the Story Comprehension and Thematic Understanding of English Proficient and Limited English Proficient Students (Center for Research on Education, Diversity & Excellence Research Reports. Paper rr06). Retrieved January 30, 2005, from http://repositories.cdlib.org/crede/rsrchrpts/rr06

Scieszka, J. (1989). *The true story of the three little pigs*. New York: Penguin.

Scollon, R., & Scollon, S. W. (1981). *Narrative, literacy, and face in interethnic communication*. Norwood, NJ: Ablex.

Scott Foresman. (1976). *The three little pigs*. Glenview, IL: Scott Foresman.

Scribner, S., & Cole, M. (1981). Unpackaging literacy. In M. Whiteman (Ed.), *Variation in writing: Functional and linguistic-cultural differences* (pp. 71–87). Hillsdale, NJ: Lawrence Erlbaum Associates.

Short, K., Harste, J., & Burke, C. (1996). *Creating classrooms for authors and inquirers* (2nd ed.). Portsmouth, NH: Heinemann.

Silva, C., & Delgado-Larocco, E. (1993). Facilitating learning through interconnections: A conceptual approach to core literature units. *Language Arts, 70*, 469–474.

Silva, C., & Kucer, S. B. (1997). Expanding curricular conversations through unification, diversity, and access. *Language Arts, 74*, 26–32.

Sims, R. (1982). Dialect and reading: Toward refining the issues. In J. Langer & R. Burke-Smith (Eds.), *Reader meets author/Bridging the gap* (pp. 222–236). Newark, DE: IRA.

Sinclair, S. (2002, July/August). Extraordinary eyes: How animals see the world. In *Arts and science for kids*, 1, pp. 6–12. Peru, Illinois: Carus Publishing Company.

Smith, F. (1977). The uses of language. *Language Arts, 54*, 638–644.

Smith, F. (1981). Demonstrations, engagement, and sensitivity: A revised approach to language learning. *Language Arts, 52*, 103–112.

Smith, F. (1988). *Joining the literacy club*. Portsmouth, NH: Heinemann.

Smith, F. (2004). *Understanding reading* (6th ed.). Hillsdale, NJ: Lawrence Erlbaum Associates.

Solsken, J. (1992). *Literacy, gender, and work: In families and school*. Norwood, NJ: Ablex.

Spinelli, J. (1990). *Maniac Magee*. Boston: Little, Brown.

Steffensen, M., Joag-Dev, C., & Anderson, R. (1979). A cross-cultural perspective on reading comprehension. *Reading Research Quarterly, 15*, 10–29.

Taylor, D., & Dorsey-Gaines, C. (1988). *Growing up literate: Learning from inner-city families*. Portsmouth, NH: Heinemann.

Teale, W. (1984). Toward a theory of how children learn to read and write naturally. In J. Jensen (Ed.), *Composing and comprehending* (pp. 127–142). Urbana, IL: NCTE.

Teale, W., & Sulzby, E. (1991). Emergent literacy. In R. Barr, M. Kamil, P. Mosenthal, & P. D. Pearson (Eds.), *Handbook of reading research* (Vol. 2; pp. 418–452). New York: Longman.

Texas Education Agency. (n.d.). Texas Essential Knowledge and Skills (TEKS). Retrieved September 24, 2004, from the Texas Education Agency Web site, http://www.tea.state.tx.us/teks/grade/grade_3.htm

Tharp, R., & Gallimore, R. (1988). *Rousing minds to life: Teaching, learning and schooling in social context*. New York: Cambridge University Press.

Thomas, M. (Vocalist). (1972). *Free to be you and me* [cassette recording, CD]. New York: Arista Records.

Tomlinson, C. M., & Lynch-Brown, C. (2002). *Essentials of children's literature*. Boston: Allyn & Bacon.

Thorndyke, P. (1977). Cognitive structures in comprehension and memory of narrative discourse. *Cognitive Psychology, 9*, 77–110.

Tolstoy, A. (1976). *The great big enormous turnip*. Glenview, IL: Scott Foresman.

Vasquez, V. (2003). *Getting beyond "I like the book." Creating space for critical literacy in K–6 classrooms*. Newark, DE: IRA.

Venesky, R. (1980). From Webster to Rice to Roosevelt. In U. Frith (Ed.), *Cognitive processes in spelling*. (pp. 9–30). London: Academic Press.

Vygotsky, L. S. (1962). *Thought and language*. Cambridge, MA: MIT.

Vygotsky, L. S. (1978). In M. Cole, V. John Steiner, S. Scribner, & E. Souberman (Eds.), *Mind in society*. Cambridge, MA: Harvard University Press.

Watson, D. (1980). Reader selected miscues: Getting more from sustained silent reading. In B. Farr & D. Strickler. *Reading comprehension resource guide* (pp. 65–70). Bloomington: Indiana University.

Weaver, C. (1996). *Teaching grammar in context*. Portsmouth, NH: Heinemann.

Weaver, C., & Brinkley, E. (1998). Phonics, whole language, and the religious and political right. In K. Goodman (Ed.), *In defense of good teaching* (pp. 127–141). York, ME: Stenhouse.

Weaver, C. (2002). *Reading process and practice* (3rd ed.). Portsmouth, NH: Heinemann.

Weber, R. (1996). Linguistic diversity and reading in American society. In R. Barr, M. Kamil, P. Mosenthal, & P. D. Pearson (Eds.), *Handbook of reading research* (Vol. 2, pp. 97–119). Mahwah, NJ: Lawrence Erlbaum Associates.

Wells, G. (1986). *The meaning makers*. Portsmouth, NH: Heinemann.

Wilde, S. (1992). *You kan red this! Spelling and punctuation for whole language classrooms, K–6*. Portsmouth, NH: Heinemann.

Wilde, S. (1997). *What's a schwa sound anyway?* Portsmouth, NH: Heinemann.

Wolfe, P., & Poynor, L. (2001). Politics and the pendulum: An alternative understanding of the case of whole language as educational innovation. *Educational Researcher, 30*, 15–20.

Wollman-Bonilla, J. (1998). Outrageous viewpoints: Teachers' criteria for rejecting works of children's literature. *Language Arts, 75*, 287–295.

Zolotow, C. (1972). *William's doll*. New York: Harper & Row.

# Indexes

# Author Index

Spinelli, J., 46, 385
Spiro, R., 33, 379
Stanley, D., 358, 361
Stanley, J., 382
Steffensen, M., 33, 385
Stokes, S., 38, 379
Sulzby, E., 52, 385
Surat, M., 163

**T**

Taylor, D., 38, 385
Taylor, M., 346
Teale, W., 49, 52, 385
Texas Education Agency, 375
Tharp, R., 55, 385
Thomas, M., 385
Thorndyke, P., 10, 386
Tolstoy, A., 61, 266, 333, 386
Tomlinson, C. M., 146, 176, 386
Turner, A., 346
Turner, J., 384

**V**

Vasquez, V., 327, 366, 383, 386
Venesky, R., 16, 386
Vygotsky, L. S., 36, 55, 56, 386

**W**

Waber, B., 320, 325
Waikowhai Intermediate School, 232
Wasik, B., 384
Watson, D., 258, 379, 386
Weaver, C., 32, 43, 82, 386
Weber, R., 30, 31, 386
Wells, G., 49, 386
Wilde, S., 5, 23, 24, 54, 386
Wildsmith, B., 88
Willows, B., 3, 381
Winter, P., 178
Wolfe, P., 5, 386
Wollman-Bonilla, J., 346, 386
Woodward, V., 36, 49, 50, 52, 53, 382

**Y**

Yaghoub-Zadeh, A., 3, 381
Young, E., 3

**Z**

Zajchowski, R., 57, 384
Zimmermann, S., 252, 383
Zolotow, C., 144, 221, 241, 320, 327, 346, 366, 386

# Subject Index

## A

Academic knowledge
  mainstream, 44
  transformative, 44
Accommodation, author's and reader's need for, 26
Action, 11
Add, Zoom, Flashback, Squeeze, X-Tend strategy lesson, 232–234
Adding (in writing process), 27
Adjective, 12
Adverb, 12
Adversatives, 10, 14
Advertisements, 365–368
Aesthetic reading, 136
Aesthetic writing, 139
Affricatives, 54
Agent, 11
Aiding the text, 113, 116–117, 307, 375
Aiding the Text strategy lesson, 113, 116–117, 307
Alliteration strategy lesson, 86–87
Alphabet Books strategy lesson, 88–89
Alternate text, creating, 160
*Amazing Grace* (Hoffman), 221, 241, 320, 327, 329, 346
*Angel Child, Dragon Child* (Surat & Mai), 163
*Animalia* (Base), 86
Antonyms, 104
Appearances, 349
Archival-related literacy, 38
Arguments, 144–145, 365–366
*Arnie and the New Kid* (Carlson), 221, 241, 327, 329, 349
Assimilation, author's and reader's need for, 26

Attributions, 10, 11
Audience
  choosing language based on, 358–362
  role of, 235
Audiences and Purposes strategies, 129, 131–147
Authority, role in language use, 359, 363–364, 367–368
Authors
  relation of author's background knowledge to reader's, 25
  relation of author's language to reader's, 24–25
  relation of author's need to assimilate/accommodate to reader's, 26
  relation of author's purpose to reader's, 25
  relation of author's strategy/availability/flexibility to reader's, 25–26
Author's Chair strategy lesson, 75, 78, 81, 235, 295
Author Studies, 241

## B

Background knowledge
  biliterate readers and, 31
  group membership and, 42
  predicting word meaning and, 280–283
  reading comprehension and, 33, 243
  reading process and, 29
  relation between reader's and author's, 25
  writing process and, 35
Beginning, Middle, End strategy lesson, 206–207
Beginning letters, 64
  perception and, 23
Beginnings, of stories, 135

**393**